THE POLITICAL ECONOMY OF WEST GERMANY, 1945–85

The Political Economy of West Germany, 1945–85

An Introduction

Jeremy Leaman

Lecturer in German Studies
Loughborough University

St. Martin's Press   New York

First published in the United States of America in 1988

Printed in Hong Kong

ISBN 0–312–00541–5

Library of Congress Cataloguing-in-Publication Data
Leaman, Jeremy 1947–
The political economy of West Germany, 1945–1985.
Bibliography: p.
Includes index.
1. Germany (West)—Economic conditions.
2. Germany (West)—Economic policy.   I. Title.
HC286.5.L4   1987   338.943   87–9458
ISBN 0–312–00541–5

Contents

List of Figures

List of Tables

Preface

This volume is intended – as the title suggests – to introduce an English-reading public to the political economy of the most powerful industrial nation in Western Europe. The approach is essentially historical, examining in turn the prehistory and foundation of the West German state, the period of strong economic growth and political continuity 1949–66 and the years of interrupted, slower growth and political (policy) discontinuity 1966–85. Within this chronological scheme the thematic structure differs, not simply because particular themes can be seen to dominate particular periods (re-militarisation, formal economic integration, 'Ostpolitik', Keynesianism, monetarism, mass unemployment, etc.) but also because a comprehensive review of all the themes in each period would not have been possible for reasons of space, nor particularly appropriate for a broad introduction. Thus the purpose of the slightly eclectic thematic structure is to stimulate further interest and raise further questions about the development of the economic relations of power and the political articulation of that power in a country which will play a major role in shaping global political and economic affairs in the future.

I wish to thank all those colleagues at Loughborough who have saved me hours of searching, by directing me straight to important sources, and contributed to the shaping of many of the arguments. I must also acknowledge a general debt to the post-war generation of critical historians and political economists who, by their commitment, questioning and, above all, rigour have done much to assist the uphill struggle for increased awareness in politico-economic affairs. I wish also to thank Campus Verlag for permission to reprint four graphs from Werner Glastetter, Rüdiger Paulert and Ulrich Spörel, *Die wirtschaftliche Entwicklung in der Bundesrepublik Deutschland 1950–80: Befunde, Aspekte, Hintergründe* (Frankfurt, 1983), in particular M. Kleinemeier who produced the excellent graphs Figs 4.1, 4.2, 4.4 and 4.11); thanks also to Verlag C. H. Beck for permission to reprint one graph (Fig. 2.1) from Dietmar Petzina, Werner Abelshauser and Anselm Faust, *Sozialgeschichtliches Arbeitsbuch, Band III Materialien zur Statistik des Deutschen Reiches 1914–45*, (Munich, 1978).

Loughborough   JEREMY LEAMAN

List of Abbreviations

apuzg	*aus politik und zeitgeschichte* (journal)
BDI	Bundesverband der deutschen Industrie
BDA	Bundesvereinigung deutscher Arbeitgeberverbände
CCG–BE	Control Commission for Germany – British Element
COCOM	Co-ordinating Committee (for Eastern Trade – within NATO)
DIHT	Deutscher Industrie – und Handelstag
DIW	Deutsches Institut für Wirtschaftsforschung (Berlin)
EStG	Einkommenssteuergesetz (Income Tax Law)
FAZ	Frankfurter Allgemeine Zeitung
FR	Frankfurter Rundschau
GM	Gewerkschaftliche Monatshefte
HWWA	Hamburg Weltwirtschafts-Archiv (Research Institute)
iw	Institut der deutschen Wirtschaft (Cologne)
Ifo	Ifo-Institut für Wirtschaftsforschung (Munich)
JG	Jahresgutachten des Sachverständigenrats (Annual report of the Council of Economic Experts)
OMGUS	Office of Military Government for Germany, United States
RWI	Rheinisch-Westfälisches Institut für Wirtschaftsforschung (Essen)
SVR	Sachverständigenrat (Council of Economic Experts)
SOPO	*Sozialistische Politik* (journal)
SDZ	Süddeutsche Zeitung
SHAEF	Supreme Headquarters Allied Expeditionary Force
WWI	Institut für Weltwirtschaft (Kiel)
WSI	Wirtschafts- und sozialwissenschaftliches Institut (Düsseldorf)

1 Political Economy and the Development of State Theory

Political economy as a branch of knowledge has experienced a marked revival over the recent years as a result of a number of developments, including the partial erosion of boundaries between traditional humanities subjects like politics, economics, sociology, history, geography and psychology. However, as a result of the process of self-adjustment within academics the concept has been stretched considerably to accommodate a wide variety of often quite different areas of study. Because of this wild abundance of 'political economies' – which include, e.g. the study of economic statecraft or of political behaviour using economic categories – it is important to define the point of departure of *this* variant. Here political economy is understood as the study of the production and distribution of social wealth, and this book is concerned with the historical reality of the politico-economic development in West Germany rather than with the development of German political economy as a (national) branch of knowledge. Within this framework particular attention is paid to the development of state policy. The following conspectus of theories of political economy thus pays particular regard to the role of the state. Even so such a conspectus can only be introductory and abbreviated in nature.

One can make a fundamental distinction between two theoretical positions within political economy: the first assumes the general efficacy of capitalism and, in line with the Smith–Ricardo–Mill tradition, addresses the problems of managing the framework for or distribution of social wealth as the *science of economic government*; the second position proceeds from a *Critique of Political Economy* (Marx) as an historical analysis of the determinate, changing nature of social organisations (notably capitalism), to develop a new tradition of political economy the categories of which presume/recommend the transcendance of capitalism.

Both traditions have developed a variety of specific theories of labour, value, production, money, distribution, interest, rent, profit, taxation, etc. but of increasing significance for both in the present century has been the articulation of (again a wide variety of) theories of the role of the state in the modern industrial economy. This increasing importance of state theory can clearly be explained historically in terms of the objective increase (within all advanced capitalist societies) of the state's share of social wealth and the economic activities of the state in the 20th century; both related developments reflected the perceived or implied need to extend the economic involvement of the state in a period of slower growth, national and international upheavals. World wars, revolutions, inflation and recession have demanded the general attention of national policy-makers and above all a reconsideration of received wisdom on the economic role of the state.

Recent bourgeois theories have proposed a variety of ways of recapturing the equilibrium which, in the first half of this century, was demonstrably absent but which is assumed to be feasible *within* capitalism. Accordingly the state is assumed to be *class-neutral*, operating according to perceptions of a *common good*. The proponents of an active guidance of and intervention in private economic activity in part reflected the historical perception of the achievements of the earlier mercantilist state and the flaws of later *laissez-faire* capitalism. Keynes and German-speaking contemporaries like Ernst Wagemann and Robert Friedländer Prechtl[1] placed the macro-economic management of demand (above all of investment demand) at the centre of their discussions on the role of the state. Their *demand theories* asserted that a flexible manipulation of state revenues and expenditure, flanked by a judicious monetary policy, was capable of neutralising the fluctuations of the business cycle and preventing the kind of disequilibrium which manifested itself in the Great Depression. Subsequently the observed weaknesses of simple fiscalism led to proposals for supplementing the economic levers of demand management with measures of social engineering (in fact implied in Keynes's work) based on theories of individual psychology (e.g. Adolph Lowe)[2] as well as for refining the instruments of economic control such that the state could assess more efficiently the appropriate means and judge more effectively the timing of their deployment (Fritz Scharpf, etc.)[3] Corresponding to these views of the feasibility of process-political, technocratic economic control are the theories of *pluralism* (Laski, Duguit)[4] which postulate a (class neutral) state apparatus which mediates *all* social tensions and threats to social equilibrium on the basis of democratic legitimacy and an unspecific notion of balance between group interests.

In contrast to these proponents of a constant, active involvement of the state as an economic agent, a revived liberalistic tradition criticised state economic intervention as inevitably flawed and hence in part responsible for the disequilibrium it sought to resolve. This new liberal tradition recommended the virtual abandonment of process-political interventions and the limitation of state economic activity to the creation of an optimal framework for the operation of otherwise self-regulating market forces. The commonest form of this (supply-side) tradition is *monetarism*, rendered fashionable more recently by the failures of fiscalism. Monetarists like Friedmann propose the radical deregulation of markets, the privatisation of state assets and services, the abandonment of exchange controls and fixed exchange rates and the limitation of the state to guaranteeing a stable domestic money supply.[5] *Ordo-liberals* (of the Freiburg School – see below Chapter 3), while affirming the privatisation of economic activity, identified the crucial significance of capital concentration, largely ignored by Keynesians and Monetarists, and proposed an extensive system of monopoly control as an indispensable means of guaranteeing the stability of the market–economic order. As theories of political economy therefore, these two liberal traditions prescribe a self-limiting function of judicial *nightwatchman* for the capitalist state, the one guaranteeing unreflectedly the rights of property disposition, the other defining the rules of 'healthy' economic activity (i.e. competition) and implying a slightly greater degree of intervention.

While the whole bourgeois tradition of political economy assumes the sanctity and primacy of a private system of production and exchange as well as the class-neutrality of the state, the *socialist tradition* seeks to overturn capitalism and identifies in the state a fortress of class rule which either has to be stormed, employed in a temporary class dictatorship of the proletariat and then abandoned (Marxism) or gradually conquered and modified as a primary instrument of working class rule (Lassalleanism, etc.). The Lassallean/statist tradition, which persists in a number of reformist social-democratic parties, cannot be said to possess an economic theory of the state of its own; rather it tended to employ selected Marxist elements in its practical agitation until these were gradually jettisoned in favour largely of forms of Left Keynesianism. While Marx and Engels had elucidated the 'laws' governing the processes of accumulation and capital reproduction, their definitive view of the state as a particular instrument of bourgeois class dominance remained undeveloped within the marxist tradition until signs of the growing split within the European labour movement made an elaboration of the hegemonic function of the state necessary (Gramsci, Luxemburg). Above all, however, it was the persistence of statist tendencies in established socialist countries, in communist as well as social democratic parties, coupled with the resilience of the bourgeois state in the first half of this century that demanded a more refined materialist theory of the state, such that emerged within the European New Left in the 1960s and 1970s.

The theory of *state monopoly capitalism*, propounded by orthodox communist parties, developed Lenin's views of the state and of imperialism, defining the state apparatus in contemporary capitalism as the power apparatus of the monopoly bourgeoisie, which through its measures reflects the collective interests of the monopolies, despite its 'relative autonomy' from individual capitals, and at the expense of small capital as well as the petty bourgeoisie and the working class.[6] The theory however does little more than dispel the views of conspiratorial capitalist politics which had dominated communist party thinking on fascism and post-war restoration and remains essentially ahistorical and mechanistic.[7]

The modification of state policies in the mid-1960s in West Germany produced a conscious challenge to the orthodoxy of *Stamokap* theories and an attempt to define more adequately the origins, development and structural functionality of the bourgeois state. An important contribution to the understanding of the historically varied state forms under capitalism was made by Bernhard Blanke and others with a theory of the *genetic derivation* of the independent institutions of the capitalist state.[8] While bourgeois theorists interpret the destruction of the personal union of political and economic power in feudalism and the emergence of a separate legal-political apparatus in capitalism as a victory of general interest over individual interest and the manifestation of general social liberty and equality, Blanke locates the root of the independent state apparatus in the *emergence of commodity relations*. Towards the end of feudalism the aristocratic administrations were increasingly obliged to guarantee the formal equality of agents of exchange. The feudal state's own interest as purchaser and collector of revenues coincided in part with the interests of the growing merchant class: neither wished to be cheated in their transactions. The uniformity of notions of equivalence (in coinage, weights and measures) can only be guaranteed by an *independent judicial apparatus* and it is this apparatus which constitutes the embryonic bourgeois state. By thus guaranteeing commodity-based relations of exchange, the feudal state hastens its own demise. The increasing complexity of exchange relations is mirrored by a corresponding expansion of the state (judicial) apparatus, the formal judicial neutrality of which allows the development of a political notion of general class neutrality which for bourgeois rule is a convenient illusion. However, for Blanke the formal equality of the agents of exchange before the law conceals the real inequality of social power behind the contractual arrangements. The commodity relationship, which is crucially reflected in the labour contract, *conceals the real extraction of surplus value.* More recently the contractual relationship between *unequal capitals* has been shown to conceal the real exploitation of small by big capital.[9] In both instances the state effectively secures real inequality by guaranteeing formal equality and compounds the contradiction between capital reproduction and democratic forms of political control, whose roots are in the political extension of the original economic guarantees.

This theory of the historical derivation of the bourgeois state allows a more refined view of the *structural functionality* of more recent state forms in terms of the attempted marriage of particular relations of production with an appropriate political apparatus (Perels, Blanke Poulantzas)[10] and also in terms of the increasingly critical role of the state in maintaining the equilibrium of social reproduction (Altvater, Hirsch, Abromeit, Läpple).[11] For the latter the Keynesian preoccupation with anti-cyclical interventions and the belief in the efficacy of equilibrium politics ignore both the meta-cyclical trend of growth rates in capitalist economies (which demands increasing remedial action from the state) and a variety of other state economic functions which are essential to the maintenance of stable capital and social reproduction and which also manifest increasing problems.

In particular more recent materialist theories of the state stress the growing significance of the *state infrastructure*[12] as an area of the national political economy in which private capital is unable or unwilling to operate (for reasons of economies of scale and/or viability) but which affects the external costs of private production considerably. Accordingly the state is obliged to maintain a system of subsidised transport, communications and other services and to finance almost exclusively a system of education and research, thereby channelling social wealth through taxation in order to sustain 'national capital' and its rate of profit. Above all the increasing role of the state in basic and applied scientific research indicates growing pressure on the rate of profit and on private research capacities.[13]

Of further significance is the state's function of *regulating social conflict*, notably the conflict between capital and labour: theories of the 'social state illusion' (Müller/Neusüß, Hartwich, etc.)[14] qualify both liberal and reformist/social democratic views of welfare institutions by stressing their *socially defensive origins and function*. As with welfare legislation, industrial law is seen as a minor concession to immediate needs but primarily also as a means of maintaining an inequitable structure of distribution. Social policy within capitalism leaves unresolved the inherent contradiction between general need and the sectional interest of capital. In addition to the system-immanent conflict of distribution, the dynamic of social need is affected increasingly by *demographic fluctuations* resulting from the military–economic turmoil of the 20th century. Such fluctuations cannot be neutralised without somehow colliding with the state's other functions, notably in maintaining the dynamic of capital reproduction. In addition the function of regulating social conflict is intertwined with the fundamental *loyalty of capital* and the *loyalty of the masses* without which the capitalist order cannot survive.[15]

Fundamental to this tradition of thought (refined considerably by the New Left in West Europe) is the view of a state which mirrors the contradictions of capitalist society and which is increasingly unable to master the combination of functions heaped upon it. Accordingly the expansion of the activities, the personnel and the resources of the state (in absolute and relative terms) is interpreted not as a sign of an increasing, overweaning strength of the state but as a sign of weakness and loss of autonomy: 'the more the state has to take on functions of economic management – both in the interests of "total capital" and by dint of its own need for legitimacy – the more it renders itself dependent upon the interests of individual big capitals, i.e. its co-ordinating activity will be limited, contrary to its own claims, to sanctioning their decisions and/or mitigating subsequent problems'.[16] Equally the quantitative increase in the state quota (state resources as a proportion of GNP) reflects not the emergence of a powerful state monolith dominated by a perceived monopoly interest (à la Stamokap) but rather the chaotic development of *partial state apparatuses*, each with particular (and often conflicting) policy priorities and 'class factions' to appease.[17]

The contradictory functions of various political institutions within the nation state are amplified by the increasing internationalisation of capital movements, where transnational corporations 'achieve a mobility and power' which 'critically limit the latitude' of all those governments in their field of operation.[18]

In summary the merit of the (admittedly often tortuous) reappraisal by the New Left in Germany and elsewhere of the political economy of capitalism consists in (a) its transcending both the questionable optimism of bourgeois theories of growth and equilibrium and the mechanistic Stamokap view of the state as a conscious agent of a general monopoly interest and (b) reasserting the original marxist perceptions of contradictory forces which are governed by structures within social relations (commodity relations, capital–labour relations etc.). As a result it is possible to outline the development of the national and international political economy of capitalism in dialectical terms, whereby the state as a definable separate apparatus is part of an integral system of reproduction. The crisis of the capitalist economy in Germany in the 20th century can thus be seen to have been diverted and absorbed by a series of state form crises. Nevertheless the new, more differentiated view of state functions indicates that the options available to the bourgeois state in this campaign of diversion and absorption are increasingly limited.

Notes

1. John Maynard Keynes, *General Theory of Employment Interest and Money, London 1936*, Robert Friedländer-Prechtl, *Wirtschafts-Wende: Die Ursache der Arbeitslosen-Krise und deren Bekämpfung* (Leipzig, 1931); Ernst Wagemann, *Geld-und Kreditreform* (Berlin, 1932).
2. Adolph Lowe, *Politische Ökonomik* (Frankfurt/M, 1965).
3. Fritz Scharpf, *Planung als politischer Prozeß* (Frankfurt/M, 1973).
4. Harold Laski, *Studies in the Problem of sovereignty and Other Essays* (New Haven, Conn., 1917); Leon Duguit, *L'état, le droit objectif et la loi positive* (Paris, 1901).
5. Milton Friedmann, *Essays in Positive Economics* (Chicago, 1953).
6. Christoph Butterwegge, *Probleme der marxistischen Staatstheorie* (Cologne, 1977). Butterwegge presents a detailed critique of New Left state theories before outlining Stamokap theory. See also Kurt Zieschang (one of the major Stamokap theorists in East Germany), 'Ursachen und Wesen des staatsmonopolistischen Kapitalismus' in *SOPO*, vol. 24, 1973.
7. For a detailed critique of Stamokap theories, see Margaret Wirth, *Kapitalismustheorie in der DDR* (Frankfurt/M, 1973); Rolf Ebbighausen (ed.), *Monopol und Staat: Zur Marx-Rezeption in der Theorie des staatsmonopolistischen Kapitalismus* (Frankfurt/M, 1974).
8. Bernhard Blanke, Ulrich Jürgens, Hans Kastandiek, *Kritik der Politi-*

schen Wissenschaft, 2 vols (Frankfurt/M, 1975); by the same authors, 'Zur neueren marxistischen Diskussion über die Analyse von Form und Funktion des bürgerlichen Staates', in *Politische Vierteljahresschrift Sonderheft* 6, 1975, 19–60.

9. See Joachim Perels, *Kapitalismus und politische Demokratie. Privatrechtssystem und Gesellschaftsstruktur in der Weimarer Republik*, (Frankfurt/M, 1973).

10. Perels, ibid.; Bernhard Blanke, 'Formen und Formwandel des politischen Systems in der bürgerlichen Gesellschaft' in *Handbuch 5 Staat*, ed. Volkhard Brandes *et al.* (Cologne Frankfurt/M, 1977) 121ff; Nicol Poulantzas, *Political Power and Social Classes* (London, 1973).

11. Elmar Altvater, 'Zu einigen Problemen des Staatsinterventionismus' in *Probleme des Klassenkampfs*, no. 3, 1972; Joachim Hirsch, 'Kapitalreproduktion, Klassenauseinandersetzungen und Widersprüche im Staatsapparat' in *Handbuch 5 Staat*, op. cit., 161ff; Heidrun Abromeit, 'Zum Verhältnis von Staat und Wirtschaft im gegenwärtigen Kapitalismus' in *Politische Vierteljahresschrift*, no. 1/,1976, 2ff; Dieter Läpple, 'Kapitalistische Vergesellschaftungstendenzen und Staatsinterventionismus' in *Handbuch 5 Staat*, op. cit., pp. 215ff.

12. Dieter Läpple, *Staat und allgemeine Produktionsbedingungen* (Berlin, 1973); Joachim Hirsch, *Staatsapparat und Reproduktion des Kapitals* (Frankfurt/M, 1974).

13. Joachim Hirsch, ibid., pp. 82ff.

14. Wolfgang Müller, Christel Neusüß, 'Die Sozialstaatsillusion und der Widerspruch von Lohnarbeit und Kapital' in *Probleme des Klassenkampfs, Sonderheft 1*, 7ff; Hans-Hermann Hartwich, *Sozialstaatspostulat und gesellschaftlicher Status Quo* (Cologne/Opladen 1970). See also Ian Gough, *The Political Economy of the Welfare State* (London, 1979).

15. Heidrun Abromeit, op. cit.; Ralph Miliband's work *The State in Capitalist Society* (London, 1973), produces valuable insights into the legitimising function of the ideological apparatuses of the state (161ff); in general, however, Miliband concentrates on political and economic élites and thus does not manage to present a comprehensive view of the position and function of the state in capitalist society.

16. Heidrun Abromeit, op. cit., p. 15.

17. Joachim Hirsch, *Staatsapparat* . . . , op. cit., pp. 375f; the 'particularisation' of state institutions refers both to individual ministries at the same level of government and to the different levels of government, particularly within a federal system.

18. Claudia von Braunmühl, 'Weltmarktbewegung des Kapitals. Imperialismus und Staat' in *Probleme einer materialistischen Staatstheorie*, Frankfurt/M, 1973, p. 89; viz also Werner Olle, Wolfgang Schoeller, 'Weltmarkt, nationale Kapitalreproduktion und Rolle des Nationalstaats', in *Handbuch 5 Staat*, op. cit., pp. 372ff.

2 The Political Economy of Germany, 1918–49 and the Formation of the West German State

It is self-evident that the first half of the 20th century determined the political economy of West Germany drastically. Two world wars resulted in the loss of millions of lives, of land and raw materials in Europe and overseas and of vast amounts of capital through military expenditure, war damage and reparations. If one adds the inflationary and recessionary crises of the Weimar Republic, Germany was exposed to four extended periods of economic instability (1914–18), (1919–23), 1929–34 and 1940–45, which together can be seen to have thrown back social and economic development significantly. Even

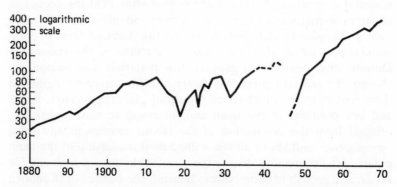

Fig. 2.1   The growth of industrial production, 1880–1970 (1936 = 100)

Source: Petzina, *et al.*, *Sozialgeschichtliches Arbeitsbuch III* (Munich, 1978).

allowing for lower rates of growth before 1913, the growth trend for net industrial production suggested irregular but constant growth for the period beyond. (See Figure 2.1) However, it was 1928 before the previous peak of 1913 was reached again, and this recovery was in turn very short-lived, with the world depression hitting Germany at the end of 1929. Measured against a putative uninterrupted trend from 1913 or against the real trade cycles of the 1920s, the recovery in the 1930s and early 1940s is not as dramatic as the legends of the Nazi economy would have us believe. As is known, it was a recovery based on rearmament and neglectful of consumer goods production; this meant that a good proportion of the industrial values produced were used to destroy other values and were destroyed themselves, and that behind the price controls strong inflationary pressures built up through state indebtedness and increased money circulation.

The instability and discontinuity of governmental institutions had up to 1933 tended to strengthen the power of capital and of executive institutions of the state – bureaucracy, judiciary and military – within which allegiance to the democratic republic was minimal. Cartelisation, monopolisation and the centralisation of pressure groups along with the traditional close integration of banking and industrial capital produced an economy dominated by a remarkably small oligarchy, which in the main also found democratic institutions both irritating and unnecessary for its purposes. The role of capital in undermining Weimar democracy and encouraging a series of authoritarian regimes is well documented.[1] It is no surprise that after 1933 the economic oligarchy strengthened its position of power and influence in German society. Mandatory cartelisation became the standard form of commercial practice in the new 'organic structure of the economy'. Despite strict controls on exports, raw materials and foreign exchange, the central figures of industry and commerce strengthened their control over branch-based industrial planning, occupied new and key positions in the main and intermediate state apparatus, profited from the destruction of the labour movement and from 'aryanisation' and above all maintained their ownership of the main pillars of the economy – despite the socialist rhetoric of rank and file Nazis, and growth of state power. Beneath the banner of 'Kanonen statt Butter' (guns before butter), the industrial structure shifted heavily towards the production of capital goods and brought about a corresponding shift in the distribution of wealth away from the working class and petit bourgeoisie to the bourgeoisie.

Industrial capacity in specific branches was expanded markedly: special steels, petrochemicals, the electro-technical industry, shipbuilding and aircraft manufacture. Much of this additional capacity

Table 2.1   Proportion of individual social classes as a percentage of the total population in Germany, 1925–39

	1925	1933	1939
Self-employed	20.9	19.8	16.2
Ancillary (within family)	9.8	9.6	9.8
Salaried employees	19.1	18.5	20.4
Manual workers	50.2	52.1	53.6

Source: C. Bettelheim, *L'économie allemande sous le nazisme.*

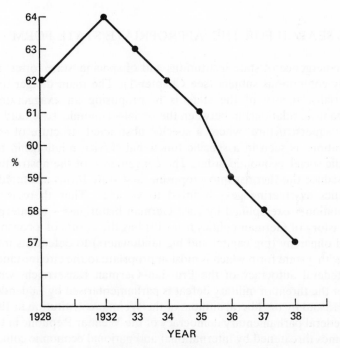

Fig. 2.2   Wages quota, 1928–38 (wages and salaries as a percentage of national income)

Source: Hennig, E. *Thesen zur deutschen Sozial- und Wirtschaftsgeschichte* (Frankfurt, 1973)

survived the war, in particular in the industrial heartlands of the Ruhr and other West German conurbations.

It is thus possible to assert that the Weimar Republic and fascism reinforced both the capital goods bias of the German economy and the command structures of its industrial oligarchy. In addition 'national socialism' accelerated the centralisation of production and the demise of the artisan, and rationalised the economic infrastructure by creating a national electricity grid and a functional road–rail network. Thirty years of German imperialism, in the two guises of 'aristocratic' and 'technocratic' butchery, bequeathed Germany and Europe a tragic mess, but a mess with a very distinct and different shape to the 'order' prior to the First World War and also reflecting a violent process of political experimentation.

THE SEARCH FOR THE 'APPROPRIATE STATE FORM'

The emergence of state institutions and of specific 'state forms' is a highly contentious subject (see Chapter 1). The main danger for a materialist theory of the state is in proposing an exaggeratedly mechanistic relationship between the social–economic 'base' and the state 'superstructure' where a specific abstracted structure of state institutions is seen in a specific functional service relationship to a specific social–economic order. The convenience of the abstractions can seduce the theorist into proposing that state forms are fitted to societies as steering gear is fitted to vehicles. Thus there is the temptation – exemplified by East German historians[2] – to interpret the history of German politics from 1914 as the efforts of a conspiratorial oligarchy (big capital and big landowners) to defend its interests with a state form which is most appropriate to the circumstances; the federal autocracy of the Prussian–German Kaiserreich, which under the threat of military defeat is parliamentarised by Ludendorff in 1918 and by the liberal authors of the Weimar constitution in 1919; the federal parliamentary democracy of the Weimar Republic in turn becomes threatened by international and national economic collapse and social chaos and has to be replaced by a centralised autocracy with a nationalist mass base (fascism) in 1933, and when this fails in 1945, the same oligarchy reverts desperately to (federal) parliamentary democracy in the form of the West German state. This scenario which concentrates on an identifiable group of German 'imperialists' reinforces the hitherto traditional view of history as the product of great actors in an historical drama and makes the sphere of politics look rather like a gents' outfitters.

This model of a conscious, coherent class conservatism is unsatis-factory, inasmuch as it reduces social history to a limited set of determinants and reduces the state to a separate, instrumental and exchangeable phenomenon. However it does draw attention to the puzzle of 20th century German history, namely the *contrast between the extreme discontinuity of the form of government and the relative continuity of the socio-economic order*: German capitalism has sur-vived, but in less than forty years has 'tried on' four different state forms. The determinants of political change have been more varied, the causal relations more complex than the vulgar-Marxist model, but the inherent problem of maintaining and legitimating capitalism is exposed as primary – and rightly so. Furthermore, even though the model of a conspiratorial oligarchy is badly flawed, it is given some plausibility by the exceptionally centralised decision making struc-tures within German capitalism. There clearly was an oligarchy of propertied interests – albeit split into sub-groups; deriving in part from the system of universal banking, the articulation of German capital interests was far less diffuse than, say, that of British or French capital; the command structures of the economy were nar-rowly enough based to allow conspiratorial behaviour, evident above all in the winter of 1932/33. However the success of conservative German politics must also be explained in terms of anonymous economic forces at home and abroad, in terms of the ignorance of rival political groups, inaction, non-decisions, and not least in terms of the failure of radical politics.

The Weimar Republic represented the first departure from auto-cratic rule in the whole of German history and can indeed be seen as an attempt to reconcile capitalism with democracy, a process which the Kaiserreich had attempted to frustrate. But as an 'improvised' democracy (*Eschenburg*), it bore the marks of a hastily constructed form of government which owed as much to the *opportunism of anti-democratic forces* as to the good will of the social–liberal alliance which made up the republican bloc; parliamentary democracy was as much the child of the pre-emptive counter-revolution of Ludendorff, as of the November uprisings. Within the constellation of social forces in Germany, democracy was in fact the real 'foreign body' and not the bureaucracy or the military or big business.[3] Apart from the demise of direct aristocratic rule and the establishment of elected national and regional parliaments and governments, the strands of continuity between the two periods were intact: the civil service, judiciary police, the teaching profession, the military, and the diplomatic corps remained as intact as the relations of production and the class structure. By June 1920 even the national parliament (the Reichstag) had lost its republican majority and was never to regain it. Significantly, however, it had been the petty bourgeoisie and not the industrial bourgeoisie that had briefly joined the working class in the promotion of democracy. Big business and big agriculture hardly took democracy seriously. The constitution(s) and the statutes passed by the various legislative assemblies, although amenable to capital and ambivalent enough to be manipulated by and for capital, became an increasing irritant to the representatives of capital (along with the negative results of defeat, the Versailles Treaty and economic instability). The German bourgeoisie had hitherto been used to low taxation, low wage costs, powerless trade unions and camarilla politics, and was thus unwilling to accept the irksome consequences of parliamentary democracy: trade union recognition, workers' participation in private and state bodies, state arbitration, higher levels of social security payments, eight-hour day, cartel legislation, etc.

More importantly the *new democratic state was unable to create and maintain stable conditions for the reproduction of capital*. Disregarding the invidious international position of the German state, its economic policies were consistently destabilising in their nature and effects:

1. deliberate inflation, based on a reckless monetary policy of unlimited, cheap discounting;
2. the 'borrowed boom' from 1924–29, based on short-term Americans loans and increased labour exploitation; and
3. a policy of deflation from 1930–32 which compounded the global recession pro-cyclically rather than alleviate it anti-cyclically.

As a result the democratic state form failed to fulfil two of its main functions: maintain mass loyalty as well as the loyalty of capital and mediate the social conflict arising from the contradiction between labour and capital; the state was powerless to prevent the radicalisation of the working class, the bourgeoisie and above all the petty bourgeoisie.

The failure of the 'normative power' of the state paralleled and reinforced the contradictions between the demands of liberal democracy and the interests of monopoly capital. The guarantee of contractual freedom and equality, while appropriate to the optimal functioning of a market based on small capital, becomes increasingly dysfunctional when the national economy is dominated by monopolies, oligopolies, cartels, syndicates and centralised pressure groups. This was the situation in Germany in 1918. Thus the German state, despite token attempts to regulate cartels in November 1923, *reinforced the power of monopolised capital merely guaranteeing the rights of property and the formal equality of contractual partners in a situation where the contractual terms between big firm and small supplier/customer were dictated by the big firm or syndicate*.[4] The level of economic concentration and centralisation increased dramatically throughout the Weimar period, contributing both to the radicalisation of the increasingly subordinated petty bourgeoisie and to the perception within bourgeois circles in general of the powerlessness and hence dispensability of democratic state forms.

Given the general disloyalty, indifference or antipathy of the ruling oligarchy in Germany to democracy, and given its relative strength and cohesion, it is *possible* to see the series of presidential cabinets from 1930 to 1933 as conscious attempts to establish a state form which was appropriate to the needs of the ruling élites, but which could also achieve some degree of mass loyalty. Brüning's cabinet failed both to stem the recession and to achieve any mass support and in the eyes of many conservatives became suspiciously 'bolshevist' in its plans for agrarian reform; Papen failed because his 'cabinet of barons' was hopelessly isolated from all but the very rich and was unable to woo a militant and uncompromising Nazi party; Schleicher, finally, failed because his brand of corporatist politics was regarded as poison by the big landowners and heavy industrialists ('Schleicher's bolshevist plan').

The 'solution' of the state form crisis in the shape of, firstly, a coalition cabinet under Hitler and subsequently a fascist one-party state, can be seen as part of this process of desperate experimentation managed through the President, Von Hindenburg. Judged according to the yardsticks of either materialist theories of the state or bourgeois criteria of economic policy success, the fascist state seemed initially to fulfil its 'function' very satisfactorily. The market economists' dream of the 'magic square' – economic growth, low inflation, high employment and healthy balance of payments – was ostensibly achieved by 1936; equally the marxist roster of state functions under capitalism – guaranteeing property rights, maintaining economic growth, the infrastructure, the loyalty of the masses and of capital, and mediating social conflict – was fulfilled, albeit with extreme means. For a short time Germany presented the image of economic stability, civic pride and resolute nationalism – manifested by full

employment, public works and the 1936 Olympiad – for which the
state form of centralised repressive dictatorship managed to claim
credit. Even into the late war years the state, with its monopoly of
information, continued successfully to conceal the major contradictions of German class society as well as the impossibility of a long-
term stable fascist state (of a 'thousand year Reich'). The strategems
of a nation in uniform, conscious political indoctrination, of the
'enemy within', of 'world conspiracies', of cheap holidays and perks
for the party faithful, were however incapable of sustaining mass
loyalty ad infinitum: by 1938 the domestic state debt was so vast that
it could only be reduced by war and plunder; the industrial structure,
with its increased emphasis on capital goods and armaments, could
only be maintained by war and the optimal utilisation of armaments
capacity which this demands; the living standards of the masses could
only be improved by annexation and pillage.

Fascism as a state form became rapidly dysfunctional. It finally
proved even more disastrous than the imperialism of the Kaiserreich,
whose adventures it attempted to repeat. German capitalism seemed
to be doomed to a long-term state-form crisis, assuming it could
survive at all. It is significant however that the state form crisis
derives both from the general and particular contradictions in the
historical development of German capitalism, in which the state form
itself has been an important determinant factor. The German economy shared the general characteristics of changing capitalism: increasing concentration, increasing capital intensity, internationalisation and capital export, falling rates of profit, etc.; it also grew under
very special circumstances: the German industrial economy developed late and under the defensive control of a resilient aristrocracy.
In the sphere of circulation the pre-unification states and later the
Reich imposed severe restrictions on banking, joint-stock companies
and trade, with the result that the capital market was far less developed than in Britain, for example, with its extremely versatile equity
market. When share-capital eventually expanded as a form of investment, it was not the stock exchange which mediated between investor
and enterprise but the increasingly powerful universal banks, centred
in Berlin (the Deutsche Bank, Dresdner Bank, Disconto-Gesell-
schaft, Darmstädter Bank, Berliner Handelsgesellschaft, National-
bank). These in turn developed uniquely close ties with industrial
firms in a formidable alliance which asserted itself aggressively in both
domestic and foreign trading against foreign competition, the state
(with its partiality for agriculture), the working class and small capital.

The state, as a defender of both aristocratic landowning interests and of a nascent industrial capitalism, developed a strongly bureaucratic form of class politics, which involved state enterprises, protectionism, support for cartels, increasing arms expenditure, trade diplomacy, diversionary ('social') imperialism, police surveillance, repressive legislation, social insurance schemes and more.

However the aristocratic regime's attempts to reconcile its landed interests with the interests of a new industrial elite and hold back the working class, tended to reinforce the class contradictions, calling for more intensive and ultimately self-destructive measures to conserve an obsolete status quo. But, while destroying itself in the First World War, the Kaiserreich bequeathed a political economy dominated by monopolistic forms of control (in banking, heavy industry and the electrical and chemical industries) and characterised by a bureaucratic, autocratic political tradition, whose efficiency and convenience was threatened by democratic participation and consultation. Weimar democracy was thus an interlude which failed to weaken the power of German social elites. However, in contrast to Britain and France, the advantages of parliamentary democracy in achieving mass loyalty were ignored, the Weimar facade was brushed aside to make way for another form of autocracy, this time more modern and ruthless. Fascism in turn strengthened monopolism, shifted the industrial structure further towards capital goods and away from consumer goods production; and, while failing in a dramatic and messy way, it bequeathed a political economy which was ostensibly unable to find an appropriate stable state form. The victorious allies were thus confronted with a perplexing combination of historical contradictions, for which there was little chance of a mutually agreed diagnosis or consequently of a jointly agreed solution.

THE COLLAPSE OF THE NAZI STATE AND THE SUSPENSION OF SOVEREIGNTY

If one postulates a normally organic relationship between the economic base and the superstructure of the state, then it is clear that the interregnum in Germany between 1945 and 1949 was both unusual and problematic. The institutions and authority of the German state had slowly disappeared behind the advancing Allied fronts from the end of October 1944. After May 1945 there was no German state. All authority passed to the occupying military powers. For four years the control of all major levels of administration, judiciary, police, trade, transport and industrial production lay in the hands of the separate military administrations in the British, French, American and Soviet zones.

The breaking of the organic connection between state and economy and the regime of total occupation have important implications for the subsequent shaping of the political economy of both East and West Germany. The temporary state bodies supplied by the victors no longer articulated the interests of Germany's social elites, let alone the interests of the German people, but represented rather the perceived interests of the Allied governments. The primary and common interest of all four allies was to destroy the political and economic potential of the German state to wage war. Thus the power to modify state institutions to the needs of economic interests and historical circumstance was wrested from the economic and political élites that had guided Germany through 1914, 1918/19, 1930–33 and beyond. Thereby, however, the solution of Germany's long-standing state-form crisis was thrust onto an unwilling and often indifferent set of military administrations.

Bereft of direct political power and influence, what was left of social power (or potential social power) was located in the ownership of productive property. Next to the problem of a future state form for Germany the question of the ownership of the main pillars of the German economy therefore became a fundamental problem of allied occupational policy. The diagnoses and solutions for both problems (which were eventually adopted) were major factors determining the final partitioning of Germany and the shape of the political economies in East and West.

THE 'ANTI-HITLER'-COALITION BEFORE AND AFTER 1945; ALLIED DIVISIONS AND THE DIVISION OF GERMANY

The alliance between Britain, the United States and Russia from 1941 onwards has been described correctly as a 'consensus of antagonistic powers'.[5] The smiling unanimity of Roosevelt, Stalin and Churchill in Casablanca, Moscow, Tehran and Yalta concealed the problematic nature of their relationship and the problems of a joint policy after victory. The alliance against Nazi Germany was a negative coalition in a very real sense, in that its only real common aim was the defeat of expansionist German imperialism. Prior to the

German attack on Russia relations between the later Allies had been extremely unfriendly. Western appeasement had in part been informed by a willingness to allow eastward expansion of the Third Reich, in the belief that Germany could provide a 'bulwark against Bolshevism'.[6] The Hitler–Stalin pact of August 1939 was a rude awakening for those who had negotiated away Czech sovereignty; conversely it manifested Russian indifference to the inevitable blood-letting in Western Europe, strengthening their hope that fascism – as the 'last stage of capitalism' – would accelerate the demise of the class enemy.

Even after June 1941 and the transformation of Soviet Russia from enemy to courageous ally, the triple alliance was little more than mutual opportunism, within which the East–West conflict persisted as a determinant factor of respective policies. The famous remark of Senator (later President) Truman spoke volumes for the cynicism of many in the American leadership: 'If we see that Germany is winning the war, we ought to help Russia, and if Russia is winning the war we ought to help Germany, and in that way let them kill as many as possible'.[7] Stalin's bitterness over the absence of a second front fostered a suspicion that the West was indeed allowing Germany and Russia to weaken each other in order to spare itself the economic and human costs of war. The eventual Normandy landings in June 1944 have in turn been interpreted as a reaction to the advance of the Soviet Army all along the Eastern front and the possibility of Russia liberating the rest of Europe single-handed. If one compares the human losses suffered by the respective allies the differences in war effort become very apparent. Russia lost some 20 600 000 dead, Britain – 326 000 and the USA 259 000. The damage to the Russian economy – with 1710 towns and 70 000 villages destroyed – was far greater than all the other European states, including Germany, put together.

Given the enduring antagonism of capitalist West and socialist East, and given the evident differences in the contribution of the individual allies to the defeat of German fascism, it was inevitable that the qualified unanimity of the three nations would be exhausted once they had achieved their common goal, and that their differences would (once again) dominate their policies both towards Germany and towards each other.

The divisions within the victorious alliance were not limited to the East–West antagonism. New tensions manifested themselves within the western camp, especially after the inclusion of France as an occupation power, tensions relating to a variety of aspects of occupation policy: reparations, denazification, industrial policy, the geographical shape and the state form of the future Germany (see below). In turn each occupation power suffered from strong differences of priority between the military administration in Germany, with its code of pragmatic expediency, and the respective civilian authorities at home who were perhaps more concerned with the realisation of the more abstract political goals of Tehran, Jalta and Potsdam – notably denazification and reparations. Increasingly there were also conflicts within the civilian authorities between those, like Morgenthau, with political priorities – punishment, restitution and economic subordination – and others in the State Department who recognised the primacy of domestic economic interests and the central role of a revitalised German economy in serving those interests. The triumph of American economic interests over the mixed interests of Britain, France and Russia was a major factor in determining the later shape of the political economy of West Germany; it reinforced the general view of the primacy of the economic within capitalism and demonstrated the strategic economic and military weakness of the other three allies.

Resolutions and National Interests – the Growing Contradictions of Allied Policies

The conferences of Casablanca (January 1943), Moscow (October 1943) and Tehran (November/December 1943) were dominated by the strategic problems of defeating Nazi Germany and preventing a resurgence of military expansionism. Apart from agreeing to pursue the unconditional capitulation of the German state there was a consensus view of the need to partition defeated Germany and to demilitarise its economy. Stalin and Roosevelt expressed a clear preference for a drastic separation of Germany (excluding Austria and the annexed territories) and the internationalisation of the North Sea ports, the Ruhr and the Saarland. Churchill preferred a less drastic division, allowing a confederation of South German states, in order, above all, to weaken Prussia.

The subsequent plan developed by Henry Morgenthau – the American Secretary of State – presented a further variation of geographical partition with the new element of a drastic de-industrialisation of the 'heart of Germany's industrial power', the

Ruhr and the North-West ports. Roosevelt's qualified acceptance of the 'Morgenthau Plan', if short-lived, reflected the peak of success for those American policy proposals which took abstract political perspectives as their point of departure – the destruction and punishment of Nazi Germany. The fact that, within days of the Quebec agreement between Roosevelt and Churchill on the basis of the Morgenthau Plan, 'both men began to beat a rapid retreat',[8] indicates the confusion within the western camp about the best way of eradicating fascism, and their ignorance of the negative effects of the destruction of a key world economy for the victorious capitalist powers. A number of groups, including state department officials, already recognized the potentially dysfunctional effects of partition and de-industrialisation,[9] but these did not assert themselves fully until late 1946 and 1947. Both the Yalta and Potsdam agreements thus retained the commitment to repressive economic and political controls.

Roosevelt and Morgenthau seem to have been influenced by an emotional, moral commitment to punish Germany which corresponded to Russian indifference to the economic future of Germany and their (justifiable) desire for considerable reparations. Russia's well-documented insulation from world trade and the vagaries of the world market made the economic survival of Germany and the rest of capitalist Europe a trifling concern compared to the restoration of a devastated Russian economy. On the other hand the interdependence of the western capitalist nations and, above all, the dependence of American post-war growth on a healthy world market for goods and capital made the Western leaders increasingly aware of the ill-considered, if unanimous, earlier agreements.

The joint communiqué after the Yalta conference (11 February 1945) contained nothing about plans for a permanent partition of Germany but some detail about the establishment of zones of occupation, including a possible French zone and general details concerning reparations. The minutes to the conference reveal that there was again agreement about the general principle of partition but disagreement between the British delegation and the other two (the USA and the USSR) about the degree of divisions. A separate minute on reparations mentioned a fixed amount of $20 billion and a 50 per cent share for the Russians; however the specific recommendation of such details was left to a Reparations Commission which would convene in Moscow.[10]

Although the partition agreements (of Tehran) were still officially valid, the British Chancellor of the Exchequer, Anderson, in a memorandum from 7 March 1945, insisted that the plan to divide up Germany was exclusively Russian in origin.[11] This fundamentally dishonest claim allowed Anderson to develop a new polarity between British good sense and Russian unreason. Using the experiences of the Allied occupation of Italy, Anderson concluded that partition would both prevent a satisfactory solution to the reparations problem and force Britain to pay for the survival of a weakened, dislocated Germany and hence indirectly pay for Britain's own share of German reparations. Anderson's recommendation was thus the abandonment of the partition plan, as a means of securing adequate reparations, with the rider that in the event of an independent Russian occupation policy a 'united West Germany' should be created 'which can be integrated into the general economy of West European countries, as part of an overall strategy to rebuild the European economy'.[12]

However, the official policy of the USA remained punitive. Directive 1067 of the Joint Chiefs of Staff (26 April 1945) specified 'that no steps are to be taken which a) could lead to the economic recovery of Germany or b) would be suitable for the maintenance or the strengthening of the German economy'.[13]

Contrary to Anderson's claims it was Stalin who was the first to officially retreat from plans to divide Germany into separate states (in a radio broadcast on 9 May 1945).[14] He confirmed this in meetings with the US special envoy, Hopkins, in Moscow (26–28 May), stressing Russian approval only for the revision of German boundaries in the West and East in contrast to British and American partition plans. The well-documented animosity between the Churchill government and the Russian leadership emphasised the increasing differences between perceived national interests, and were not dispelled by the Labour victory in July 1945 or the run-up to the Potsdam Conference.

Potsdam was the only peacetime summit of the three major Allies. Even though agreement was reached on the general principles of occupation policy – the four D's: democratisation, demilitarisation denazification and dismantling (reparations) – the methods for achieving these goals remained significantly unresolved. Reparations were to be taken primarily from the respective zones of occupation, although the Russians were accorded the right to extract 15 per cent of their reparations from the Western zones, in exchange for deliveries of foodstuffs, and a further 10 per cent without reciprocation. However such percentages were virtually useless in the absence of an agreed total sum of reparations. Despite Russian demands for a confirmation of the $20 billion proposed in Yalta, Edwin Pauley, the US representative in the Reparations Commission, refused every attempt to fix a specific amount.[15] No decision was made on the possible partition of Germany. The Control Commission (the joint allied supervisory body) was given the task of determining a plan for dismantling German industry and for reducing industrial capacity.

The Potsdam agreements were a recipe for confusion and further dissent, as the subsequent months revealed. Lucius Clay, deputy military commander of the US occupation zone, saw in the Potsdam Accords a mandate to rebuild the German economy,[16] whereas the First Industrial Plan of March 1946 imposed controls on production and a dismantling scheme which 'would have reduced Germany to a condition which the Morgenthau-Group had found desirable':[17] all military-related production was to be abandoned, the production of ball-bearings, tapered and ordinary roller-bearings, machine tools, tractors, rubber, petrol, oil and ammonia banned; the overall capacity of German industry was to be reduced to 67 per cent of that of 1938.

Above all, the reparations question rapidly became the main issue of dissent between the Russians on the one hand and the USA as the increasingly dominant exponent of a 'western line' on the other. The predicted economic/financial burden of military occupation[18] became rapidly apparent: in 1946 the US and British governments were forced to organise food imports at their own expense in order to maintain a dangerously low level of nutrition among the population (roughly half accepted levels of viability). Added to this the abrupt reduction of military production in the USA, as well as Britain, threatened to produce both a slump and an inflationary capital surplus in the United States. Consequently, in view of the relative unimportance of reparations to the USA – spared from the physical ravages to war – there was a gradual shift away from the primacy of punishment and restitution of losses to a new primacy of national economic interests within the international economy.

In view of the Russians' massive war losses, the sum demanded of $10 billion was hardly excessive, although it was perceived as of vital importance to the rebuilding of the Russian national economy. American insistence on the use of the respective zones as source of reparations and their refusal to consider reparations in detail with fixed sums, was perceived as a clear snub of a country that had borne the greatest burden in defeating Germany. More galling to the

Russians perhaps was the apparent preference given to German post-war needs over Russian reparations claims. The attitude of the British and American authorities towards German *balance of payments problems* was highly contradictory. It presupposed an improvement in general economic conditions in order to sustain necessary imports from German funds, but denied the Germans the means of achieving that improvement, by imposing severe production quotas in the First Industry Plan. Russia proposed a rise in the production quotas and the increased use of current production as a source of reparations in contrast to dismantling.[19] The Americans claimed that the confiscation of goods as opposed to means of production was in contravention of the Potsdam Accords,[20] although no such interpretation can be made of the text of the Potsdam communiqué, while the Yalta conference specifically allowed such confiscations. The dismantling of whole factories or factory plant proved a very unsatisfactory source of reparations. Both the British and the Russians recognised that the dismantled plant often had no productive value but only scrap value. Consequently the use of current production was more lucrative to the occupying power and far less damaging to the German economy, a fact born out by the better levels of industrial production in the Soviet zone in the first year after the end of the war compared to the situation in the Western zones. However after Lucius Clay's abrupt decision to end reparations deliveries to the Eastern zone in May 1946, the Russian authorities had no alternative but to plunder their zone of occupation more intensively, reversing their initial economic and political successes and badly handicapping the East German economy.

The subsequent establishment of the Bi-Zone by the British and American zonal authorities was extolled as the triumph of reason and conciliation over unreason and revenge, but was little more than the coincidence of self-interest with the short-term interests of West Germans in sustaining economic production and supplies of basic foodstuffs. The luck of the Western allies in having borne a far smaller proportion of the war effort and the need to avoid a post-war slump and post-war inflation could be sold as the virtue of liberalism selflessly restoring a vanquished enemy. However the chaos of Western planning and the changing priorities of British and, above all, American national economic interests reveal a position more of cynical opportunism than of moral good will.

Economic Conditions in the Western Zones, 1945–48

The economic history of the immediate post-war years in the western zones is still a subject of controversy. For a long time West German academic views of the post-war period remained ideologically flawed, reinforcing popular views of a unique West German achievement in rebuilding the economy from nothing – the double myth of the *Stunde Null* and the *Wirtschaftswunder* – and only more recently have more differentiated analyses attempted to confront these myths.

Much of the controversy is centred around the material and structural preconditions for economic recovery in the Western zones. The expression *Stunde Null* implies at the least the destruction of the greater part of productive capital assets,[21] but logically would also imply a drastic reduction in the quality of human resources. The most cursory glance demonstrates that neither implication applied. Although the economic preconditions were by no means optimal, they came nowhere near the irremediable condition implied by the mythology of miracles. If one examines major categories influencing economic progress a more realistic and differentiated picture emerges.

1. The immediate *factors of production* were clearly affected by war and by defeat. The general level of fixed capital (productive potential) was reduced by wartime bombing, land operations and by post-war dismantling and plunder in all four zones. However the degree of capacity losses is the subject of some disagreement. Apart from the *tabula rasa* views there a good number of authors who state global figures of 20 per cent or more for capacity losses through war damage for the Western zones.[22] Werner Abelshauser, on the other hand, estimates a global figure of 17.4 per cent of 1936 capacity, but qualifies this significantly by pointing out the high level of investment between 1936 and 1945 (equivalent to 75.3 per cent of 1936 capacity), so that even after total accumulated depreciation of 37.2 per cent is taken into consideration, gross fixed assets were still over 20 per cent higher in 1945 than in 1936. Furthermore he relativises the level of destruction by quoting American Bombing Survey figures which stated that in 1944 only 10 per cent of the damaged plant was irreparable, and by pointing out the low level of damage to the vital coal and steel industries.[23]

Similarly global figures for post-war losses through reparations range from 12 per cent (of 1939 capacity)[24] to 6.6 per cent of 1936 capacity[25] with a variety of estimates in between. The most reliable figures (in Baade, Harmssen and Abelshauser) set the level of reparations losses far lower than the upper estimates. Thus a realistic assessment of both war and reparations losses still allows a net gain in industrial capacity by 1948 of over 10 per cent over 1936 (See Table 2.2).

Table 2.2   Gross industrial fixed assets in the Western zones, 1936–48
(1936=100)

(1936 = 100)	per cent
Gross investments (in real terms), 1936–45 as a percentage of gross assets, 1936	+75.3%
Depreciation (in real terms), 1936–45 as a percentage of gross assets, 1936	−37.2
Capacity losses as a result of war damage as a percentage of gross assets, 1936	−17.4
Gross industrial assets, 1945	120.6
Gross investments (in real terms), 1946–48 as a percentage of gross assets, 1936	+8.7
Depreciation (in real terms) 1946–48 as a percentage of gross assets, 1936	−11.5
Restitution (in real terms), 1945–48 (per cent of 1936)	−2.4
Dismantling losses (in real terms, 1945–48 (per cent of 1936)	−4.4
Gross industrial fixed assets, 1948	111.1

Source: W Abelshauser, *Wirtschaftsgeschichte der Bundesrepublik Deutschland 1945–1980*, p. 20.

The very low level of investments after 1945 indicates both the virtual non-existence of a capital market between 1945 and 1948 and the uncertainty over the present and future latitude for expansion. Overall however West Germany inherited a 'remarkably large and modern capital stock' from the war[26] – modern in terms of both technological refinement and the age structure of the plant.

The position of labour – as the vital factor of production – was overall not unfavourable. The sudden influx of Germans from the confiscated territories and increasingly from the Russian zone was by no means equally distributed regionally,[27] and initially it represented a net burden to both the Allied and German (local) administrations.

Nevertheless the age structure and the levels of skills of the potential working population became more favourable and because the supply of labour far exceeded the demand for it, wage and thus production costs could be reduced and the surplus labour force slowly absorbed into existing capacity.

Nevertheless the 'productive potential' of labour was significantly reduced agricultural land, animal stock, fodder, fertilizer and seed, West German farmers were only able to achieve production levels of some 72 per cent of 1936 levels in 1947 and 1948;[28] as a result the Western allies were forced to import foodstuffs into their zones and in the case of Britain to maintain rationing at home. Despite this the productivity of German coal-miners slumped, which both handicapped industrial production and hit the living standards of the working population still further, especially in the miserable winter 1946/47. In the short term the situation of the working population was poor; potentially, however, labour was plentiful and enjoyed a relatively high level of qualification and skill.

Raw materials, the third major factor of production, were in very short supply for both industry and agriculture. Low domestic productivity coupled with the almost total absence of foreign assets or currency and gold reserves, as a means of financing imports and a badly damaged transport system affected production more severely than the disadvantages relating to either fixed capital or 'human capital'. Even when coal could be produced in reasonable quantities – in the winter of 1946/47 – the collapse of the transport system prevented supplies reaching corporate or household customers.

2. The second major category determining the pre-conditions for growth, the *infrastructure*, thus showed real weaknesses. The *transport system* was more severely affected by bombing than industry during the war. The railways suffered from a bad shortage of rolling stock and intact stretches of line, which meant that effective transport was limited to local services for the first few post-war years. The *circulation process* was further hindered by a currency which lost its convertibility on the foreign exchanges and was rapidly losing its value and its usefulness domestically. The massive expansion of the *money supply* to sustain the war was controlled by low consumption and price controls (which continued under the Allies), but in the absence of price-controlled goods after May 1945, the black market dominated the budgets of private households and indicated the real effects of the sudden end of an armaments' economy.

Monetary inflation was fuelled further by *a higher rate of money*

Table 2.3   Prices of selected basic commodities, 1938–47

| | Official prices | | Black market | |
	1938 RM	Nov. 1945 RM	Apr. 1947 RM	(British zone)
1500g Rye bread	−.47	−.52	25.0 (approx)	
500g Wheat flour	−.22	−.23	30.0 (approx)	
500g Sugar	−.38	−.44	70.0–90.0	
500g Butter	1.57	1.80	240.0–250.0	
500g Beef	−.83	−.87	60.0–80.0	
500g Pork	−.82	−.92		
5kg Potatoes	−.44	−.56		
1 Egg	−.12	−.12	15–20 (Berlin)	
1 Pair men's shoes		16.00	750.0	
1 Man's suit		75.00	1000.0	
1 Ladies' dress		31.90	800.0	

Source: Grebing *et al.*, *Die Nachkriegsentwicklung in Westdeutschland 1945–1949*, vol. I (Stuttgart, 1980) p. 38.

circulation and by the introduction of an *Allied Mark*[29] (ostensibly a means of controlling inflation) but after the money supply had increased by some 12 billion marks between May 1945 and early 1946 the Allies issued no more and allowed both the destruction of the Reichsmark as a serious official currency and the dominance of the American cigarette as means of exchange. Money savings lost their value slowly (as in the Weimar inflation) and *banks* were no longer able to fulfil their central function of mobilising investment capital.

3. Property relations in the Western zones are a further category for assessing the preconditions for subsequent economic development. The ownership and control of productive property had undergone a slow process of concentration through the twenties and particularly through the period of Nazi rule. The Potsdam agreements included the pledge to deconcentrate monopolised sectors of the economy (banks, heavy and chemical industry, etc.)[30] but this pledge was pursued in quite different ways in the Russian and the Western zones. Whereas the Russian military administration spread landownership far wider through the expropriation of big landowners and redistribution to small farmers and confiscated the industrial and commercial property of Nazi businessmen, Western land reform plans were gradually abandoned by the other occupation powers, and the control of the big banks, the chemical giant IG Farben and of heavy industrial firms was merely suspended and placed under Allied trus-

teeship. Apart from the restitution of some property to a few of the victims of the Third Reich, there was virtually no redistribution at all in the Western zones. The temporary suspension of proprietorial control proved to be a farce (see below Chapter 3). However the natural process of inflation effected *a slow shift of wealth distribution in favour of the owners of material assets*, which was compounded still further by the currency reform of June 1948, where old savings in Reichsmark were converted by a ratio of 10:1, whereas the debts of industrial, commercial and agricultural enterprises were reduced by the same ratio. The policies of the Western allies thus reinforced the power potential of the traditional economic elite and partly determined the future shape of productive relations. The situation on the labour market meanwhile brought a further shift in the distribution of income to the disadvantage of poorer households:

Table 2.4   Income distribution, 1928 and 1950

Per cent of income earners	Per cent of income	
	1928	*1950*
0–50	23.2	16 .0
50–90	39.6	48.3
90–95	10.0	8.7
95–98	9.5	9.2
98–99	4.8	3.2
99–100	12.6	14.6

Source: Huster *et al.*, *Determinanten der Westdeutschen Restauration*, op. cit., p. 102.

Thus it is fair to say that the distribution of productive and private wealth and of income created favourable conditions for those large enterprises which could rely on export sales and not so much on domestic consumption.

4. The creation of separate zones of occupation and the ultimate partition of Germany created special structural problems for the economies of both East and West Germany. The respective *branch structures* of each economy displayed serious disproportions – the abrupt destruction of a unitary economy with a very rational regional division of labour left East Germany with a highly developed manufacturing sector but no ready source of raw materials, fuel and heavy machinery and left West Germany with a huge primary industrial

sector, whose capacity far exceeded the domestic consumption of the new zone and the foreseeable foreign demand. However, the regional distribution was less critical in the West than in the East where industry was concentrated almost wholly in the South and in Berlin, with Mecklenburg and Pommern enjoying few of the infrastructural and social advantages of an industrial economy. On balance, the state of the Western zones – as a headless body – was less critical than the bodyless head of the East German economy, in that, in the West, the foundations of an expanding economy existed. The relatively higher pre-war level of industrialisation in the East could never compensate for the dangerous lack of this primary base.

5. The *trade structures* of both emerging states were similarly affected by partition. Domestic 'trade' between the Soviet zone of occupation and the Western zones slumped from a turnover of 300–400 million RM before the war to 45 million RM in 1947.[31] Long-standing sources of basic materials, components and semi-finished goods started to dry up; the reciprocal dependence of the weaving industry in Saxony on the spinning industry of Westfalia, of the West German camera on optical glass from the Russian zone, etc. had to be altered to suit the new circumstances. Foreign trade structures posed new problems of varying weight for the two states. Despite attempts under Hitler to minimise the dependence of the 'Reich' on Western trade, the developed industrial economies of the West remained its most significant trading partners (see Table 2.5). The quality of trade with Western countries had been significantly different than with the less developed economies of Eastern Europe, the Middle East and South America. Thus the preconditions for the intensified reintegration of a capitalist West Germany into a capitalist world economy were in the main far better than those governing East Germany's new dependence on the less developed economies of Eastern Europe. Equally, the Western economies needed West Germany as a trading partner and a market for capital exports more than Russia needed East Germany. Nevertheless the geographical dislocations of both states created considerable short-term trading problems which compounded the difficulties of stimulating growth in the immediate post-war years.

6. The final major category of factors determining the economic development of the Western zones is that relating to the *structure of decision-making* (and the nature of major decisions made). The hierarchy of decision-making was dominated by the powers of occu-

Table 2.5   The shift in German trade, 1929–38

	Share of total exports in per cent				Share of total imports in per cent			
	1929	1932	1935	1938	1929	1932	1935	1938
South Eastern Europe	4.3	3.5	5.9	10.3	3.8	5.6	7.7	9.8
Egypt, Turkey & Middle East	1.4	1.3	3.4	5.4	1.4	2.5	3.8	3.8
Latin America	7.3	4.1	9.1	11.7	11.7	9.6	13.1	14.9
Northern Europe	10.2	9.4	11.4	12.0	7.3	6.4	9.9	11.4
Total	23.2	18.3	29.8	40.3	23.9	23.5	34.5	39.9
Western Europe	26.2	31.9	26.1	20.8	15.7	15.1	14.1	11.9
Great Britain	9.7	7.8	8.8	6.7	6.4	5.5	6.2	5.2
USA	7.4	4.9	4.0	2.8	13.3	12.7	5.8	7.4
Others	33.5	37.1	31.3	29.4	40.7	43.2	39.4	35.6
Total	76.8	81.7	70.2	59.7	76.1	76.5	65.5	60.1

Source: R. Erbe, *Die nationalsozialistische Wirtschaftspolitik* (Zürich, 1958) p. 76.

pation, but after the creation of the Bizone in 1947 it was opened up increasingly to German influence. Initially the decision-making structures were chaotic, lacking internal national coherence and a satisfactory degree of cohesion and co-ordination between the various occupation powers.

The supreme Allied body of government should have been the Control Council, based in Berlin,[32] Allied differences made this impossible. Thus effective political control was exercised by respective military administrations. The senior staff of the British and American administrations (CCG–BE and OMGUS) were generally senior field officers with no political experience. They were faced with tasks which would have taxed seasoned politicians, i.e. not just the execution of the political decisions of the Potsdam Conference, but also the maintenance of civil order, food supplies and basic services. A vital matter for all the occupation administrations was the recruitment of German staff to fill the lower echelons of the temporary apparatuses. This process, as much as the policies implemented, had a significant effect on subsequent economic developments.

The first occupation handbook produced by SHAEF stated that

'under no circumstances shall active Nazis or ardent sympathisers be retained in office for administrative convenience or expediency'.[33] Yet the practice of both American and British military governments was to do just that: Nazi or ultra-nationalist Mayors were appointed in Aachen, Hamburg, Wuppertal, Bremen, Hannover, Kiel and many other smaller communities, who in turn chose staff of like kind. Nazi managers were confirmed in their posts in private enterprises and state bodies, despite workers' protests. The chief adviser on rebuilding the US zone railways was, for a brief period, Dr Dorpmüller – Hitler's Minister of Transport – and the British in turn appointed Dr Fritz Busch (who was on the mandatory removal list) as general manager of the British zone railways. In contrast to the general disinterest of the British (Labour) government, Eisenhower was appalled: 'What in the devil is the American Army doing in Germany, if not to denazify the German government and administration? The Russians killed their Nazis; the Americans put them in office.'[34]

The main defence of both British and American administrations was that of 'indispensability', where they referred to a number of accepted amendments to the global ban on the employment of ex-Nazis and to the lack of alternative appointees. It is on record, however, that political refugees from Nazi Germany, who were all too willing to help, were deliberately excluded from consideration.[35] The major group of anti-Nazis within Germany, Socialists, Communists and trade unionists, were also ignored.[36] Both these exclusions indicate an ideological filtering of potential governors of liberated Germany, whereby anti-capitalist elements were assumed to be unacceptable. The recorded plausibilisations of British and American selection policy stressed the importance of a 'liberal and pro-democratic' outlook.[37] However, 'liberal democrats' were remarkably thin on the ground within the ranks of the German bourgeoisie and petty bourgeoisie, so that the choice of Nazi and non-democratic technocrats was virtually inevitable. It made a mockery of the war effort and the commitment to denazify Germany, but inasmuch as anti-fascism implies anti-capitalism (namely Horckheimer), it was logical that the West should retreat from the historical implications of purging Germany's élites: namely creating a vacuum which could be filled by the Left. The retention of experienced bureaucrats and managers thus established some degree of continuity and, if the claims of economic expediency are correct, helped to maintain a minimum level of civil order and thus avoid the social unrest which could itself fuel anti-capitalism. It also gave ex-Nazis the chance to prove their competence and hence their 'indispensability'.

For the first two years after the war the decision-making structures were dominated by local priorities, because of communications problems, partition and also because of American preferences for decentralised modes of government. The creation by OMGUS of the regional states Bavaria, Württemberg/Baden and Hessen in September 1945 pre-figured the later imposition of federal structures. While maintaining a commitment to the Potsdam agreement to treat Germany as a unitary economic territory, the creation of Länder with extensive powers in economic policy, law, transport, education and communications allowed the development of relatively weak partial apparatuses which could resist private economic pressure less effectively than centralised state institutions but at the same time could develop their own spheres of interest. Lines of communication within the decentralised structure were initially less effective than in the Russian zone, certainly up until the creation of the Bizone – as demonstrated by the sluggish economic recovery in the West compared to the the East in the immediate post-war period.

Overall the picture of economic conditions immediately after the war shows a confusing state of affairs. Subjectively this picture was dominated by hunger, homelessness, urban desolation and the black market. Objectively the pre-conditions for recovery were not unfavourable: a ready supply of surplus, skilled labour and huge surplus capacity could be exploited once the transport crisis was resolved. The rebuilding of the towns, the roads and the railways represented a potential dynamic boost to growth with the customary multiplicator effects, which only required an initial infusion of capital.

The official mythology of the West German state would have us believe that recovery only began after the implementation of the currency reform, the Marshall Plan and the introduction of the 'social market economy', i.e. after deliberate acts of well-considered policymaking. Recently these claims have been severely questioned, particularly by Werner Abelshauser, who in contrast claims that official statistics give a misleading view of pre-1948 economic development. According to his own calculations there are clear indications of sustained growth before June 1948, particularly after the transport crisis was overcome in 1947.

The currency reform clearly boosted industrial production but

Table 2.6 The development of industrial production in the American and British Zones of Occupation, 1945–1949 (1936=100)

Year/ quarters	American Zone	Bizone	British Zone
1945 III	12		15
IV	19		22
1946 I	31		30
II	37		33
III	46		37
IV	50		37
1947 I		34	
II		44	
III		46	
IV		50	
1948 I		54	
II		57	
III		65	
IV		79	
1949 I		86	

Source: Abelshauser, *Wirtschaftsgeschichte*, op. cit., p. 34.

within a cyclical upturn and partly through the liberation of previously horded products; indeed it was the 'upturn of the Autumn of 1947 which facilitated the currency reform'.[38]

The significance of the *Marshall Plan* cannot be denied: it provided foreign currency for importing vital goods; with its mechanism for rechanneling repayment monies it allowed the mobilisation of capital for specific (infrastructural) investments and it helped to reintegrate West Germany into the world economy.[39] Its quantitative significance – providing an average of 3.5 per cent of gross investment finance between 1949 and 1953 – was 'not small',[40] particularly for certain key sectors, but was outweighed according to some by its politically symbolic effect:

a. in virtually ensuring the maintenance of capitalism,[41]
b. allowing the US-government a certain influence over German economic policy with investments financed by the 'counter-value funds' conditional on US approval;[42] and
c. as a 'placebo' restoring/reinforcing German confidence in a secure economic future.[43]

The introduction of the so-called 'social market economy' cannot be judged as vital for subsequent growth of the West German economy, because we have no means of verifying any such causal connections. However, the vagueness of the 'new' order's terms of reference and the subsequent unremarkable shape of its policies and results suggest that the 'social market economy' was an elaborate confidence trick (see below), or at most that it played 'a much smaller role than other growth determinants which are independent of economic systems'.[44]

One of the decisive factors which ultimately allowed the sustained exploitation of West Germany's dormant productive potential was the shift in occupation policy, led by the Americans.

American Economic Interests and the Shaping of Western Germany

The creation of the Bizone in January 1947 was more than an administrative convenience; it represented the first formal step towards partition and the adoption of West Germany by the US-government as a junior partner within a broad western economic block against the USSR. On 19 January 1947 Dulles spoke openly of the need to create a West European federation so that 'the industrial potential of West Germany can be securely built into the economy of Western Europe',[45] because he saw real dangers of an independent, unified centralised German state, which might not be so committed to a Western Alliance. Dulles and his Republican colleagues were becoming increasingly worried not so much about Russian policy in the satellite states (which had been allotted to the Soviet sphere of influence at Yalta) but about independent successes of communist movements and parties in Greece, Italy and France, which were supposed to stay within the 'western sphere'. West German Social Democrats supported neutralism and reunification, and with the likelihood of a left majority in a re-united Germany, American economic interests in Europe could have been in some danger. Partitioning off the Western zones with the industrial jewel of the Ruhr and Rhine basins became a real strategic option, which would leave the new Soviet bloc isolated, economically empoverished and, because of the American monopoly of nuclear weapons, strategically weaker. America's determinant influence and dominance over France and, in particular, Britain became more and more apparent. Britain was heavily in debt to the US as a result of the lend–lease system and its domestic debt was worsened by the costs of occupation. The Bizone administration began by being shared equally between OMGUS and CCG–BE, but in September 1947 the British government was forced to ask the USA to take over a large portion of the burden of occupation. This in turn gave the United States a voting majority in both the Joint Export–Import Agency and the Joint Foreign Exchange Agency. Britain was thereby 'eliminated as a determinant factor in Germany'.[46] France, which maintained a slightly more independent line, was nevertheless heavily dependent on American aid and thus never seriously endangered American plans, especially after the Marshall Aid Programme had begun.

American policy goals of restoring normal economic activity in Western Europe and thereby maintaining a capitalist economic order and controlling the US business cycle were achieved with relatively little difficulty. A portion of the US capital surplus was syphoned through bond issues into the ERP and thence to the 18 recipient nations, including the Western zones, later the Federal Republic. This improved the zonal balance of payments situation, alleviated occupation costs and tied the economies to their US creditor. At the same time monetary stability was achieved through the currency reform of June 1948, though convertibility for the new Deutschmark was not introduced until 1958. The US also used openly repressive means of maintaining a capitalist order. All German initiatives to introduce public ownership of key sectors of the economy were nipped in the bud. Demands for socialisation came not just from the Left in the western zones but also the old Centre Party and the early CDU groupings. Despite this, General Clay suspended both the Socialisation Article of the Hessen Constitution and the implementation Law of Article 160 of the Bavarian State Legislative. In Hessen, the Americans insisted on a referendum on the issue, but when 72 per cent voted in favour of public ownership for key sectors of industry, the Military Government simply forbade the implementation of the Article. Beyond this OMGUS made the British Military Government suspend the Law on the Expropriation of the Coal Industry in January 1947. The stance of the Labour government on public ownership was very favourable, but it was a great disappointment to the West German labour movement when Bevin finally capitulated to US pressure in August 1947 and reluctantly withdrew his political support for nationalisation in the Western zones. Similar action by the Americans was taken to suspend laws governing workers' participation in controlling the commercial policies of enterprises, in Hessen (3 September 48), in Würtemmberg/Baden and in Bremen. In Baden, the French were forced to ban similar Land legislation in September 1948 after protests from General Clay.[47] The only minor success for progressive industrial policies was the introduction of co-determination in the supervisory boards of the Ruhr Coal and Steel enterprises in the British Zone from 1947.

The land reform plans in the West bore little comparison to the extensive redistribution of big estates (including state holdings) in the East. Land reform laws (OMGUS 15 October 1946, British Military Government 4 August 47 and French Military Government 21 October 47) affected only a small portion of the land holdings of estates of more than 100 or 150 hectares, and the expropriation was well-compensated. The results were marginal, such that the proportion of total land owned by units over 100 hectares altered by 0.4 per cent between 1939 and 1949 from 27.9 per cent to 27.5 per cent. Its value was at most propagandistic.

Working class action in support of socialist alternatives was dealt with summarily in all three Western zones. In early 1947 there were a whole series of strikes in all three zones demanding improved rations and the expropriation of the coal mines and other large firms. As a result, the three military governments banned all protest strikes and demonstrations. The US governor, Colonel Newman, threatened a universal withdrawal of food supplies, the cutting of rations for strike ringleaders and even the death penalty.[48] Communist newspapers were consistently banned or censored, reducing further the latitude of the labour movement to mobilise against the restoration of the status quo ante.

At the political level the US confirmed their dominance over Great Britain by imposing their model for the future constitution of a separate Western zone. For reasons of convenience and ideological preference the British Labour government favoured a centralised state structure along British lines with a parliamentary rather than presidential government. The French preferred a decentralised structure as a means of avoiding the potential threat of a strong unified centralised German state. The Americans favoured federalism with a weak central state as the system least capable of threatening a 'private market economy'. The US government not surprisingly held sway. On 1 July 1948 the Minister Presidents of the Länder received copies of the so-called 'Frankfurt Documents' in which the Western occupying powers called for the convening of a constituent assembly which would draft a constitution for the Western Zones. The constitution would 'create a form of government of the federalistic type',[49] subject to the approval of the three military governments. They were also ordered to respond to a draft 'statute of occupation' and redraw the Land boundaries. The response of the Minister Presidents and the public at large was largely negative, notably on the question of partition and the impossibility of *legitimacy for a separate West German constitution*.[50] Clay spoke of 'sabotage', as the cool reply of the Minister Presidents was received. He argued that their response would weaken the US position against the USSR and this could reduce US commitment to Berlin.[51] After several meetings the Military Governors did accept the reduction of the constitution to a provisional status pending reunification and it was agreed that the Parliamentary Council (as a constituent assembly) would convene on 1 September 1948.

The work of the Parliamentary Council was dominated by the problem of federalism. While there was no complete rejection of federalist elements, there were major differences of opinion; the SPD was the strongest proponent of a more centralised structure, with some autonomy for the Länder, but with the important demand for central fiscal control; the CDU favoured a Land-based fiscal structure. The Allies were asked to 'mediate' and their unbending insistence on highly decentralised government with a weak central state was finally pushed through despite 'a serious crisis',[52] and the draft Basic Law was passed by the Parliamentary Council on 8 May 1949.

A federal structure, above all a decentralised fiscal structure, can be interpreted as a means to obviate a resurgence of German expansionism (corresponding to French fears), but for the Americans it clearly served the purpose of weakening the potential for (socialist) change by strengthening private and regional (public) self interest. Linked to a strong independent central bank, it was to prove a potent means of frustrating democratic endeavour.

The Development of Social Forces in the Western Zones up to 1949

The activity of interest groups and political parties was subject to strict control by the Military Governments of all three zones. Because of the predominant view of an individual responsibility of all Germans for the Third Reich and the Second World War, there was programmatic resistance to the sanctioning of any political or quasi political organisations or even the employment of acknowledged resistance groups (e.g. within trade unions, the SPD and the KPD). The only exception were the churches which were allowed to continue without hindrance and which were used as sources for political advice by the British and American military governments – often with embarassing results,[53] given their anti-democratic past and the high measure of support they accorded the Nazi dictatorship. The fact that the only untarnished social forces were from the Left explains why the Western allies imposed a blanket ban on all organised groups after May 1945. Had the Left been given favoured status and thus a head start in political and industrial organisation, the chances of preventing radical change would very probably have been diminished. Thus the various Anti-Fascist Committees (Antifas) and the Works Committees (composed largely of left oppositionists) were stripped of the limited responsibilities they had accrued between the invasion of Germany and capitulation. Local administration and commercial management was transferred to nominees of the military governments. Organised groups were not surprisingly secretly active, sometimes with the tacit approval of the local military commanders but official sanction for political and industrial pressure groups was only given after mid-August 1945 and then on the basis of strict control. Activity was restricted initially to the local level and was only licensed after a process of application.

Trade unions were regarded with considerable suspicion by the military authorities; Montgomery observed signs of 'subversion by Russian communists' among certain unions[54] and argued that the longer one delayed the sanctioning of complete freedom of activity, the better would be the chance of a 'moderate' union leadership.[55] The strategy was sound. The initial strength of communist trade unionists, particularly in the British zone, was slowly weakened by military decree, by the failure to achieve a united front with social democrats, by the ultimate improvement in economic conditions in the Western zones and by the unimpressive beginnings of Stalinism in the Russian zone.

The trade unions were active at local and regional level above all in restoring production and communications but also in campaigns for rigorous denazification of administration and management and for the socialisation of industry and banking. The union structures which emerged were a conscious attempt to avoid the sectarianism of the Weimar Republic. Both the American and the British military governments resisted the attempts to establish a unitary model of trade union (the *Einheitsgewerkschaft*) with subordinate industrial and professional groups, but by 1949 the old craft unions had been transformed into 16 industry-based unions with a relatively high level of membership. Interzonal co-operation was difficult and it was only in November 1947 that a joint trade union council of the unions of the British and American zones was established. The ambitions of the trade union leadership were initially very high: German capitalism was finished (Böckler); it was only just a question of stepping into the power vacuum, socialising industry and banks, reforming agriculture and establishing a system of socialist planning under the aegis of the Allies and the working class state would be in the bag. In fact the unions emerged from the four-year occupation as a powerless and frustrated force.[56] They were hamstrung and largely ignored by the military governments. Even demands for effective participation at factory level and regional and national level were brushed aside – it is significant, for example, that the trade unions played no part in the interzonal Economic Council (established in 1947). Nazi managers continued to manage. The old monopolies were broken up temporarily and their owners' control suspended, but both measures were reversed soon after the establishment of the Federal Republic. The bargaining power of the unions was weakened by the massive flow of skilled refugee labour into the labour market and they were confronted by increasingly resilient employers' organisations, restored from the low point of 1945.

The Chambers of Industry and Commerce resumed their work at local level 'in the first few days after the occupation'[57] with the blessing of the occupational powers. According to Simon, the previously dominant 'monopolists' were no longer in evidence but the important monopoly groups were still represented and, by implication, still strong.[58] After the founding of the Bizone the IHKs of the two zones formed a joint 'working group' which was the basis of the Convention of German Chambers of Industry and Commerce created in October 1949.

The restoration of branch-based regional and national employers' groups was equally a matter of course, as was the rebuilding of representative bodies for industry. The latter were perceived as particularly important by the Allies for both the general restoration of production and for the specific skills involved in the continuation of wage–price controls from the Nazi regime – but also for the implementation of dismantling orders, against which there was concerted opposition and considerable lobbying of the military governments. It is only fair to speculate that the modification of the First Level of Industry Plan in the Second (Western) Plan of August 1947 and its reduction of dismantling plans was in part due to this effective lobbying.

There are two major facts about the emerging industrial interest groups which need stressing here:

a. heavy industry played a dominant role in the formation of the bizonal Iron and Metal Federation, which before 1950 functioned as a kind of 'trustee for all industry'[59] in national politics, thus preparing its later dominance of the Federation of German Industry, restored in 1950 on the model of the old Imperial Federation of German Industry;

b. In contrast to the Trade Unions, the Iron and Metal Federation was consulted by top Allied and German administrative bodies, including the Economics Council in Frankfurt, on important economic issues, setting the pattern for the 1950s.

The differing evolution of employers' and workers' organisations is mirrored in the emergence of a new order of *political parties* after the war. Of the parties which had survived fascism and the war there were objectively only two with an unblemished record of opposition to the Third Reich, the SPD and the KPD. All the other parties (including the Centre Party and the Liberals) had voted for the Enabling Act of March 1933 which was the 'legal' basis for the establishment of a dictatorship of the Nazi Party. Subjectively, too, SPD and KPD felt themselves to be the rightful heirs (jointly or separately) of the throne of post-war politics. In particular the exiled leadership of the SPD and the survivors from the underground movement had high hopes of a large majority in a democratised Germany. In the Autumn of 1945, when parties were legalised, the traditional efficient party organisation was re-mobilised and began campaigning for support with a nationwide set of local newspapers, etc. But in the regional elections of 1946 and 1947 the SPD failed to achieve a 50 per cent share of the vote anywhere, gained an absolute majority of seats in only Schleswig-Holstein and Hamburg and was beaten into second place in six out of eleven Länder – by a completely new party, the Christian Democratic Union. And yet this was the pinnacle of the SPD's achievement up until the late 1960s. The reasons for the failure are too numerous to describe in detail here but they include: the accident of (Western) occupation and of iron fist

Table 2.7   Elections for the Regional Parliaments in the Western zones, 1946–47

	Baden 18.5.47		Bavaria 1.12.46		Bremen 12.10.47		Hamburg 13.10.46		Hessen 1.12.46		Lower Saxony 20.4.47		North Rhine Westphalia 20.4.47		Rheinland-Pfalz 18.5.47		Schleswig Holstein 20.4.47		Wurttemberg Baden 24.11.46		Wurttemberg Hohenzollern 18.5.47	
Electoral Roll participation	0.695 m 67.8%		4.211 m 75.7%		0.338 m 67.8%		0.968 m 79.0%		2.380 m 73.2%		3.957 m 65.1%		7.861 m 67.3%		1.668 m 77.9%		1.595 m 69.8%		1.875 m 71.7%		0.616 m 66.4%	
Total votes cast	0.428 m		3.048 m		0.219 m		0.808 m		1.609 m		2.459 m		5.029 m		1.161 m		1.073 m		1.269 m		0.378 m	
	Seats	% of votes	Seats	% of votes	Seats	% of votes	Seats	% of votes	Seats	% of votes	Seats	% of votes	Seats	% of votes	Seats	% of votes	Seats	% of votes	Seats	% of votes	Seats	% of votes
CDU/CSU	34	55.9	104	52.3	24	22.0	16	26.7	28	30.9	30	19.9	92	37.5	48	47.2	21	34.0	39	38.4	32	54.2
SPD	13	22.4	54	28.6	46	41.7	83	43.1	38	42.7	65	43.4	64	32.0	34	34.3	43	43.8	32	31.9	12	20.8
KPD	4	14.3	–	6.1	10	8.8	4	10.4	10	10.7	8	5.6	28	14.0	8	8.7	–	4.7	10	10.2	5	7.3
FDP	9	7.4	9	5.6	15	13.9	7	18.2	14	15.7	13	8.8	12	5.9	11	9.8	–	5.0	19	19.5	11	17.7
DP	–	–	–	–	3	3.9	–	–	–	–	27	17.9	–	–	–	–	–	–	–	–	–	–
NAV	–	–	13	7.4	–	–	–	–	–	–	–	–	–	–	–	–	–	–	–	–	–	–
SSV	–	–	–	–	–	–	–	–	–	–	–	–	–	–	–	–	6	9.3	–	–	–	–
DKP	–	–	–	–	–	–	–	0.3	–	–	–	–	–	–	–	–	–	3.1	–	–	–	–
DRP	–	–	–	–	–	–	–	–	–	–	–	0.3	–	0.5	–	–	–	–	–	–	–	–
Zentrum	–	–	–	–	–	–	–	0.7	–	–	6	4.1	20	9.8	–	–	–	0.1	–	–	–	–

Source: Klaus-Jörg Ruhl (ed.), *Neubeginn und Restauration* (Munich, 1982) pp. 502–3.

politics in the Eastern zone in the name of socialism; the delusion of leaders like Schumacher that 'capitalism had collapsed' with the end of the war; the subsequent refusal to entertain the idea of a united front with the revolutionary KPD (when revolution was not needed); the immobility of the SPD in responding to changed circumstances; the refusal of the SPD leadership to chair any of the important committees in the bizonal Economic Council – this merely allowed the CDU appointees to demonstrate their indispensability, whereas the SPD's 'constructive opposition' was barely comprehensible to the ordinary voter; the failure of the British Labour party to acknowledge the needs of the SPD and to support its own scheme for nationalisation; finally the residual influence of Nazi anti-socialist propaganda, and the widespread distrust of any 'collectivist' solutions of social crises after fascism, in the face of the rude self-reliance imposed by the post-war years of hunger and re-consecrated by a 'benevolent' US government and its German allies. The SPD in 1949 found itself once more in the position of resigned paralysis, yet unable to draw adequate theoretical conclusions from its plight.

The political victor of the post-war years was the CDU (and its sister party from Bavaria, the CSU). The CDU was a shrewdly conceived creation; it dubbed itself a catch-all-party (*Volkspartei*) aiming notably at a synthesis of the working-class and the petit-bourgeois vote under the banner of the Christianity of the few within the Catholic and Protestant Churches that had opposed fascism. The CDU that finally emerged at the August elections in 1949 was a slightly different beast from the initial prototypes in 1945. The early regional programmes of the CDU acknowledged the anti-capitalism of the mass of the population with the appropriate commitments to a *complete reorganisation* of the economic order,[60] the Berlin Christian trade unionist, Jakob Kaiser, went as far as formulating a view of Christian socialism which proclaimed the greatness of Marx and Engels' Communist Manifesto and the end of the 'bourgeois epoch'.[61] Organisationally, however, the CDU was slowly adopted by the professional politicians of Weimar's bourgeois parties, the strident socialism of Kaiser and others was pushed aside and, with the increasingly positive stance of the USA, a 'new' programme was developed based on the 'social market economy'. This magic new formula evoked social justice and solidarity as counterweights to the normal market economy; the only actual concrete measure proposed to counteract the vicissitudes of the market was a (grand-sounding) institution of monopoly control. The formula, though quite unproven and seemingly very flawed, was nevertheless effective. It united bourgeois and *petit-bourgeois* inside and outside the party; it caught a good chunk of the working class vote by damning both monopolism and collectivism which were associated for many with Hitler and Stalin.

The rise of the CDU/CSU represented an exceptionally effective reorganisation of bourgeois politics in West Germany. Its electoral opportunism was mirrored by the party's adaptation to the primacy of American politics. Konrad Adenauer, with his power base in North Rhine Westphalia, was prepared to surrender the party's commitment to the 'unity of the Empire' in favour of a separate West German federal state from the very beginning. Adenauer, who also had strong connections to Rhineland industrialists and bankers from his days as mayor of Cologne, steered the party safely into the arms of the Americans as the guarantors of social continuity and as golden egg producers. The tactical victory over the conservative nationalists and centralists in the party was well engineered, even if he was swimming with the tide.

The CDU demonstrated the extreme flexibility and adaptability of German conservative politics. It was helped on its way by a labour movement in the Western zones which was unable to re-organise itself at all at party level and whose continuing divisions merely reinforced that grim paralysis so common in left-wing parties in the West. The significance for the political economy of the Federal Republic is that its new political élite achieved a very rapid integration of Germany's most important economic resources into the Western block, effected an optimal degree of social continuity in the administrative and industrial apparatuses, while maintaining political legitimacy. For this CDU-politicians could only claim some of the credit; historical circumstance and the Western Allies did the rest.

Notes

1. See R. Kühnl/G. Hardach (eds), *Die Zerstörung der Weimarer Republik* (Cologne, 1977); David Abraham, *The Collapse of the Weimar Republic: Political Economy and Crisis* (Princeton, 1981); George Hallgarten/Joachim Radkau, *Deutsche Industrie und Politik* (Cologne, 1974).
2. E.g. Manfred Nussbaum, *Wirtschaft und Staat in Deutschland während der Weimarer Republik* (Vaduz, 1978); Eberhard Czichon, *Wer verhalf Hitler zur Macht* (Cologne, 1967); Kurt Gossweiler, *Großbanken, In-*

dustriemonopole, Staat. Ökonomie und Politik des staatsmonopolistischen Kapitalismus in Deutschland 1914–1932 (Berlin, 1975).

3. Conversely, Wilhelm Hoegner, (in *Der politische Radikalismus in Deutschland 1919–1933*, Munich/Vienna, 1966, p. 65), asserted that it was an anti-democratic bureaucracy that was the 'foreign body' in the democratic society of Weimar Germany, a view which misread the nature of political culture in general in this period.

4. Joachim Perels, *Kapitalismus und politische Demokratie*, op. cit., p. 10.

5. Ernst-Ulrich Huster, Gerhard Kraiker, Burkhard Scherer, Friedrich-Karl Schlotmann, Marianne Welteke, *Determinanten der westdeutschen Restauration 1945–1949* (Frankfurt, 1975) p. 9.

6. Viz. the account of the meeting between Anthony Eden, Sir John Simon and Hitler in Berlin in 1935 in Alan Bullock, *Hitler, a Study in Tyranny* (London, 1952) p. 334.

7. Senator Truman, quoted in D. F. Fleming, *The Cold War and its Origins 1917–1960*, vol. I (London, 1961) p. 135.

8. Tom Bower, *A Blind Eye to Murder. Britain, America and the Purging of Nazi Germany – a Pledge Betrayed* (London, 1981) p. 161.

9. Memorandum of British Chancellor of the Exchequer, Anderson, 7 Mar. 1945, reprinted in Klaus-Jörg Ruhl (ed.), *Neubeginn und Restauration, Dokumente zur Vorgeschichte der Bundesrepublik Deutschland 1945–1949* (Munich, 1982) pp. 52ff; Memorandum of the Economic and Industrial Planning Staff (US State Department), 2 Sept. 1944, ibid., pp. 27ff; US State Department Report for the Yalta Conference, Nov. 1944–Jan. 1945, ibid., pp. 29ff.

10. Crimea (Yalta) conference, 4–11 February 1945: Protocol of the proceedings, press release, 24 Mar. 1947, in *United States Department of State Publication 3556, Germany 1947–1949, The Story in Documents* (Mar. 1950) p. 44.

11. Anderson Memorandum, 7 Mar. 1945, op. cit., p. 56.

12. Ibid., p. 58.

13. Directive JCS 1067, 26 Apr. 1945, Part II, section 16, in: *Germany 1947–1949: the Story in Documents*, op. cit., p. 26f.

14. Stalin's broadcast to the Russian people is reprinted in: Ruhl, *Neubeginn und Restauration*, op. cit., pp. 89f.

15. Pauley's view is cited in Bruce Kuklik, *American Policy and the Division of Germany* (New York, 1972) pp. 131f; see also Huster *et al.*, *Determinanten der westdeutschen Restauration*, op. cit., p. 30.

16. Jean Edward Smith (ed.), *The Papers of General Lucius D. Clay* (Bloomington/London, 1974) vol. I, pp. 237ff; Clay was also adamant that rebuilding the German economy would save it from communism, ibid, p. 391.

17. Huster *et al.*, *Determinanten der westdeutschen Restauration*, op. cit., p. 34.

18. See note 9 above.

19. See Molotov's speech in Paris, quoted in: Huster *et al.*, *Determinanten . . .*, op. cit., p. 37.

20. Viz. Secretary James F. Byrnes' speech in Stuttgart, 6 Sept. 1946, reprinted in *Germany 1947–1949: the Story in Documents*, op. cit., p. 4.

21. Alfred Müller-Armack asserts Germany's 'total . . . economic collapse', in Ludwig Erhard, Alfred Müller-Armack, *Soziale Marktwirtschaft. Manifest 72* (Frankfurt, 1972) p. 29.
22. E.g. the West Berlin Deutsches Institut für Wirtschaftsforschung in its *Handbuch DDR* (Hamburg, 1977), p. 19, cites a figure of 21 per cent capacity losses through war damage in the Western zones, using 1939 as the data base.
23. Viz. Werner Abelshauser, 'Rekonstruktion der deutschen Wirtschaft' in: Scharpf/ Schröder (eds), *Politische und ökonomische Stabilisierung Westdeutschlands 1945–1949* (Wiesbaden, 1977) pp. 7f; also Abelshauser, *Wirtschaftsgeschichte der Bundesrepublik 1945–1980* (Frankfurt/M 1983) pp. 20ff.
24. DIW, *Handbuch DDR-Wirtschaft*, op. cit., p. 19.
25. Werner Abelshauser, *Wirtschaftsgeschichte*, op. cit., p. 20.
26. Ibid., p. 22.
27. The population of Schleswig-Holstein, for example, had increased by 63 per cent between 1939 and 1946, that of Lower Saxony and Bavaria by 38.3 per cent and 24.9 per cent respectively, whereas it fell in the major cities of Hamburg and Bremen and in the most populous area of North-Rhine Westfalia (Source: Huster *et al.*, *Determinanten* . . ., op. cit., p. 100).
28. F. W. Henning, *Das industrialisierte Deutschland 1914 bis 1972* (Paderborn, 1974) p. 191.
29. Huster *et al.*, *Determinanten* . . ., op. cit., p. 87.
30. Protocol of the Proceedings of the Potsdam Conference, press release of 24 Mar. 1947, reprinted in *Germany 1947–1949*, op. cit., p. 49 (IIB, para. 12)
31. Werner Abelshauser, *Wirtschaftsgeschichte*, op. cit., p. 28. His example only considers trade between the Russian zone and the 'Bizone'.
32. Potsdam Conference Protocol, op. cit., p. 48 (IIA, para. 1).
33. Source: Tom Bower, *Blind Eye to Murder*, op. cit., p. 163.
34. Ibid., p. 174.
35. Ibid., p. 170.
36. Ute Schmidt, Tilman Fichter, *Der erzwungene Kapitalismus* (Berlin, 1975) pp. 108f.
37. Tom Bower, *Blind Eye to Murder*, op. cit., p. 165.
38. Werner Abelshauser, Rekonstruktion der deutschen Wirtschaft', op. cit., p. 10.
39. Manfred Knapp, 'Deutschland und der Marshall-Plan', in *Politische und ökonomische Stabilisierung Westdeutschlands 1945–1949*, op. cit., p. 43.
40. Werner Abelshauser, 'Rekonstruktion der deutschen Wirtschaft', op. cit., p. 12.
41. Manfred Knapp, 'Deutschland und der Marshall-Plan', op. cit., p. 43
42. Abelshauser, 'Rekonstruktion . . .', op. cit., p. 12.
43. Ibid., p. 12.
44. Ibid., p. 17.
45. J. F. Dulles, quoted in: Badstübner/Thomas, *Restauration und Spaltung. Entstehung und Entwicklung der BRD 1945–1955* (Cologne, 1975) p. 215.

46. Huster *et al.*, *Determinanten* . . ., op. cit., p. 44.
47. Viz. two secret memoranda on Co-determination in South Baden, in *The Papers of General Lucius D. Clay*, op. cit., vol. II, pp. 981 and 989.
48. Colonel Newman in a radio broadcast 16 May 1947, quoted in *Frankfurter Rundschau*, 17 May 1947.
49. Instructions from Military Governors of US, UK, and French Zones to German Minister-Presidents (Frankfurt, 1 July 1948), reprinted in *Germany 1947–1949*, op. cit., pp. 275ff.
50. See Peter Hüttenberger, *Die Entstehung der Bundesrepublik Deutschland* (Informationen zur politschen Bildung), (Bonn, 1974) p. 25.
51. Lucius Clay, quoted in Wolfgang Bergsdorf, 'Besatzung und Wiederaufbau Deutschlands', in *aus politik und zeitgeschichte*, B/20 (1979) p. 23.
52. Peter Hüttenberger, *Die Entstehung der Bundesrepublik Deutschland*, op. cit., p. 28.
53. See Tom Bower, *Blind Eye to Murder*, op. cit., pp. 173, etc.
54. Montgomery, *Memoirs*,
55. Ibid., p. 464.
56. See Theo Pirker, *Die blinde Macht* (Munich, 1960); Eberhard Schmidt, *Die verhinderte Neuordnung* (Frankfurt, 1970).
57. August Küster, quoted in Walter Simon, *Macht und Herrschaft der Unternehmerverbände, BDI, BDA und DIHT* (Cologne, 1976) p. 47.
58. Ibid., p. 47.
59. Walther Hermann, quoted in Simon, ibid., p. 50.
60. Thus ends the first paragraph of the Ahlen Economic Programme of the CDU in North-Rhine Westfalia (3 Feb. 1947), reprinted in full in: Huster *et al.*, *Determinanten* . . ., op. cit. pp. 424ff.
61. On 31 Oct. 1945, Adenauer wrote to the Mayor of Duisburg, Weitz, that the division of Europe and Germany was an unchangeable 'fact' and that the 'creation of a centralistic unified state will not be possible, nor desirable' [sic]. The letter is quoted in Badstübner/Thomas, *Restauration und Spaltung*, op. cit., p. 179.

3 The 'Economic Constitution' of West Germany

The Federal Republic has a provisional political constitution, which is clearly defined in the statutes of the Basic Law (*Grundgesetz*). In addition however the term 'economic constitution' (*Wirtschaftsverfassung*) has become part of accepted ideological currency, even though there is no document of state law which contains the specific statutes of such an Economic Constitution.

For the pragmatic Anglo-Saxon tradition, with its continuity of state form, economic relations have been circumscribed largely by state guarantees for the rights of property, for the formal equality of agents of exchange (in contract law, e.g.) and for the standard values of weights, measures and currency. These guarantees represent an inalienable essence of capitalist state law. There has been a welter of additional legislation but none of it has been elevated to the status of unalterable constitutional law.

In Germany however there had been an extreme discontinuity of state form, as well as a tradition of legalism, which had encouraged the formalisation of social relations and the creation of separate branches of judicial control, including labour law and administrative law. The misuse of economic and industrial law under fascism strengthened the desire to establish a strict framework of laws which could prevent both economic and political abuses and guarantee some degree of legal continuity. Above all the new political leadership of the Federal Republic clearly perceived the need both to demonstrate its economic loyalty and 'creditworthiness' to the Western occupying powers and to justify the social order to the West German electorate. As a result a great deal was made of the proposal for a 'new economic constitution' which would plough a *'middle course' between monopoly capitalism and socialist planning*, the one compromised by two world wars and the social disasters of the 1920s and 1930s, the other eschewed by the leaders of the United States and rendered unpalatable for many by the excesses of Stalinism. The middle course, the 'third way', could be presented as both expedient and desirable, thus the concept of the 'social market economy' was elevated to a central position in the official doctrine of the Christian democrats and their allies. The 'economic constitution' of their social market economy, in addition to the customary guarantees of capitalist states, proposed to freeze economic relations within the economic order at a level of optimal competition by means of variety of legal sanctions, notably by monopoly control, and by implication to maintain that order *ad infinitum*.

From the outset there was some confusion as to the actual *constitutional status* of the economic constitution. There was an extensive debate about whether the Basic Law prescribed a specific economic order for West Germany: for Maunz and Krüger the Basic Law was economically neutral,[1] for E. R. Huber it ruled out *laissez-faire* capitalism and socialist planning and therefore by elimination implied 'a social market economy' as a middle way,[2] and for Nipperdey the Basic Law represented in a formal sense a constitutional decision for the social market economy.[3] This debate was a large extent disingenuous, not simply in that it demonstrated the actual ambivalence of certain clauses of the Basic Law, but also in that it ignored a number of important factors. Firstly any debate about the legal or constitutional status of the economic order was academic in that western integration meant the de facto maintenance of a capitalist economy in West Germany, which constitutional lawyers were powerless to alter; secondly, in 1949 there was nothing about the 'new' economic order which distinguished it clearly from previous market economies; thirdly, in addition to the Basic Law, the West German state acknowledged earlier economic and social legislation and in the course of time introduced further statutes, which *together* were supposed to define more closely the constitutional framework of the economic order. The Basic Law cannot in fact be seen as prescribing any 'social market economy'. Nor, however, was it economically neutral, since it contains in a very unelaborated form the guarantees normally granted by a liberal capitalist state: the right to own and dispose of productive property (means of production) (Art. 14), freedom of movement (Art. 11), free choice of occupation (Art. 12), freedom of assembly and association (Arts 8 and 9), equality before the law (including contractual relations) (Art. 3).

What is interesting about the extensive debate surrounding the economic constitution is not so much that it demonstrated any real changes in the West German economic order, but that illustrated the efforts made by its proponents to present that economic order as a state-guaranteed 'third way'. The subsequent growth of the West

German economy increasingly made such efforts less urgent, but it also highlighted many real contradictions between the claims of the original 'social market' theorists and the real economy, i.e. between the theoretical and the real 'economic constitutions' of West Germany. This in turn raises the question of the actual validity of the idea of a prescriptive economic constitution, given the difficulties of theoretical definition and practical maintenance. The concept may only be valid as a heuristic fiction, with which one can illicit a *given* framework of legal and power relations, within which an economy functions at any point in time.

THE THEORY AND PRACTICE OF THE 'SOCIAL MARKET ECONOMY'

'Ordo-Liberalism' and relations of exchange – the 'Düsseldorf Principles' of the CDU

Competition is the greatest and most genial means of reducing power in history. You only need to invoke it and it does the rest of the work by itself. (Franz Böhm)[4]

A severe dilemma for liberal market economists in Germany in the first few decades of the 20th century was reconciling their espousal of capitalism with the political and social havoc it was wreaking. At the centre of this dilemma was the phenomenon of concentrated economic power in the hands of monopolies, oligopolies, cartels, trusts and syndicates. By accident or by design these various forms of concentration were contributing to the distortion and often complete neutralisation of competition; those enjoying concentrated economic power took advantage of that power at the expense of weaker economics agents, thus disturbing the so-called self-regulating mechanisms of the market and compounding cyclical fluctuations, particularly in the Great Depression. Despite attempts at legal control in the Weimar Republic, Germany remained the 'land of cartels', of price-fixing and monopoly power. Above all primary sectors of the economy (heavy industry, big agriculture) were able in part to avoid the vagaries of the market and impose on the rest of society, including smaller businessmen, their inflexible and inequitable regime. Whereas large sections of the bourgeoisie turned to a strong dictatorial state in

1933 as economic saviour, a minority of academics and politicians remained committed to competitive liberalism and anti-collectivism. The 'Freiburg school' of Walter Eucken and Franz Böhm, which emerged around 1930, proposed a reassertion of competition through rigorous state anti-monopolism, the school's later periodical ORDO gave the theory its name of *ordo-liberalism*.

Under 'national socialism', private monopoly power was the main organisational principle within each branch of the economy, where 'mandatory cartelisation' subordinated smaller agents of production to the authority of dominant firms in each branch; the cartelised branches ran a system of order allocations, production quotas and price regulation akin to that of the earlier coal, steel and iron syndicates. The process of accumulation was thereby accelerated, the big banks and the monopolies of the heavy, chemical and electrical industries benefited disproportionately from both peace and war, while the mass of the German population experienced the consequences of the policy of 'guns before butter'. As a result the loyalty of the German population to the economic order became increasingly strained.

With the collapse of fascism, the emergence of cold war tensions and the scotching of socialist initiatives in the Western zones, the ordo-liberals successfully stepped into the forefront of post-war West German politics. They presented their new economic model under the title of the 'social market economy', a name which rapidly became common currency. The organisational basis of the 'social market' programme was a union between ordo-liberals, social liberals and Christian democrats, some of whom were free from the odium of Nazi connections, but many of whom were not. The programme's first extensive public manifesto was the CDU brochure entitled the *Düsseldorf Principles*, which was published in July 1949.

These 'principles of economic policy' reveal an economic strategy which is in fact barely distinct from the manifestos of the republican middle class parties of the Weimar Republic, except for the *increased stress on statutory monopoly control*. The central pivot remains the idyll of perfect competition based on the dynamic but socially responsible small businessman.

The Düsseldorf Principles were understood as an extension of the earlier Ahlen Programme with its famous first sentence – 'the capitalist economic system has not done justice to the vital interests of the German people in state and in society'.[5] The Ahlen Programme was however to be 'supplemented and further developed in the direction of the market economy'.[6] The Düsseldorf Principles define the 'new economic order' as follows:

> The 'social market economy' is the socially bound constitution of the commercial economy, in which the endeavours of free and able people are set in an order which yields a maximum of economic advantage and social justice for all. This order is created by freedom and obligation, which in the 'social market economy' express themselves through genuine competition and independent monopoly control.[7]

The text clearly indicates that monopoly control is the main 'social' component of this economic order and reflects the belief of ORDO-liberals that an optimal *competitive order* would create increasing amounts of wealth and an equitable distribution of that wealth, reducing the need for economic and welfare intervention by the state. 'Social' here does not mean primarily a policy which would involve a wealth-transferring welfare state apparatus, but rather a policy of competition which *indirectly would allow the formation of private social security funds*. State redistribution measures thus would become less important. The presentation of the 'principles' puts the reader in no doubt as to the primacy of market economics as the basis for social justice and the secondary importance of actual redistributory social policy. Sixteen principles for the 'realisation of the Social Market Economy' are elaborated, none of which are social-political in nature:

1. Competition guaranteed by monopoly control.
2. Increase in the commercial responsibility and liability of businessmen.
3. Increased public accountability of joint stock companies, etc.
4. Central supervision of the monetary system.
5. Freedom from state influence on price formation – prices must be determined by the market.
6. Improved purchasing power through reduction of prices, not through wage rises.
7. Wages and conditions of labour to be decided by wage contract system – modest wages essential for economic recovery.
8. Science and technology to be encouraged as sources of reduced production costs.

9. Freedom of choice for career, place of work and profession.
10. Private property to be affirmed as the basis for economic independence. The Social Market Economy allows as many able people as possible to own property. Broad property ownership reduces the urgency of nationalisation.
11. 'Savings capital' to be encouraged as a primary source of investment capital.
12. Taxation system to be simplified, above all to allow capital formation.
13. Effective crisis management policies to be established – above all through credit and monetary policy, but also through an effective policy of public investment.
14. Foreign trade to be encouraged 'with all means'.
15. A merchant fleet to be recreated.
16. Representatives of the workforce to be involved in factory level and national supervision of economic life in order to achieve the essential trust of all social strata.

There then follow the 'principles of the CDU for future agricultural policy' and finally 12 'social political principles of the CDU':

1. There is a natural right to work. Women should have equality of opportunity.
2. Free choice of career and workplace with job security.
3. Appropriate remuneration – pay must correspond to productivity. Equal pay for women for same type of work.
4. Six-day working week – maximum hours not fixed.
5. Safety protection at Work; particular protection of young workers and women workers (unelaborated).
6. Social insurance as the basis of general social security.
7. Aid for war victims and returnees.
8. Integration of displaced Germans.
9. Welfare provision for proven need from public funds outside social insurance.
10. Compensation for war victims and refugees; land reform.
11. Social housing to be developed.
12. International Social Policy as basis for solidarity between nations.

The concluding remarks of the section confirm the subordination of Social Policy to the primacy of economics: 'It must however be particularly stressed that the basis for a healthy social order is a successful economic policy'.[8]

The principles of social policy are also not innovative. Apart from the specific compensation and aid for war victims (8 and 10) and the vaguely worded demand for international social policy (12) the essential elements of social policy were found in the Weimar Constitution or earlier.[9] Above all the principle of social insurance lays stress on self-help through a system of specific contributions and removes the state from responsibility for all but extreme cases. This is consistent with the anti-collectivism of ordo-liberalism. *The only real innovative element of the principles is the commitment to monopoly control and the creation of optimal competition*, and it is this element, the primary social component of the 'social market economy' which is made the centre of the programme.

The picture of perfect competition which emerges from the text is one of startling naïveté. The feasibility of effective monopoly control is assumed; the instruments of that control are thus barely elaborated beyond the demand for the legal proscription of cartel agreements.[10] Given, therefore, that the state has successfully de-monopolised the economy and created a situation of 'equal opportunities and fair conditions of competition',[11] it can withdraw to the sidelines to observe and supervise the dynamic interplay of market forces.

> The state is thus freed from the worry of central direction. There remains the task of making and protecting the law, of encouraging competition and organising monetary affairs.[12]

According to the guidelines monopoly control *allows the consumer to become 'master of the economy'*,[13] since in the market 'a competitive struggle for the favour of the consumer 'takes place and the consumer rewards the good producer with his custom'.[14] This dream of a state of dynamic equilibrium – the 'idyll of the petit bourgeoisie', as Welteke describes it[15] – reduces economic activity to the abstract metaphor of competitive sporting combat: a generalised consumer judges the performance of competitors on a unitary market with uniform conditions of competition, like a princess judges jousters at a mediaeval tournament.

Disregarding the fact that the Düsseldorf Principles were conceived as a political manifesto with the normal requirements of simplified mass appeal, there is little doubt that central advocates of the 'social market economy' like Erhard, Röpke, Böhm and Josten considered their model of optimal competition to be adequate and feasible. Röpke summarised this belief appropriately:

By setting ourselves against monopolism, concentration and colossal capitalism in the name of a genuine market economy and by declaring ourselves for a reduction of hardships and conflicts in favour of the weak, in the name of a positive economic policy which is guided by reason and humanity, we have already made our choice in favour of the small and medium-sized firm in all branches of the economy, in favour of all that is moderate, self-contained, easy to survey and suited to human dimensions, in favour of the middle classes, in favour of the restoration of property to the widest number of people, in favour of that kind of politics which can be summarized under the headlines of deproletarianisation and decentralisation in the national economy.[16]

This belief defied Weber's widely accepted theoretical position of the rationality of capital concentration as a function of the *economies of scale*, as well as Marx's forecast of inexorable concentration as a *function of a law of accumulation*. But it also defied the reality of increasing concentrations of economic power worldwide, which had at no time been checked, and most evidently the reality of market economies as such.

The actual absence of a unitary consumer on a unitary market, assessing equally matched moderately sized competitors, indeed the absence of free competition at any time in German history, did not seem to disturb the ordo-liberals. Then as now sceptics asked: How should/could the state control a large national company, if it represented a monopoly on the domestic market but a mere competitor on the international market? How could the state weaken a company which attracted high export earnings back into the domestic economy and employed thousands of German workers? How could an international corporation be controlled when its operations depended on complex transnational transfers and minimisation of local costs and therefore exploitation of local conditions? How could parcel industrial holdings of medium-sized companies by wealthy individuals, holding companies or big banks be controlled, given the guaranteed rights of ownership and disposition of productive assets? Above all, how was an effective control of cartel agreements feasible, given the severe 'deficit of information' of state bodies concerning the private economy?

Given that West Germany was firmly locked into the capitalist west, a *number of factors made the nurturing of large companies by the state a necessity rather than a crime*:

a. the reality of world market competition;
b. the laws of economies of scale;
c. the structural and regional importance of large companies as employers, earners of foreign currency and suppliers of strategically vital goods (armaments, energy, primary industrial products).

Thus the pledge to 'devote special attention and support to the nurturing of middle-sized and small firms'[17] could only have been a pious declaration of faith.

The conception of a guaranteed competitive order thus ignored a number of insuperable problems. Above all by proposing to freeze an economic order in a state of optimal competition it presented a fundamentally ahistorical position, which was attempting to defy the historical reality of capital concentration and thus to defy the very dynamic of profit-based accumulation which it wanted to preserve.

It is only reasonable to suspect that, alongside the 'believers' in the CDU, there were a large number of agnostics who regarded the new banner of the 'social market economy' as a fig-leaf, behind which they could conceal *the primary intention of maintaining and rehabilitating capitalist relations of production*, in the same way that all bourgeois parties historically hide behind the image of the pioneering dynamic small businessman. After the second world war the image of a self-reliance, which defied the vicissitudes of mass society and state politics, was a very potent one. National Socialism could be presented as the child of both monopolism and collectivism, thus frightening away all ideas of rational collective solutions which included large scale production and planning.

However in 1949, both believers and agnostics would have been aware that the constitutional framework for the 'social market economy' (monopoly control) had not been created by the Basic Law, nor by the earlier monetary reform of 1948 – the Basic Law doesn't even mention competition – but still needed to be created by additional government legislation (see below). Relations of exchange were circumscribed simply by the formal guarantees of property and contractual rights and by monetary law. At the real level of circulation the *currency reform* of June 1948 had made conditions of competition not more but less equitable by reducing the value of Reichsmark money savings to 10 per cent of their previous value, thus reinforcing the advantage of the owners of larger accumulations of real assets. The apparently equitable issue of DM 60 per head of the population (para. 6 of the Currency Reform Law) helped to conceal the real inequitable shift in the distribution of wealth. Furthermore the important issue of the future of the heavily concentrated coal, steel and chemical industries and the big banks had yet to be resolved under German law. The logical implication of these facts was that the 'social market economy' would only exist when its 'constitutional' framework was established, since its fundamental features could only be achieved by the provision and maintenance of strict rules of play. And yet in some people's minds the mysterious 'social market economy' already existed.

However, there was one further aspect of economic concentration which exercised the minds of the authors of the 'guidelines', namely that of interest groups and above all of trades unions. While the guidelines, in line with the Basic Law, recognise the legitimacy of trade unions, this recognition is qualified by the requirement that 'trade unions and trade associations' remain 'within the limits of their appropriate tasks as institutions of public life'[18] and reference is made to earlier 'group struggles and the exploitation of the interested parties'.[19] When Röpke talks of the 'rabble of interest groups hungry for intervention' and Müller-Armack of 'group egoism',[20] they are clearly implying trades unions, given that the unions had been in the forefront of the struggle against restoring German capitalism, demanding socialisation, economic planning by the state and union participation in commercial and state affairs. The political response to the threat posed by the trades unions were the proposals in the 'guidelines' for workers' participation at factory level, first mooted in the Ahlen Programme, and in certain state supervisory bodies governing labour law, monopoly control, monetary affairs, etc.[21]

'Codetermination' was conceived as means 'to overcome existing polarities and develop new forms of co-operation in the sense of genuine partnership bonds of communal endeavour and mutual responsibility for the common enterprise'.[22] Without looking at the real results of the codetermination legislation in West Germany, it seems reasonable to regard the mere proposal with extreme scepticism along with the proposal for monopoly control. The fundamental difference between employers, for whom wages represent costs to be minimised, and workers, for whom wages represent income to be maximised, cannot objectively be described by notions of 'genuine partnership' and 'common enterprise'. Semantically partnership implies commonality and equality of interest. The state of the labour market at the beginning of the new republic benefited employers inordinately; with over two million unemployed and hundreds of thousands of refugees and prisoners of war joining the job queues every year, labour costs could be held low for many years (as the guidelines implied)[23] and organised labour neutralised by the economics of the market. It is a commonplace that an economically and politically weakened German labour force was a vital precondition for the restoration both of the capitalist order and bourgeois prosperity, which in turn allowed the investment-led booms of the 1960s and 1970s. Talk of 'co-determination' and 'partnership' within this framework was at the very least specious, nothing more than an ideological flank for the sacrifices demanded by the market.

The theory of the 'social market economy', the 'new' economic constitution as outlined in the Düsseldorf guidelines, was remarkable not so much for its innovatory substance but for its semantics, for its way of selling old lamps as new ones and of reasserting the myth of the perfectly competitive economy. The ultimate failure of the model cannot be blamed on the politicians, who somehow perverted the purity of otherwise adequate principles, as Müller–Armack insisted'[24] but on the model itself. This model defies the reality of an internationalised market dominated by highly concentrated blocks of capital which are essentially immune to the isolated tinkering of individual nations.

From the Allied Decartelisation Laws to the Cartel Law of 1958

The Potsdam Agreement included the pledge to 'decentralise German economic life with the aim of destroying the present excessive concentration of economic power represented especially by cartels, syndicates, trusts and other monopolistic organisations'.[25] Accordingly the Western Allied Powers issued blanket decrees forbidding the formation of cartels and monopolies.[26] In addition however, the twelve largest heavy industrial firms were broken up into 28 separate legal entities under Allied trusteeship, the chemical giant IG-Farben was controlled by Allied trustees right up until 1953 when a final decision was made to split the infamous firm into 4 units; the three big banks, Deutsche Bank, Commerzbank and Dresdner Bank were each split into ten separate units based on the ten Länder excluding Berlin.

Much has been written about the motives behind such rigorous attempts at deconcentration. Many German commentators, like Borchardt and Wurm, assume a desire by the Western Allies to weaken German competition on world markets,[27] others talk of a concerted attempt by the West to conceal the restoration of capitalism and to outflank demands for immediate socialisation.[28] British and American historians tend rather to emphasise the strategic importance of weakening the economic potential for military production. What is certainly clear is that none of the three Western occupying powers had similarly rigorous formal controls on economic concentration, not even the USA, the pioneer of anti-trust legislation. It is thus reasonable to conclude that Allied deconcentration was fuelled by an expedient combination of retribution and commercial cynicism.

The Decartellisation laws remained in force until 1957. One of the conditions of the transfer of sovereignty to the West German state was the introduction of similar German legislation to replace it. The 'Law against Restraints on Competition', which was passed in July 1957 and came into force on 1 January 1958, represented the fulfilment of this condition. Ludwig Erhard stressed the importance of this law to the economic constitution of West Germany by dubbing it 'The Basic Law of the Economy',[29] its 'Magna Charta' no less.[30] However, although the law was held up as 'the most modern and progressive cartel law in the world',[31] it has never become an essential part of political and economic practice, nor was it ever likely to.

From the start, few, apart from the Ordo-Liberals themselves, showed much faith in cartel legislation. The Federation of German Industry (BDI), in a restrospective survey of cartel-control, noted with amused satisfaction that under the original decartellisation statutes 'the allies were extremely cautious in the prosecution of violations and the German authorities limited themselves likewise to modest prosecution activity'.[32] In 1950 E. Nölting, the Economics Minister of North Rhine Westphalia, stated that the West German Economy was 'covered in a spider's web of illicit pricing agreements . . . illegal cartels growing profusely as in greenhouse'.[33] Quite apart from failing to prosecute cartels effectively, the Americans in their zone also failed to abolish the restrictive practices of tradesmen and artisans, whereby both certificates of qualification and proof of (local) need for particular trades were required before a new business could be sanctioned by the Chamber of Trade.[34]

The fact that it took eight years to devise the 'Basic Law' of the social market economy to replace Allied Law is both an indication of the lack of real urgency involved as well as as the severe opposition to any such legislation on the part of German industry and commerce. The history of the passage of the law is itself illuminating: in July 1949, the Economics Ministry produced a draft bill for 'securing competition' and the creation of a monopolies office, which has become known as the *Josten draft*. This draft proposed a strict ban on *all* cartel agreements and other restrictive practices, to be backed up by severe legal sanctions. The Josten Draft thus corresponded to the strict but vague proposals of the Ahlen Programme and the Düsseldorf Guidelines but was never seriously debated because of outraged opposition from industry, representatives of which described the draft as 'nothing short of catastrophic'.[35] The first formal bill was drafted in May 1951 and debated in June 1952 in a first reading by both houses of parliament and then passed on to the Economics Committee of the Bundestag. This draft allowed three exceptions to the general proscription of cartels: cartels designed (a) to counteract economic crises, (b) to facilitate 'rationalisation' and (c) to encourage exports. Over the following two years Erhard was able to 'use the opportunity once more of discussing the most important proposals of the draft with interested economic circles, especially with the Federation of German Industry',[36] in the course of which he is reported to have made a number of concessions.[37] In January 1955 however the original 1951 draft was represented to the Bundestag, but was challenged by a counter-draft from Höcherl (CSU), which would have virtually permitted all cartels. The ordo-liberal member of the Bundestag Franz Böhm (CDU) presented yet another draft which reasserted the principle of a blanket ban on cartels, repudiating any suggestions of an arrangement with big business. After the first reading of these drafts at the end of March 1955, all three were presented to the Economics Committee which produced a number of amendments; these were debated in 1957 and the 'Law against Restraints on Competition' was passed in 27 July.

In its final form the law contains a general ban on cartels in par. 1, but then proceeds to outline those cartels which were *generally permissable* (1. agreements on conditions of sales, etc. 2. discount cartels, 3. rationalisation cartels) and others which could be *permitted on application* (import and export cartels, cartels for combatting structural crises). There were some eight exceptions in all. The Law provided for the creation of a cartel office, independent of the Federal government, to supervise the maintenance of its statutes, but even so the Federal Economics minister has the power, according to par. 8, to permit any other cartels if he considers them acceptable. Furthermore certain sectors of the economy are totally excepted from the purview of the law: the public sector, including post and railways, the commercial banks, agriculture and the coal and steel industry in as far as the latter was covered by the statutes of the ECSC. This means that the exceptions effectively made proscription the exception.[38]

However what is most significant is that this law, which represented fulfilment of the original pledge to introduce monopoly control, did virtually nothing to control the formation of monopolies as such. There was solely the requirement to *register* mergers with the cartel office, if the merger produced a 'market share of 20 per cent or more for a particular kind of commodity or commercial service, or if one of the enterprises involved already has a market share of this magnitude' (para. 23 GWB), in which case 'the cartel authority can call on the participants to take part in oral negotiations or to submit a written statement on the merger' (para. 24 GWB). Even then the law provided for no meaningful sanction against mergers. The Economics Minister was also empowered to overrule any recommendation of the Cartel Office and sanction any merger if national economic advantages were considered to outweigh the danger to competition (para. 24.3). For firms that already enjoyed a position of market dominance, the law provided only for the control of the *misuse* of this power and the Cartel Office was empowered to forbid certain actions or declare certain contracts null and void; however 'the stipulations remained so unclear that in the early years of the law's operation they were not applied to any case of major importance'.[39]

The 'Magna Charta' of the Social Market Economy, was in fact a mere 'caricature of an anti-monopoly law',[40] in which 'the original idea was barely discernable'.[41] Franz Böhm noted wryly in the cartel debate: 'If these proposals become law, then industrialists in every single branch of production will be able to sue the general secretary of their trade association for compensation, if he doesn't manage to persuade the cartel authority to allow their cartel.'[42] The law was less of a 'compromise solution',[43] but more clearly a capitulation to those very interests which it was seeking to control, as the historical development of capital concentration in West Germany shows.

The Development of Economic Concentration in West Germany after 1949

Economic concentration is a central feature of twentieth century capitalism; it has developed for a variety of reasons: technical rationality (economies of scale), natural commercial success, private and governmental convenience and, not the least, greed. The trend towards ever increasing concentration is unbroken, implying a *law of accumulation*, such as Marx had proposed. Concentrated economic power is located in personal fortunes but increasingly in anonymous blocks of parcellised capital holdings, exemplified by the world's giant joint stock companies. The function of concentrated economic power – be it intended or not – is to neutralise competition, the ideological cornerstone of the market economy, and thus to allow greater latitude for the maximisation of profits. Economic concentration takes several forms and concentrated economic power expresses itself in a variety of ways.

Collusion between competitors is most often sparked off by the threat of stagnation or recession and the possibility of murderous price wars, but frequently persists after recovery and through subsequent trade cycles; it can take the form of a simple *cartel*, of a more formalised *syndicate* or a *trust*. These forms of collusion have been historically very effective, but were often unstable subject to pressures resulting from the perceived unfairness of fixed production quotas, fixed geographical allocations of markets etc.

A more obvious form of concentration can be seen in the development of *vertical and horizontal oligopolies*, where individual large companies achieve a large share of particular markets either through natural expansion or through mergers and takeovers. *Horizontal concentration* infers the extension of control over a particular range of like products, *vertical concentration* the unification of several stages in a chain of production (from raw-material through production goods to consumer products). A more recent but less obvious form of ownership-based concentration is that of parcel-holdings, so-called *diagonal concentration*, whereby a private individual, a public company or a financial institution accumulates sizeable shareholdings in formally and technically separate companies. This is a formalised and extended system of share speculation which allows greater flexibility for profit maximisation through retention of only those holdings which are profitable and the hiving off of the least profitable; this form of concentration also avoids the public opprobrium which results from a famous public company ending or reducing its operations in a particular region or country.

In West Germany all three forms of concentration have thrived despite the state's ideological commitment to competition. Indeed there are many who argue that the West German state has aided and abetted concentration (see below).

In September 1955 *Economist* declared that 'Germany had once more become a land of price fixing' and this, despite a definitive ban on all cartels in Allied Law. In 1958, with the introduction of the 'Law against Restraints on Competition' there are no indications of any change in this situation. Up to the end of 1964 there were some 260 applications for formal cartels, of which 136 were sanctioned.[44] From 1958 there were six cement syndicates within the building materials industry; there were three big coal syndicates in the Ruhr area, as well as syndicates for nitro-chalk, potash, petrol and tar. Borchardt assumes that, apart from the 136 official cartels, there were many more unofficial, illegal ones, given that in 1930 there were 3000 or so cartels in Germany.[45] This is implied if not confirmed by the fact that in the first ten years of the 'cartel law's' operation the cartel office in Berlin instituted proceedings in 4546 cases, where there was suspicion of the law having been violated. However it is perhaps more significant for the practice of anti-monopolism in West Germany that in only 7 of these 4546 cases was a fine imposed, of which only 5 were enforced.[46] Even if this incredibly low conviction rate (compared to criminal law) is not the result of judicial or official unwillingness to prosecute commercial malpractice – and that is by no means certain – it does illustrate, if nothing else, the difficulty of proving the suspicion of collusion when this takes the form often of mere verbal agreements. The convenience and profitability of cartels has clearly not diminished, as more recent cases show. Apart from those domestic cartels, which are generally permissable or sanctioned by the authorities in West Germany, a number of illicit cartels have succeeded in functioning despite the threat of prosecution and fines. These include a cartel of 12 West German telephone producers which was broken up in 1976 by the Cartel Office, resulting in a severe price war led by Siemens; a cartel of the five main producers of industrial batteries and a cartel of fork-lift truck producers were broken up in 1977; in 1979 the eleven main producers of welding rods were fined nearly DM 600 000 for price fixing – these included subsidiaries of Krupp (2), Hoesch, Hoechst, Thyssen, as well as of GKN (Britain), Neuss (Sweden), Oerlikon (Switzerland) and the Austrian Vereinigte Stahlwerke; in 1982 fines of DM 11 million were imposed on the five main producers of glass containers for fixing production quotas, and in 1983 77 building firms were fined a total of DM 54 million for operating a rotating bid cartel for mainly large public contracts – the long list of firms includes Philip Holzmann, Bilfinger & Berger, and Moll & Kunz.[47]

Internationally there have been long-standing cartels in the electrical and chemical industries. A vast electro-cartel numbering 49 west European and six Japanese firms has existed for some time – it includes the German firms AEG, Siemens, Voith, Kraftwerk Union and Transformatoren Union. Their collusion was brought to light as is often the case by a disgruntled cartel member, Kurt Rudolf Mirow, and involved price fixing in contract tenders for steam turbines, generators, water turbines, switch gear, transformers and gas turbines.[48] The international chemical industry, dominated by some 25 large western firms (including Hoechst, Bayer and BASF) has employed market collusion programmatically for years, according to a recent UNCTAD study, notably for fertilisers and industrial chemicals, but also for man-made fibres.[49] (In the latter case a European 'crisis cartel' has been approved by the EEC authorities). Both chemicals and electrical international cartels function at the expense of Third World customers in particular and are still immune to prosecution by national anti-monopoly bodies.

Price-fixing and the other restrictive practices of cartels and syndicates have clearly thrived in West Germany as elsewhere, and the success of these mechanisms has to a certain extent obviated the need for more organic forms of concentration, since they maintain the illusion of separate competitive firms while allowing the benefits of collusion. The '*Law against Restraints on Competition*' has to a degree *reinforced the cartelisation process*, merely by advertising the legality of certain cartels and thereby possibly allowing illicit collusion to hide behind legal forms. Conversely it has also reinforced tendencies towards organic concentration in those cases where cartels are not sanctioned. Where two firms fail to establish the legality of their cooperation as separate legal entities, they may choose by means of a merger to circumvent the cartel ban, and in a situation where the cartel office virtually sanctions all mergers, this is to be expected.[50] There is evidence for such a process in the building industry, recently hit by prosecutions for collusion, where the largest firms – like Hochtief, Philip Holzmann and Dyckerhof & Widmann – have exchanged parcel holdings in one another.[51]

It is thus not surprising perhaps that organic capital concentration has become an increasingly dominant feature of commercial life in West Germany. The half-hearted and ill-considered attempts by the Allies to deconcentrate the heavy industrial, chemical and banking sectors, were almost all reversed. The only deconcentration measure to stick was the division of IG-Farben into the original three companies, Hoechst, Bayer and BASF. However one glance at turnover statistics for the world chemical industry shows how farcical such measures were, since all three companies are at the top of the league as oligopolies in their own right and under firm suspicion of collusion anyway.[52]

It is in fact a commonplace that in West Germany today, as in other Western countries, larger industrial and commercial concerns have come to dominate national economies, many of them being multinational in character. This domination is articulated in a number of different ways and must therefore be assessed using different indicators.

Firstly, using the general coefficients of turnover and workforce, it is possible to assess the *general influence of large firms* on the national and regional economies, as well as on the respective branches of industry. In 1954 the 50 largest industrial firms in West Germany had a collective turnover of DM36 800 million which represented some 25.4 per cent of total industrial turnover. By 1960 the top fifty firms turned over some DM92 300 million or 33.5 per cent of total industrial turnover and by 1967 DM160 500 million or 42.5 per cent. In other words of the 101 089 industrial firms in 1967 50 registered 42.5 per cent and the remaining 57.8 per cent of turnover. More recent figures for the top 10 industrial firms reinforce the picture of an unbroken trend towards increased concentration. Already in 1965 the top ten registered 15.6 per cent of total industrial turnover, in 1980 the figure stood at 20.7 per cent and in 1982 at 22.13 per cent. The same ten firms employed 1 131 800 people in 1965 or 13.4 per cent of the total industrial labour force which rose to 1 737 260 in 1980 (22.7 per cent) or 7.6 per cent of the total labour force of 22 986 000!

These and other top companies thus represent considerable economic and political power. Many of them are major export earners; they all contribute a great deal in taxation and underpin directly or indirectly national and regional prosperity as purchasers of goods and services and providers of wages and salaries. Their well-being is not identical to the 'national well-being', but national prosperity is increasingly dependent on their commercial operations. It is therefore not surprising that these large companies have been nurtured throughout the history of the Federal Republic in a way which medium-sized and small firms have not (with the possible exception of agricultural units). Their views have been considered far more than those of small businesses.[53] The state allows many thousands of small and medium-sized firms to go bankrupt, but has provided

Table 3.1 Industrial concentration, 1965–82

	Turnover (DM million)			Workforce		
	1965	1980	1982	1965	1980	1982
Volkswagen	9 268	33 288	37 434	122 700	257 930	239 116
Siemens	7 179	31 960	40 106	257 000	344 000	324 000
Daimler Benz	5 125	31 054	38 905	108 000	183 392	1–5 687
Thyssen	6 899	27 128	30 610	94 200	152 089	144 715
Hoechst	5 236	29 915	34 986	72 900	186 850	182 154
BASF	4 050	29 171	33 978	56 000	116 518	115 868
Bayer	5 389	28 825	34 834	81 700	181 639	179 463
AEG/Telefunken	4 638	15 151	13 267	143 000	145 200	92 730
Krupp	5 007	13 919	16 720	112 000	85 706	78 201
Veba	5 510	39 970	49 281	84 300	83 936	80 474
Total	58 301	280 381	330 121	1 131 800	1 737 260	1 622 408
Total industrial turnover	374 612	1 350 500	1 491 700[a]			
Share of top 10 firms in per cent	15.6	20.7	22.13[a]			
Workers in industry				8 460 000	7 661 000	7 239 000
Share of top 10 firms in per cent				13.4	22.7	22.4

Sources: Statistisches Jahrbuch der Bundesrepublik; Die Zeit (Aug. 1980; Aug. 1982): own calculations.
[a]approximate figures

billions for the salvage and maintenance of large firms that are threatened with insolvency. A few examples will suffice:

1. Ruhrkohle AG. The crisis in the West German Coal Industry in the late 1950s and early 1960s, which arose both from the development of excess capacity and from the glut of cheap oil, was remedied initially by the subsidised closure of certain pits and later by the creation of a large parent company for Ruhr pits, called Ruhrkohle AG; the Bund guaranteed the owners' debts (which meant paying most of them) and took only a minority share holding in the parent company, which was thus controlled collectively by the mine owners. Not only were plans to nationalise the mines thus avoided, but a vast private monopoly concern was created with state aid.
2. The iron steel industry, apart from being protected by the European Coal and Steel Community, had been sustained directly by the state through subsidies on coking coal (which also helped to maintain the income of coal producers); the Bavarian state has had a direct shareholding in the Maxhütte, the Bund in the Peine-Salzgitter works; the ARBED steelworks in the Saarland has recently been salvaged with considerable support from the Bund amounting to DM307 million so far. The Bund is also offering support to a merger of at least two of the three threatened Ruhr firms of Hoesch, Thyssen and Krupp.
3. AEG/Telefunken: in 1982, a year in which there were some 16 000 bankruptcies in West Germany, the electrical giant AEG was saved from collapse by massive injections of state monies.

West Germany's *largest firms have been allowed to grow at a far faster rate than the economy as a whole*. They have grown disproportionately fast in boom periods and have survived economic crises far better than smaller firms. Indeed such crises appear to encourage the accumulation process, not simply because size guarantees survival, but also because smaller weaker competitors sell up more cheaply. Large firms seek to diversify their operations, and the collapse of competitors on a reduced market may in fact increase the relative market share of the surviving large company. Certainly the history of mergers and takeovers in West Germany would confirm both this and the ineffectiveness of state merger control, ostensibly strengthened by four revisions of the 'Law against Restraints on Competition'. The main agents of such mergers are the large companies,

Table 3.2   Mergers in the Federal Republic, 1963–81

1963	1965	1967	1969	1971	1973	1975	1977	1979	1980	1981
29	50	65	168	229	243	448	554	602	635	618

1966 1st revision of GWB

1967 Recession

1973 2nd revision of GWB

1974 Oil crisis/recession

1976 3rd revision of GWB

1980 4th revision of GWB

1981–82 Recession

their main objects of accumulation – medium- and small-sized firms. In the energy sector Veba and German BP between them took over 333 companies between 1973 and 1981; these transactions included the controversial purchase by BP of Veba's subsidiary Gelsenberg (oil and natural gas) which was vetoed by the Cartel Office in 1978

Table 3.3   The ten largest takeover operators in West Germany, 1981

	No. of takeovers between 1973 & 1981		Development of turnover		
			1973 (DM billion)	1981 (DM billion)	per cent increase
Veba	196		12.5	49.4	+295%
Deutsche BP	137		4.8	24.3	+406%
RWE	112		7.8	20.5	+280%
Haniel	74		1.9	6.2	+226%
Shell	72		7.1	19.7	+177%
Ruhrkohle	61		8.5	18.2	+114%
Estel Hoesch	53		6.2	8.0	+ 29%
Thyssen	53		11.9	28.2	+137%
Salzgitter	53		5.3	9.2	+ 73%
Dresdner Bank	53	Total Balances:	56.6	131.5	+132%

Sources: *Der Spiegel*, 13 Dec. 1982; own calculations.

but approved by the Economics Minister Lambsdorff, in 1979 in accordance with Art. 24 of the GWB. The large oil companies have a long tradition of aggressive operations which include increasingly the use of localised or general price wars to put smaller firms in the petrol or heating oil trade out of business.[54]

Finally, the absolute and relative increase in the power of the largest companies is confirmed by statistics on the development of the workforce, which show that whereas the total German working population (and the industrial labour force) declined after reaching a peak in 1965, the workforce of the top 10 and top 50 companies increased to peak in 1980, after which rationalisation and recession have produced a slight fall.

Beyond the general influence of large firms, the wave of mergers reflects the increased importance of the *specific influence of branch-based oligopolies*. The development of the *concentration ratios* in separate branches of the German economy is a common indicator of increased monopolisation.

Table 3.4 Concentration ratios in West Germany's chemical, electrical, steel and car industries, 1961 and 1969

Large firms	*Share of branch turnover (per cent)*		*Share of branch workforce (per cent)*	
per branch	*1961*	*1969*	*1961*	*1969*
3 Firms in the chemical industry	38	49	41	46
8 Firms in the electrical industry	60	68	62	68
4 Firms in the steel industry	61	65	66	60
5 Firms in the car industry	76	92	61	76

Source: Urs Jaeggi, *Kapital und Arbeit in der Bundesrepublik* (Frankfurt, 1969).

Even these broad figures of branch dominance do not reveal the true levels of concentration, since they cover a wide range of products in each branch. Each firm does not produce the whole range, indeed the production of specific products is often concentrated in very few hands. Large steel pipes are produced solely by Mannesmann after taking over Thyssen's pipe producing interests, the aircraft industry is dominated by the enlarged Messerschmidt–Bölkow–Blohm, over 90 per cent of the production of lorries and of typewriters is in the hands of three firms.

Table 3.5   Share of domestic production of Selected Goods by the three largest producers in 1980 (per cent)

Televisions	40.8
Photo equipment	42.9
Petrol	51.1
Refridgerators	55.5
Cigarettes	62.2
Batteries	62.3
Cars	66.8
Car tyres	68.1
Washing machines	69.9
Detergents	73.8
Lorries	90.3
Typewriters	91.1

Source: *Der Spiegel*, 13 Dec. 82.

Market dominance of the producers of particular products does not simply facilitate price leadership on the one product market, but more significantly perhaps it produces a situation where competition between smaller suppliers of components, services etc is exploited by the *monopolised demand* of one large firm. In 1965 details were published revealing the scale of this dependence with examples of the number of suppliers of certain large firms:

Table 3.6   Monopolised demand

	no. of suppliers
AEG:	30 000
Siemens:	30 000
Krupp:	23 000
Daimler-Benz	18 000
Bayer:	17 500
BASF:	10 000
Opel:	7 800

Source: J. Huffschmid, *Die Politik des Kapitals*, p. 70.

The formal independence of supplier firms can in reality be a situation of virtual subordination to the larger customer firms, especially if the latter is the main or sole customer. The contractual arrangements between large and small firms are rarely publicised but there is considerable evidence for widespread malpractice. This primarily involves the dictation of prices and discounts, through which firms' profits are maximised and the profit margins of smaller firms are correspondingly squeezed.

In 1977, for example, AEG wrote to its suppliers stating its expectation of a 3–5 per cent reduction in component prices. 'in order that in future we will be able to place our orders with you without interruption'.[55] In 1974, when general inflation in West Germany stood at around 7 per cent p.a. and factory gate prices rose by 13.4 per cent, the Volkswagen company imposed the previous year's prices on many of its 6 000 suppliers but proceeded to raise its own prices twice the following year on grounds of rising costs.[56] The electrical firm Bosch introduced a clause into its contracts which allowed it to withdraw if it received lower price quotations from other sources *after the contract was signed*.[57] In particular the retail trade giants in West Germany have succeeded in imposing increasingly stringent conditions on their suppliers, even on multinational food companies like Unilever and Nestle. These conditions go beyond simple price discounts and include free delivery and free price-labelling. It is also quite common that suppliers are charged both and 'entry fee' for access to a retail chain and then a retainer to prevent the discontinuation of a particular line.[58] This 'naked extortion'[59] yields higher profits for the retail oligopolies like Tengelmann, Aldi, Allkauf, Edeka and Rewe and reduced income for those smaller retailers who cannot impose similar conditions in their operations. The result of the process is that virtually half of West Germany's food retail shops disappeared between 1960 and 1980, leaving two thirds of food retail turnover in the hands of only 2 per cent of the retail firms. Another result is the increase in bankruptcies among supplier firms,[60] which can easily be hastened by the punitive extension of periods of payment.[61]

A generalised picture of the relative advantages of branch-based oligopolies in West Germany has been given by Herbert Schui, who has demonstrated the correlation between branch concentration ratios and price rises. He reveals that those branches with a higher degree of concentration have been able to increase price (and by implication profits) at a higher rate than branches with lower degrees of concentration, particularly in periods of declining rates of growth.[62]

Monopolised supply and monopolised demand are features of concentration, the nature and effects of which can be fairly easily grasped. The same cannot be said for the more recent phenomenon of *diagonal concentration*. This misnomer is a maladroit attempt to distinguish a company with diverse holdings from horizontally and vertically concentrated companies; 'diagonal' implies a degree of coherence in the firm's interests which rarely exists; the only import-ant common feature of the various holdings of such a company is their absolute commodity form. The holding company, like *Flick*, *ITT* or *Interversa*, is simply a big investor in corporate form; it is largely anonymous in that it is not identified with a specific product or service, and it is free of the managerial responsibilities attached to a specific product range, specific suppliers and a specific work force. Its assets are in the purest sense mere instruments of accumulation, yielding an assorted income, be it from dividends or interest or from sales of holdings. In West Germany 'diagonal' concentration is less advanced than in Britain, or the USA; this is probably due to the developed tradition of corporate investment through the banking and insurance sector rather than through individual portfolios managed by stock-brokers. However increasingly, diversified holdings have been identified as valuable hedges against the weaknesses of specific markets and as lucrative sources of accumulation as such. The relative strength of conglomerate holding concerns is demonstrated by the fact that they have a generally higher ratio of net added value to turnover; in the 1982 merit table of the top 100 industrial enterprises in West Germany, *Flick* is 28th in the turnover league and 21st in the net-added-value league, *VIAG* – 40th/30th, *ITT* – 66th/49th and *Interversa* – 76th/60th.[63] It is therefore no surprise that traditional branch-based oligopolies have begun to diversify into unrelated areas of the economy.[64] The three big universal banks have maintained considerable and widely diverse holdings: the *Dresdner Bank* in Mining, Engineering; Cement, Electrical, Nuclear Energy, Shipping and retailing; the *Commerzbank* in Civil Engineering, Building, Cement, Retailing, Films, Engineering; the *Deutsche Bank* in Elec-trical companies, Shipping, building, heavy engineering, retailing and sugar.

It is extremely difficult to survey the complex web of parcel holdings in West Germany; it is equally difficult to assess the econ-omic and political influence of conglomerates. It is only possible to make generalised assertions, based on known cases. It is clear that *Flick*, with its 38 per cent holding in Daimler-Benz, or *Quandt*, with

40 per cent of BMW, 14 per cent of Daimler-Benz and 50 per cent of Varta (batteries), exert considerable influence over the car industry. Flick also controls major sections of the armaments industry (Buderus, Krauss-Maffei, Dynamit Nobel) and the paper-milling giant Feldmühle AG. Flick's political influence has been demonstrated by the revelations of the 'Flick Affair', indicating political bribery of government ministers, CDU/CSU and FDP members and influence over government appointments, notably that of Wolfgang Kartte, the present head of the cartel office (!).[65]

The flexibility, anonymity and profitability of holding concerns would seem to indicate that they will continue to increase and expand.

The *role of the state in the increased concentration of West German capital* is the object of considerable discussion.[66] As was observed above, the reality of international trade and technical rationality has effectively forced the West German state to nurture concentration while paying lip service to anti-monopolism. There are one or two examples of *direct state influence* in the creation of large domestic monopolies and oligopolies: the creation in 1968 of a parent company for coal mining in the Ruhr area, Ruhrkohle AG, has been described above (p. 67); the same year, the Bund promoted the concentration of the aircraft industry with the merger of Bölkow, Messerschmidt and in 1969 Blohm, and more recently it virtually forced the merger of MBB with the Krupp-owned Flugtechnische Werke GmbH, by making a DM300 million subsidy for the Airbus project conditional on the marriage.[67] It is also very likely that the government will make steel subsidies conditional on the creation of a 'Ruhrstahl AG', which would involve some form of merger between anyone of Thyssen. Krupp, Hoesch or Klöckner. Beyond these direct measures of concentration, the Bonn government has, on five occasions, lifted the Cartel Office proscriptions of mergers, even though such proscriptions are extremely rare (see above).

The *indirect furtherance of concentration* has taken various forms. The encouragement of self-financing[68] as a primary instrument of investment in the early 1950s through differential taxation, is one example which was virtually unavoidable, given the absence of an adequate capital market. *Cumulative turnover tax*, which was retained until 1967 is generally recognised as having encouraged vertical concentration, since it made separate firms in a productive chain pay 4 per cent tax on each transaction, but allowed firms which combine a number of those stages, to pay 4 per cent only once.[69]

More recently the introduction of *Keynesian policies* has, in the view of some, encouraged concentration, firstly by giving priority to the global management of demand, rather than to differentiated demand management and secondly by consulting only the representatives of big business.[70] As was suggested above, cartel legislation combined with few merger controls have made mergers often more worthwhile. Above all, however, *state inactivity has allowed capital concentration to proceed as if there were no countervailing legislation*, let alone a commitment to anti-monopolism.

THE REDEFINITION OF THE 'SOCIAL MARKET ECONOMY'

Anti-monopolism, the 'social' cornerstone of Ordo-liberalism, has failed in West Germany. It would therefore seem appropriate that the appellation 'social market economy' with its two pillars of 'freedom'/competition and 'obligation'/monopoly control would have been withdrawn discreetly from official usage in West Germany – but not a bit of it. All the major parties in West German political life, most industrialists and a number of trade union leaders employ the catchword 'social' in a seemingly conscious attempt to demarcate the West German economy positively from other market economies, and yet the West German economic order cannot be distinguished essentially from that of other advanced capitalist societies. The legal framework, the 'economic constitution', does not set West Germany apart from other states, many of whom have likewise token monopoly control. *However what West German state ideologues now emphasise is not monopoly control as the 'social' attribute of the economic order, but the social security system*. Thus, whereas in the 1950s the primacy of monopoly control as the social component was stressed by government and its academic supporters more recent state and academic publications ignore anti-monopolism completely: in 1978 under the sub-heading 'the social component of the economic system', the government press office wrote exclusively in terms of the 'dense net of social security surrounding the Federal Republic'.[71] Karl Thalheim, describing the difference between 'free' and 'social' market economies, states:

> social guarantees are built into the economic system of the Federal Republic to a considerable degree and the state intervenes with

numerous measures – e.g. through cyclical policy – in economic affairs. In the social field regulations have been created which are quite often foreign to the *free* market economy, among others through employment protection, the Works Council Law, as well as the co-determination of workers in the Coal and Steel industry and in a great part of the other large industrial plants.[72]

These two examples reflect a general shift in the definition of the 'social market economy' within the West German establishment, which entails at the least intellectual sloppiness and at worst plain dishonesty. Firstly the social legislation perceived now as the distinguishing feature of the West German economic order is common to many western capitalist democracies; it had in part already been in existence in the Wilhelmine Empire (sickness, accident insurance and old age pensions) or the Weimar Republic (works councils, unemployment insurance, employment protection, etc.) – it was thus not innovative in the way a guaranteed order of near perfect competition would have been. Secondly, *protective social legislation is not an attribute of the functioning of a market economy*, but of normal state activity which is essentially apart from the market process but subordinate to it in terms of a) the particular social instabilities resulting from market fluctuations and b) the material resources with which the state attempts to neutralise those instabilities. Thirdly, the very function of the 'social state' is a matter of some controversy in relation to the primary interests it serves (see below). The attribute 'social' (be it attached to the *market economy*, 'partnership' between employers and workforce, or the state) is clearly being exploited as an ideological catchword, but at the same time it is being sorely tested by the divisiveness of social expenditure cuts and mass unemployment. It could therefore mean that the 'social' market economy might need yet further redefinition, if the social state were seen to fail after the failure of monopoly control.

CONSTITUTIONAL IDEOLOGY AND CONSTITUTIONAL REALITY

The 'Economic Constitution' as proposed by the Düsseldorf Guidelines does not exist. The ideology of a state-guaranteed competitive order has been confounded by its own theoretical contradictions, by the concerted opposition of the organised business community and by the impotence of the instruments of legal sanction created to realise the ordo-liberal dream. The Cartel Office, which administers those sanctions, has become little more than a registry for the increased concentration it was supposed to check; the fatalistic tone of its regular reports bears witness to that.

The *constitutional reality* of economic life in West Germany is very different from the theoretical model, being the corollary of the failure to realise any adequate form of monopoly control. This reality reflects the critical position of West Germany and other nation states in the face of internationalised market forces, which are borne by large oligopolies with numerous national bases for their operations.[73] The position of the sovereign state of early capitalist societies, which guaranteed and enforced the formal contractual equality of agents of exchange, has been weakened by the development of monopoly power within its jurisdiction. This monopoly power has subordinated locally based small capital into a serf-like status, such that the *weaker contractual partner is obliged to accept discriminatory conditions* (see above pp. 5f) *and the state is obliged to enforce those conditions in any subsequent litigation, as if they were the expression of fair competition.*

It is this ability of the oligopolies to determine discriminatory contractual conditions which has led some commentators to talk of a *process of refeudalisation*[74] in which the industrial giants increasingly *set their own legal frameworks* in order to avoid the influence of competitive market forces. The concept is primarily polemical but it illustrates vividly the erosion of the nation state as an important pillar of high capitalism. The old state was seen to referee the fair interplay of individual capitals in the interest of national capital in general. However, national capital – as a geographically limited and 'patriotic' entity – has become (or has always been) a fiction, and the nation state is increasingly the handmaid of internationalised capital. A statement by Wolfgang Kartte, the present head of the Cartel Office in Berlin demonstrates the totally contradictory position of the isolated state body in an environment which has outgrown the nation state system:

> We don't want to do anything against those concentrations which assist technical progress or which are necessary to maintain the exporting ability of the German economy. . . . We do however want to take in hand those acts of concentration which would in fact lead to a questionable accumulation of economic power, to an economic power which would in fact suspend the competitive mechanism.[75]

This fine distinction between good and bad concentration defies the reality of West German economic life, where *technical and national economic rationality coincide with the suspension of competition*. The technologically most advanced, export-intensive oligopolies – in the electro-technical, automative, chemical, steel and energy industries – are usually the main culprits in restraints on competition and it is naive to assume it could be otherwise.

It might be concluded that the development of supra-national institutions of monopoly control could more effectively counteract the abuse of economic power by the multinational oligopolies. Thus far, however, EEC competition policy has been directed towards the impovement of 'European Competitiveness' in the triangular rivalry of the USA, Japan and Europe. This has meant the direct encouragement of concentration and co-operation, the sanctioning of cartels and the strengthening of nationally based oligopolies.[76] The EEC's commitment to combatting restrictive practices is thus largely a token one and mirrors the contradictions embodied in West German and other national competition policies: all assert the sanctity of competition while deliberately subverting it nationally and regionally. The EEC Commission's attempt to unify the concentration process is even then distorted by individual and rival national policies which seek extra advantages for 'national' capitals – the European steel industry is a prime example.

The embarassment of the contradictions of competition policy can only be dispelled by the abandonment of that policy and the exclusive encouragement of national or European capital as putative entities. The actual contradictions between small and big capital will remain, as will the anarchy of particularised nation states who attempt to employ their fiscal resources more or less independently in order to maintain the interests of particularised blocks of capital. But these, it has to be stressed, have long since broken the umbilical cord to one nation.

Notes

1. Theodor Maunz, *Deutsches Staatsrecht* (Munich, 1973) p. 169; H. Krüger, 'Staats-Verfassung und Wirtschafsverfassung' in *Deutsches Verwaltungsblatt*, 1951, pp. 361ff; their view was supported by the Federal Constitutional Court in 1954 in its deliberations on the Investment Aid Act (cited in: *Freiheitliche demokratische Grundordnung*, ed. Erhard Denninger (Frankfurt, 1977) vol. I, p. 320).

2. E.R. Huber, *Wirtschaftsverwaltungsrecht*, vol. I (Tübingen, 1953) pp. 30f; H. Krüger, 'Wirtschaftsverfassung, Wirtschaftsverwaltung, Rechtsstaat' in *Betriebsberater* (1953) p. 565.
3. Hans Carl Nipperdey, 'Freie Entfaltung der Persönlichkeit', republished in *Freiheitliche demokratische Grundordnung*, op. cit., pp. 251ff.
4. Franz Böhm, 'Demokratie und ökonomische Macht' in F. Böhm, *Kartelle und Monopole im modernen Recht* (Karlsruhe, 1961) p. 22.
5. Das Ahlener Wirtschaftsprogramm der CDU für Nordrhein Westfalen, 3 Feb. 1947, republished in Huster *et al.*, *Determinanten der westdeutschen Restauration*, op. cit., pp. 424ff.
6. Düsseldorfer Leitsätze der CDU, 15.7.1949, republished in Huster *et al.*, ibid., p. 433.
7. Ibid., p. 430.
8. Ibid., p. 448.
9. Die Verfassung des Deutschen Reichs (11 Aug. 1919), Reichsgesetzblatt S.1383, arts 7, 111, 109, 161, 9, 10.
10. Düsseldorfer Leitsätze, op. cit., p. 433.
11. Ibid., p. 430.
12. Ibid., p. 433.
13. Ibid., p. 433.
14. Ibid., p. 431.
15. Marianne Welteke, *Theorie und Praxis der sozialen Marktwirtschaft* (Frankfurt, 1976) p. 38.
16. Wilhelm Röpke, *Die Gesellschaftskrisis der Gegenwart* (Erlenbach, 1948) p. 80.
17. Düsseldorfer Leitsätze, op. cit., p. 434.
18. Ibid., p. 445; see Grundgesetz (Basic Law), Art. 9, para. 3.
19. Düsseldorfer Leitsätze, op. cit., p. 441.
20. Röpke, as quoted in Welteke, *Theorie und Praxis*, op. cit., p. 39; Alfred Müller-Armack, in L. Erhard/A. Müller-Armack, *Soziale Marktwirtschaft – Manifest 72* (Frankfurt, 1972) pp. 44f.
21. The problematic relationship of the trade unions to the 'social market economy' is the subject of an extensive section in: Erhard/Müller-Armack, *Soziale Marktwirtschaft*, op. cit., pp. 101ff.
22. Düsseldorfer Leitsätze, op. cit., p. 441.
23. Ibid., p. 445.
24. Erhard/Müller-Armack, *Soziale Marktwirtschaft* op. cit., pp. 192ff.
25. Protocol of the Proceedings of the Potsdam Conference, press release, reprinted in: *Germany 1947–1949: the Story in Documents*, op. cit., p. 49 (Section IIB, para. 12).
26. See Law Nr. 56 of the American Military Government, Nr. 78 of the British Military Government and Nr. 96 of the French Military Government.
27. Knut Borchardt, in Gustav Stolper *et al.*, *Die deutsche Wirtschaft seit 1870* (Tübingen, 1964) p. 291; Franz F. Wurm, *Wirtschaft und Gesellschaft in Deutschland 1848–1948* (Opladen, 1975) p. 276.
28. Rolf Badstübner/Siegfried Thomas, *Restauration und Spaltung, Entstehung und Entwicklung der BRD 1945–1955* (Cologne, 1975) pp. 438ff; Karl Neelsen, *Wirtschaftsgeschichte der BRD* (Berlin, 1973) pp. 53ff.
29. Thus Erhard, quoted in Knut Borchardt, op. cit., p. 291.

30. Erhard, *Wohlstand für alle* (Düsseldorf, 1957) p. 168.
31. Ludwig Erhard in a Broadcast on Bavarian Radio, 5 July 1957.
32. Der Bundesverband der deutschen Industrie, *10 Jahre Kartellgesetz, 1958–1968. Eine Würdigung aus der Sicht der deutschen Industrie* (Bergisch-Gladbach, 1968) pp. 445ff.
33. Ernst Nölting, quoted in *Frankfurter Rundschau*, 8 May 1950.
34. Borchardt, op. cit., p. 293.
35. BDI, *10 Jahre Kartellgesetz*, op. cit., p. 446.
36. Erhard, *Wohlstand für alle*, op. cit., p. 171.
37. Neelsen, *Wirtschaftsgeschichte der BRD*, op. cit., p. 58.
38. Ibid., p. 58.
39. Borchardt, op. cit., p. 292.
40. Neelsen, *Wirtschaftsgeschichte der BRD*, op. cit., p. 58.
41. Borchardt, op. cit., p. 292.
42. Franz Böhm in 76th session of the Second Bundestag, 24 Mar. 1955, quoted in: Huffschmid, *Die Politik des Kapitals* (Frankfurt, 1972) p. 149.
43. Thus Günter Elsholz, *Die Wettbewerbsordnung in der Bundesrepublik* (Informationen zur politischen Bildung 121), (Stuttgart, 1967) pp. 12ff.
44. Borchardt, op. cit., pp. 292f.
45. Ibid., p. 293.
46. Huffschmid, *Die Politik des Kapitals*, op. cit., p. 150.
47. See *Der Spiegel*, 47/1977, *Frankfurter Rundschau*, 19 Jan. 79, 26 Feb. 82, 7 Sept. 83.
48. *Frankfurter Rundschau* (FR), 26 June 1980, *Der Spiegel* 50/1979.
49. UNCTAD, *The structure and behaviour of enterprises in the chemical industry and their effects on the trade and development of developing countries*, UNCTAD/ST/MD/23, United Nations 1979.
50. Thus Elsholz, *Die Wettbewerbsordnung*, op. cit., p. 15.
51. *FR*, 15 Dec. 1982.
52. UNCTAD, *Structure and behaviour of enterprises*, op. cit., pp. 14f.
53. See Hallgarten/Radkau, *Deutsche Industrie und Politik*, op. cit., pp. 508ff.
54. See *Der Spiegel*, 28/1983, p. 51; c.f. also the price war in the telephone equipment industry between Siemens and smaller firms, *Spiegel*, 47/1977.
55. Quoted in *Der Spiegel*, 46/1977.
56. Ibid.
57. Ibid.
58. *Der Spiegel*, no. 10 (1980).
59. Thus Nestlé Manager, Helmut Maucher, ibid.
60. See Huffschmid, *Die Politik des Kapitals*, op. cit., pp. 71ff.
61. In 1980 Tengelmann apparently doubled its payment periods from 10 to 21 days and included a 3 per cent discount in its delayed payment, see *Der Spiegel*, 10/1980.
62. Herbert Schui, 'Die hohe Wirtschaftskonzentration trägt die Schuld an der Wachstumskrise' in *FR*, 25 Nov. 1978.
63. Statistical Source: *Die Zeit*, 12 Aug. 1983.
64. Viz. Lutz Dreesbach, *Die kleinen Seitensprünge großer Unternehmen* (Düsseldorf, 1983).
65. *Der Spiegel*, 31/1983.

66. Viz. Dieter Grosser (ed.), *Konzentration ohne Kontrolle* (Opladen, 1974); Helmut Arndt, *Die Konzentration in der westdeutschen Wirtschaft* (Pfullingen 1966); Huffschmid, *Politik des Kapitals*, op. cit., pp. 109ff; Welteke, *Theorie und Praxis*, op. cit., pp. 79ff.

67. Huffschmid speaks of 'massive pressure' from Economics Minister Karl Schiller in forcing through the Messerschmidt–Bölkow deal, stresses the large financial inducements for the Ruhrkohle amalgamation and cites Schiller's (in the event unnecessary) encouragement to the oil companies to effect an 'organisational amalgamation of all economic forces', *Politik des Kapitals*, op. cit., pp. 59, 57f, 58; the MBB merger with the Flugtechnische Werke was dealt with more or less in the open, with few qualms about the creation of a monopoly, see *FR*, 1 Dec. 1980.

68. C.f. Borchardt, op. cit., p. 288, Welteke, *Theorie und Praxis*, op. cit., p. 76ff.

69. C.f. Friedrich Bloch, 'Steuern und Konzentration' in *Konzentration ohne Kontrolle* (ed. Grosser), op. cit., pp. 160ff; Helmut Arndt, *Die Konzentration in der westdeutschen Wirtschaft*, op. cit., p.00.

70. See Huffschmid on the composition of the tripartite discussion ('Konzertierte Aktion'), *Politik des Kapitals*, op. cit., pp. 126f.

71. Presse–und Informationsamt der Bundesregierung, Tatsachen über Deutschland (Bonn, 1978) pp. 138f.

72. Karl Thalheim, *Die wirtschaftliche Entwicklung der beiden Staaten in Deutschland* (Berlin, 1978) p. 13.

73. The chemical firm Farbwerke Hoechst has subsidiaries in 36 different countries, Bayer AG has subsidiaries in 33. See *Yearbook of International Organisations*, 12th ed, pp. 1203–4.

74. Joachim Perels, *Kapitalismus und politische Demokratie*, op. cit., pp. 57ff.

75. Wolfgang Kartte, Radio Interview with Westdeutscher Rundfunk, 19 May 1971, concerning the revision of the Cartel Law.

76. See Joachim Lau, 'Die Wettbewerbspolitik der EWG', in: F. Deppe (ed.), *Europäische Wirtschaftsgemeinschaft* (Hamburg, 1975) pp. 312–37.

4 The Role of the State in the Expansion of the West German Economy, 1949–66

FOREIGN POLICY

The consideration of foreign policy before domestic policy as factors affecting economic development is a deliberate choice, not because foreign policy can generally be considered primary when approaching an advanced industrial economy, but because West Germany occupied a very special position within the Western community which required far greater attention to foreign political and economic relations than any other nation of its standing. Nevertheless there is a sense in which, with the emergence of two major federations of states after the Second World War, individual nation states are obliged to consider bloc allegiances and foreign relations as a contribution to their primary task of guaranteeing a particular constitutional order. This is reinforced in West Germany's case by specific dependencies: *state sovereignty* was not achieved until 1955 and was conditional on the approval of the USA, Britain and France, whose forces remained on German soil as armies of occupation; as a recipient of ERP monies and as a member of the OEEC the West German state was formally bound to aid conditions which were determined by non-national interests intent on the maintenance of the post-1949 status quo; outside any formal obligations the recovery of West Germany's industrial economy demanded both a high level of foreign trade with countries where 'goodwill' was in many cases minimal and had therefore to be nurtured, and the abandonment of hitherto strong trade links with Eastern Europe.

It is thus possible to talk of the *primacy of Western integration* in the central state policy of the first two Adenauer governments at least until 1955. Beyond this the actual achievement of sovereignty cannot be seen as eliminating the general international constraints on state policy, but the concentrated effort of (re-)integration can be seen to recede, particularly after the Rome Treaties of 1957. After this West

German foreign policy is less urgent but no less vital to the maintenance of the politico-economic status quo and to economic growth.

One important difference between West German foreign policy after 1957 and that of similar states lies in the fact that the 'German question' continued to remain unresolved, such that the partition line between East and West Germany continued to represent the partition line between the two major power blocs and the two Germanies play vital roles in the struggle to maintain the respective orthodoxies of each bloc. It can be argued that this limits the latitude of the West German state to adopt an independent line (in both foreign and domestic policy) in the face of its perceived strategic importance to the USA and other NATO governments; these limitations are apparent in part in West Germany's status within NATO. The *formal* sovereignty of the West German state after 1955 thus perhaps diverts attention away from the persisting block dependence, the dominance of the USA and the lack of *effective* sovereignty.

Foreign policy nevertheless has to be seen as subordinate to domestic interests, whether it is the subject of greater or lesser concern in a state's day to day work. This qualification is necessary because some historians and political scientists do not simply identify a primacy of foreign policy in West German politics beyond 1955 and 1957 but define that primacy in terms of pursuing international (European) political goals; when Thilo Vogelsang states that Adenauer pursued his 'Europe-policy for the sake of Europe'[1] he implicitly denies that basic chain of interest which is rooted in the modern (West German) capitalist state. He implicitly denies that foreign policy and domestic policy are no more than means to represent the dominant domestic economic interests. This chapter in contrast accords foreign policy primacy over domestic policy only as a means of furthering domestic national interests as the primary goal.

Military Integration and Economic Development

The integration of West Germany into the Western bloc was achieved formally in two distinct though related ways: through its membership of the NATO military alliance and through its membership of Western Economic Organisations – the EEC, OEEC (1961: OECD), IBRD (World Bank), the IMF and others. It is problematic to accord military integration greater importance than formal economic integration as the order of sections here implies, but in one sense the rearmament of West Germany and its membership of

NATO were vitally important; they represent moves to *guarantee the fundamental economic order* over and above the nation state's constitutional guarantees of property and entrepreneurial rights. The organisations of economic integration, while concerned with the maintenance of capitalism as such, directly address problems of *economic processes* within the capitalist system (rates of profit, global competition, rationalisation of production, circulation and development). Military integration reflects a *fundamental* function of the state (although increasingly also process-political functions) while economic integration fulfils other functions which are *contingent* on particular stages of development within the general system.

One thing is certain: the re-militarisation of the Federal Republic has influenced the nature of its political economy significantly. In Potsdam the Allies had decreed the "complete disarmament and demilitarisation of Germany" and the elimination of its armaments industry.[2] The perceived German tradition of military imperialism was to be ended once and for all. Equally the fatal dynamic of escalating arms production was to be neutralised along with the possibility that rearmament could be used by any future German state as an instrument of economic recovery as in the 1930s. Ten years after Potsdam however the remilitarisation of West Germany was under way, indicating the final abandonment of the chief pillar of the Potsdam conference and the full blossoming of cold war attitudes in the Western alliance.

According to Badstübner and Thomas, discussions concerning the remilitarisation of West Germany had already begun within Western military groups in the spring of 1948.[3] With the creation of NATO, the development of a Russian nuclear bomb, the Chinese revolution and the outbreak of the Korean War, the 'normal' western pre-war stance of anti-communism was resumed, only more vigorously. NATO took over from the fatally unreliable Anti-Comintern Pact as the vanguard of 'containment' or 'roll-back', as the 'policeman of the West'. In addition to the increasingly ineffective policy of isolating socialist countries, a more thorough-going system of group solidarity was established within the developed capitalist world which helped, in part, to offset the effects of de-colonisation in the developing world. The spectre of German militarism, although not completely evaporated, was now less important than the spectre of 'Soviet imperialism'. Moreover three overriding reasons seem to have moved the Western Allies, above all the USA, to reverse the Potsdam decision on demilitarisation:

1. The Germany economy, notably German heavy industry, was of strategic importance to any West European defence effort.

2. The costs of maintaining both an army of 'occupation' in West Germany and a standing army with sophisticated weapon systems in Europe were increasingly high with possible consequences for the balance of payments and the rates of economic growth in the USA and elsewhere.

3. It was tactically more sensible to absorb a West German military apparatus into a Western alliance rather than attempt military operations in a country whose population was not involved either militarily or logistically and was potentially hostile or unco-operative; should not an economic ally contribute to its own defence?[4]

The stages of re-militarisation are well known. Despite considerable mass opposition within Germany – epitomised by the 'Ohne Mich' movement – and Adenauer's acknowledgement that rearmament was 'extremely unpopular',[5] official discussions on a modest West German programme of rearmament began in earnest in 1950.[6] American proposals in September 1950 to integrate West German military units into NATO immediately were rejected by Bevin and Schumann. As an alternative, in October 1950 the French premier, Renée Pleven proposed the formation of a European Army, including subordinate German forces, which was approved by the French National Assembly, by the Bundestag and by NATO ministers. The 'Pleven-Plan' for a European Defence Community was then developed in detail and given official approval in an appropriate treaty on 27 May 1952 between the Federal Republic, France, Italy, Luxemburg, Belgium and the Netherlands. The EDC treaty was linked to the 'German Treaty' of the previous day between West Germany, the USA, Britain and France, governing the end of the Statute of Occupation and the granting of partial sovereignty. Both treaties were rendered null and void however in August 1954 when the French National Assembly rejected the EDC project. Nevertheless within two months West Germany's 'defence contribution' was transferred into the full framework of NATO in the shape of the 'Paris Treaties' (23 October 1954) which came into force on 5 May 1955. West Germany was accorded armed forces of 500 000 which, in contrast to all the other NATO partners, would be subordinate to NATO command. In addition no German production of A, B and C weapons, heavy weapons and large warships would be allowed. With membership of the West European Union and NATO, the Federal Republic also received its 'full sovereignty' as a nation state.

The moves to rearm West Germany were primarily the responsibility of the American government. There was no serious pressure from within Germany, not even from the potential armaments industries. The labour movement was solidly against remilitarisation, a number of employers' bodies expressed 'unease',[7] individual exponents of commercial interests argued that rearmament could have a more destabilising effect than in the 1930s.[8] There was no unanimity within Adenauer's cabinet; Heinemann (CDU) resigned as home secretary in October 1950; Adenauer's failure to consult his cabinet on many occasions (particularly in the case of the famous Soviet note of March 1952) reflected the fear of internal opposition and the need to create faits accomplis – either as an expression of tactical good behaviour towards the USA or as a desire to cement the identity of the West German state. In this connection it can be argued that the rearmament of West Germany was the final nail in the coffin for the chances of reunification and as such *sealed the geographical identity* of West Germany's political economy as well as its internal structure.

The effects of rearmament and NATO membership on the shape and development of West Germany's political economy can be demonstrated reasonably clearly:

Structure

1. Between 1956 and 1964 the proportion of military expenditure to the total federal budget rose from 10 per cent to 32 per cent. This represented a considerable redistribution of national resources to sustain a military apparatus which consumed social wealth without (directly) producing any more.[9] This can be seen to have reduced budgetary allocations for other purposes, fuelling the indebtedness of state authorities, and building up the potential for subsequent fiscal crises.

2.

a. Rearmament recreated an industrial and commercial substructure, producing military software and hardware and servicing military equipment and installations, which rendered some sectors of the economy partly or heavily dependent on state demand: aircraft manufacturing: 75 per cent, shipbuilding: 10 per cent, car industry: 3 per cent, building industry: 3 per cent.[10] To this degree they were in part freed from the constraints of market forces, in costing, development, etc.

b. Because of the demands for standardisation nationally (Bundeswehr)

and internationally (NATO) there has been direct state encouragement for firms to co-operate and, because of economies of scale, to
merge (see above, Chapter 3) – the notable example here being the
aircraft industry.

c. There is evidence of a tightly knit decision-making structure within
the whole field of arms development and procurement, involving
military, industrial and ministerial personnel. The particular role of
military officers in German industry has been the subject of considerable interest.[11]

3. Arms production is one of the most research intensive branches of
industry. This requires highly skilled staff, trained in highly developed institutes in higher education, and often high levels of direct
state financing for research projects, whose costs are difficult to
control, thereby reducing the latitude for other state expenditure.

Development

The 'economic miracle' was well under way before rearmament took
place (even though it was on the cards from 1950). It has been
asserted that German industrial production benefited from the
nation's very *non-commitment* to a military apparatus after the outbreak of the Korean war, since it was possible to expand into the
market gaps left by militarily committed nations. Certainly in the first
half of the 1950s the growth rates and export earnings were quite
sufficient to absorb surplus capacity and surplus labour without the
perceived need for state–military induced demand.[12] In addition no
investment into new advanced armaments capacity took place before
1955. It is not surprising that an under-capitalised industrial sector
was not greatly concerned about great tranches of arms expenditure,
when foreign suppliers would probably mop up the markets for
military hardware anyway; only a few branches with structural problems – like textiles, shoe-manufacturing and shipbuilding – were
actually interested in armaments orders, according to one observer.[13]
Nevertheless as early as 1955 the Federation of German Industry
(BDI) recognised the possible advantages of such orders inasmuch as
it expressed concern over the possibly excessive levels of arms
imports.[14] Linked to this perception was the view that Germany's
industrial economy as a whole would benefit not much from the
production of (low grade) supplies for a basic conventional German
army of 500 000 men, but rather from the capital intensive development of technically sophisticated weapon systems – an area domi-

nated by foreign arms manufacturers. Radkau claims that 'industry' began to show a 'noticeable strengthening of interest in armaments contracts' as soon as the recessionary signs emanating in particular from the Ruhr coal crisis became apparent in 1957 and 1958.[15] Interestingly this coincided with the appointment of Franz Josef Strauss as defence minister.

Strauss' predecessor, Theodor Blank, had been criticised for a particular arms deal with the USA which involved spending some DM3.3 billion on American arms which were said by some to be out of date. This highlighted the nature of military procurement by the Defence Ministry/Bundeswehr, since it appeared that the equipping of West Germany's new armed forces was conducted not according to military but to politico-economic criteria. The Federal Republic was the junior partner within NATO with high manpower and limited low-grade weaponry. Without a domestic source of supply it was thus dependent on the senior partner's hand-me-downs which, by definition, were not specifically developed for use by the Bundeswehr. More importantly a number of factors, including the hitherto 'civilian' bias of German industrial production and export trade, gave the Federal Republic an embarassingly *healthy balance of payments*, which contrasted strongly with other western countries. The importing of foreign armaments was thus one method of assuaging economic rivals and easing pressure to revalue a heavily underpriced Deutschmark. This national economic argument did not however neutralise the increasing desire of German industry to change the structure of military procurement 'in favour of domestic contracts'.[16]

At the same time a number of German politicians and industrialists were beginning to identify the value of state arms contracts as an *instrument of anti-cyclical economic policy*: a publication by CEPES, whose board included Ludwig Erhard and Fritz Berg (BDI), speculated on the 'greater elasticity' in military procurement afforded by the new range of goods which could allow 'purchases to be boosted or limited according to when and where private demand was stronger or weaker'.[17] This view indicates *the disapperance of military behind politico-economic considerations* in Germany and within NATO in general at that time, reflecting the artificiality of the 'threat' which informed military strategy, as well as the potentially dangerous dynamic of an armaments policy which is detached from political realities and corresponding military requirements.

The policies of the Strauss' ministry reinforced this dichotomy. The 'New Look' approach was a military farce but appropriate to a particular politico-economic logic. Fighting forces were to be reduced from 500 000 to 300 000 and their technical equipment modernised. The heart of the 'New Look' was the project to incorporate into the West German airforce the F104 Starfighter, 554 of which would be built under licence in West Germany. This was intended to satisfy American demands for arms exports to West Germany and domestic demands for a greater share of arms contracts and for an appropriate technological boost to industrial research. The addition of numerous technical 'refinements' to the F-104 was intended to give it a multi-purpose role compensating the relative inadequacy of the original for the Bundeswehr, and to give a particular stimulus to advanced aerospace research, involving co-operation between under-utilised aircraft manufacturers and the electrotechnical and chemical industries. Strauss later claimed that the Starfighter project had promoted 'the return of our people [sic!] to a high scientific technological position in the modern industrial world'.[18]

The appalling accident record of the Starfighter was however not allowed to reverse the New Look policy, the economic results of which speak for themselves. Within a rising military procurement budget the domestic input increased from 36.2 per cent (1957) to 52.5 per cent of the total (1963) (DM1.47 billion to 4.2 billion), while the foreign input still rose in absolute terms.

Table 4.1   Material and equipment procurement for the Bundeswehr, 1957–63

	Domestic input (DM billion)	Foreign input (DM billion)
1957	1.47	2.59
1958	2.58	1.09
1959	4.88	3.36
1960	3.11	2.83
1961	4.43	5.59
1962	5.76	4.51
1963	4.21	3.80

Source: Vilmar, F., *Rüstung und Abrüstung*, (Hamburg, 1973).

More significantly the proportion of imports in weapons procurement was reduced from 60 per cent in 1957 to 22.7 per cent in 1969.[19] Of the DM84 billion spent on armaments between 1955 and 1969 DM6.8 billion went on research, development and testing (DM4.8 billion on aerospace research alone). By 1971 the total military apparatus comprised some 650 000 personnel (476 000 active service-men, 169 000 civilian staff) or 2.5 per cent of the working population. The turnover of the aerospace industry increased by 57 per cent between 1959 and 1964 (from DM760 million to DM1.2 billion),[20] of which 76 per cent represented military production. The fact that the industry remained 90 per cent dependent on state funding and had little to show for the expensive research programme,[21] indicated the long-term political and economic risks involved in developing a national aerospace industry in a capital intensive and highly competitive market where the economies of scale demanded ever increasing concentration. Vilmar suggests that even politico-economic logic was less important than heavy state commitment to one of the 'holy cows of economic nationalism'.[22] However, in a period of economic growth and rising gold reserves the idea of over-commitment was less plausible to the political planners. It was only after the 1966/67 recession that a serious rationalisation of the aerospace industry took place.

Before 1967 there was no perceived need to employ arms expenditure as an instrument of global anti-cyclical policy. Nevertheles there is clear evidence that the 'New Look' policy was used to *compensate structural weaknesses* in the shipbuilding and heavy vehicles sector (as well as in the senescent aircraft industry). The spare capacity in shipbuilding which was left after the boom of the 1950s was mopped up in 1964 and 1965 by Defence Ministry orders for over DM1 billion: submarines at the Howaldts yard in Kiel, destroyers, frigates and corvettes at Blohm and Voss in Hamburg and torpedo boats at Lürssen in Bremen. The ailing locomotive manufacturer Henschel (Kassel) was one of the main beneficiaries of the Leopard Tank project, along with Hanomag and Rheinmetall. The order for the serial production of 1400 tanks saved Henschel, at least, from financial collapse.[23]

There is little evidence to show that arms expenditure has been employed subsequently as a flexible stimulus to growth, particularly in the three recessions since the 1960s; in part as a result of fixed NATO expenditure commitments, military expenditure shows a constant rising trend. More clearly the politico-economic commitment to arms production in general and to structurally ailing branches in particular has *limited the latitude of the state* to respond to other problems, notably to cyclical and demographic fluctuations. It is also difficult to assess whether Strauss's 'New Era' has functioned as the 'entry ticket' to the technology-led growth of the last two decades. Military block membership and arms production significantly determined West German economic development up until 1966 and established a framework which would be very difficult to alter subsequently. It does not seem reasonable yet to talk about a 'militarisation' of the economy[24] or the emergence of a military industrial complex along American lines (with the possible exception of Bavaria), but the requirements of group solidarity within NATO and the Federal Republic's particular geographical position and particular 'slavish subordination to the USA',[25] provide a programme which could make West Germany the victim of a military-industrial logic willy-nilly, whether home produced or not.

The Integration of West Germany into Western Europe

Preconditions for Integration

The Federal Republic of Germany didn't have the choice of determining its own foreign economic strategy. It had to adopt the role which it was allotted by the occupation powers within the framework of the re-organisation of the world economy after the Second World War (Abelshauser).[26]

By stressing the subordination of the new West German state to Western/American economic strategy, Werner Abelshauser helps to underline one important feature of Germany's formal integration into Western Europe: it cannot be explained in terms of an organic natural development of Germany's national political economy. Its future development was pre-programmed by foreign interests in a way quite distinct from the usual effects of increasingly internationalised market forces. Quite apart from the lack of political choice, the partition gave West Germany an economic structure which objectively demanded a considerable modification of its trading patterns and a stronger orientation towards the West. Whereas before the war Germany needed to import only 20 per cent of its foodstuffs, the loss of the Eastern Territories rendered the Western Zones 50 per cent dependent on food imports. This implied the need for a corresponding intensification of industrial exports to compensate for the pressure on the balance of payments. At the same time German capital's 'drive to the East' and the expectations of rich pickings in the industrialising nations of Eastern and South Eastern Europe had been abruptly halted by the partition of Europe. The need to increase its export quota was made even more urgent by the Nazi's previous policy of autarky, whereby Germany's export dependency was reduced by more than a half from the 1920s.

Table 4.2   Export quotas, 1910–80 (share of exports to net social product in Germany/Federal Republic)

1910/13	17.5	1950	9.3
1925/29	14.9	1960	17.2
1930/34	12.0	1970	23.8
1935/38	6.0	1980	26.7

Source: Abelshauser, *Wirtschaftsgeschichte*, op.cit. p. 148 – the figures for the Federal Republic do not include 'intra-German' trade. See also above Table 2.5

These arbitrary effects of war and defeat acted to compound the natural law of development common to all the developed capitalist nations: capital concentration, saturated domestic markets, rising labour costs, falling rates of profit, surplus capacity, volatile trade cycles, etc. and therefore reinforced the common need for extended markets, international concentration, cost reductions and profit maximisation. The response of most nation states to the Great Depression of the 1930s was to erect protective trade barriers and, even though the effects were sluggish rates of growth in GDP and trade, protectionism re-emerged after the Second World War and threatened the trade expansion which was demanded by the logic of capital concentration and over-capacity. In the period immediately after 1945, however, protectionism was seen as an imperfect but appropriate means of defending national economies, upset by war, from the competition of countries like the USA whose economy, far from being damaged, had flourished, expanded and been modernised through the war. The war had in fact reinforced the unequal development of the capitalist economies, which had been favouring the USA anyway, and the British, French and other Western economies seemed destined to be further weakened by American penetration into world markets and the effects of decolonisation. The contradiction between the increasing internationalisation of capital movements and the law of unequal development was only resolved, in the short term by the dominant but far-sighted self-interest of American capital and its aggressive pursuit of free trade.

The American decision to help the capitalist economies of Western Europe was the first important act of reintegration for West Germany and other economies, but was potentially contradictory, in that the ERP, as well as presenting new markets for US goods and capital, also strengthened the industrial competitors of the US. Nevertheless 'the USA preferred to rebuild competitors in Western Europe and Japan than lose these countries for the capitalist world system'.[27]

It is important to emphasise here that there were two distinct phases and qualities of economic integration for the West German state. The first phase involved the relocation of the West German economy into the framework of an American-led western economic bloc, and the general *reduction of trade barriers*; the second phase included the formal integration of West Germany with the other economies of the EEC and the *creation of specific trade barriers and trading preferences*. In the first phase West Germany has been described as a virtual passive tool of American policy, as the 'ice-breaker of anti-protectionism'.[28] In the Paris agreement on the ERP, West Germany was singled out and required to reduce customs tarifs to its western trading partners (whether these reciprocated or not).[29] The general inducements to liberalise trade which were contained in the statutes of the IMF, the World Bank (IBRD) and the OEEC and in the other conditions of the ERP and European Payments Union, prepared the ground for the creation of GATT (General Agreement on Trade and Tarifs) which West Germany joined in October 1951 and which rapidly produced over 5500 concessions on customs tariffs. The liberalisation process was facilitated greatly by the Bretton Woods system of stable exchange rates, based largely on Dollar equivalence, and by the considerable upturn in world industrial production and trade in the wake of the Korean War, which compensated for the relative disadvantages of many European economies exposed to American competition. Table 4.3 in facts shows that the American-led re-integration of the European economies produced relative advantages for the continental economies in terms of their rising share of world industrial production; and yet the relative reduction of the American share was offset both by the general absolute rise of world production and by the increasing importance of its own service sector as a contributor to GNP.

The liberalisation of world trade was an important pre-condition for the *formal institutional integration* of West European economies in two distinct ways: it reduced trade barriers within Europe and increased the movement of goods and capital between them, but it also revealed the structural weaknesses of these economies when

Table 4.3   Share of selected western industrial countries in world
industrial production, 1948 and 1969 (per cent)

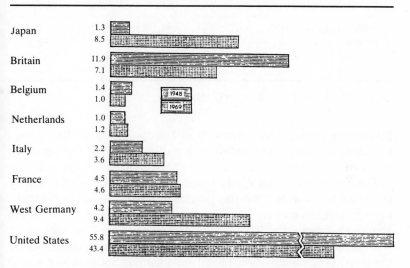

Source: Autorenkollektiv, *Der Imperialismus der BRD* (Berlin, 1973).

exposed to the harsh winds of cheaper competition. General weaknesses were the lower levels of investment as a proportion of GNP in
Europe compared to the USA and the resulting wide gap in labour
productivity:

Table 4.4   Comparative labour output per hour in selected countries,
1959 ($)

FRG	France	Neth.	GB	USA
1.17	1.09	1.02	1.12	3.6

The countries which later made up the EEC also displayed a less
advanced sectoral structure than the USA, with many more people
still employed in the primary sector (agriculture, forestry and fishing)
and far fewer in the tertiary/service sector.

In West Germany specific structural weaknesses afflicted agriculture (uncompetitive, under-capitalised small units), coal-mining
(low-cost open-cast competition from USA, Australia, etc.), steel

Table 4.5   Proportion of employees in economic sectors, 1960 (per cent)

	EEC	FRG	USA
1. Agriculture/forestry/fisheries	20.2	13.7	8.0
2. Manufacturing	41.4	47.9	32.3
3. Services	29.1	30.3	43.8
4. State	9.3	8.1	15.9

Source: F. Deppe (ed.), *Die EWG* (Hamburg, 1975).

production (general over-capacity in Europe), shipbuilding (over-capacity, low cost competition) and textiles (low-cost foreign competition).

The process of formal West European integration was informed by the need to address both the general problem of world competitiveness and some of the specific structural weaknesses of individual European economies. The *formal* nature of European integration was characterised not just by the erection of a customs union but by the creation of supra-national fiscal and planning bodies which would attempt to intervene in market processes and unify legal structures, in order to rationalise the processes of production and exchange. The EEC was thus an extension of liberalisation insofar as it attempted in a more refined way to rectify the contradictions within and between the law of unequal development and the internationalisation of capital.

From the 'Montan-Union' to the EEC

The American plans to create a European customs union within the framework of the OEEC foundered against the general opposition of most of its 16 member states. In any case it seems unlikely that it could have developed beyond a protected free-trade zone to an effective interventionist force, because of the extreme breadth of the countries' individual structural problems. It is no surprise that the first formal act of European integration was the establishment of the European Coal and Steel Community, the scope of which was limited to one sector, heavy industry, and only six countries (France, West Germany, Holland, Belgium, Luxemburg and Italy). It can also claim to have had a precursor, namely the international steel cartel of the 1920s between Germany, France, Belgium and Luxemburg.[30] The treaty governing the foundation of the ECSC (18 April 1951)

Table 4.6   Heavy industrial production in ECSC countries as a proportion
of total production, 1951 (per cent)

	Coal	Iron ore	Raw steel
West Germany	51.4	20.5	35.8
Saarland	7.0	–	6.9
France	22.8	66.9	26.1
Belgium	12.8	0.2	13.4
Netherlands	5.4	–	1.5
Luxemburg	–	10.7	8.5
Italy	0.5	1.7	8.1
ECSC	100.0	100.0	100.0

Source: Statz, Albert, 'Zur Geschichte der westeuropäischen Integration bis
zur Gründung der EWG', in F. Deppe (ed.), *Die EWG* op. cit., p. 129.

envisaged the subordination of national heavy industries to a supra-
national 'high authority' in Brussels which would endeavour to regulate both production and distribution of coal, iron ore, steel and scrap
metal, through a system of agreed quotas and selective investment.
The 'high authority' had fiscal powers of both levying revenue from
individual firms and financing selected ventures.

This scheme first emerged under the name of the French Foreign
Minister as the Schuman-Plan in 1950 against the background of
world-wide over-capacity in steel, distorted coal markets in Europe
(as a result of mandatory German coal exports to pay for reparations)
and worries over foreign import penetration in general. It was
presented within a moral-political framework of long-term goals to
unite Europe, sustain peace, etc.,[31] but the real motives were trans-
parently self-interested, involving common but also contradictory
features. Table 4.6 shows the marked disproportions of the later
ECSC members' share of heavy industrial production, as well as the
overall dominance of West Germany (even discounting its huge
surplus capacity in raw steel production). All things being equal, in a
natural market situation West German heavy industrial firms (which
combined coal, steel and heavy goods production in the main) would
have dominated the continental market, especially in coking coal and
raw steel. However as a result of the war the Ruhr concerns manifested considerable 'weakness and insecurity':[32] a number of its
prominent owners and managers were serving prison sentences as
war criminals, control had been temporarily transferred to Allied

trustees, they had been demonopolised horizontally and vertically (notably steel from coal interests) by the Allies' decartelisation measures (see above Chapter 3) and severe production limitations had been imposed by both 'Level of Industry' plans and by the Ruhr Statute. There had also been great pressure from the labour movement, but also from sections within the CDU, to nationalise heavy industry, pressure which was only partly relieved by the awarding of unique participation rights for trade unions in the British Zone coal and steel concerns (*Montanmitbestimmung*). The 'fundamentally positive attitude (of the Ruhr industrialists JL) to the Schuman-Plan' (thus Günter Henle, CDU and head of the Klöckner concern) has to be understood against this background and in terms of their hopes that within a supra-national body they could at the very least assert their rights of ownership and also end production restrictions, re-emerge and reestablish their dominance in Europe. The Adenauer government warmly endorsed the Schuman Plan from the outset and clearly regarded it, parallel to industrial views, as a lever to restore some degree of economic and political sovereignty.[33]

The attitude of the French government and of French capital was informed by a desire to protect its economy from American but notably from German competition and German dominance.[34] French dependence on German coking coal had proved a source of considerable economic concern in the 1920s and especially in the 1930s; the French plans to annex the Saarland after 1945 had been motivated in part by the desire to appropriate its coal and steel capacity (7 per cent of total ECSC production in each case) and thereby redress the disadvantage with West Germany. Above all the expectation of controlling West German heavy industry through a powerful supra-national authority played a vital role in the formulation of the plan, because it was hoped that, through a system of production quotas and controlled marketing, the traditionally aggressive policies of the Ruhr concerns could be neutralised.

Thus both French and German exponents of the 'Montan-Union' envisaged it primarily as an instrument for future national economic (sectoral) dominance, rather than as a means of politico-cultural unification. Objectively, too, there was a greater need to restrict market forces in this sector through supranational supervision than in other sectors, since market mechanisms had already been heavily distorted by high capital concentration and by private cartel agreements.[35]

The results of the ECSC treaty were the almost universal fulfilment of West German hopes: the Ruhr Statute was suspended, limits on production and capacity were lifted and the gradual remonopolisation of heavy industry under private control was made possible. The French did not get their hands on Saarland steel and coal and above all the relative advantage of German heavy industry was reinforced by the agreed steel quotas and by subsequent levels of production. German steel production rose from 11.8 million tons in 1950 to 21.3 million tons in 1955. In France steel production rose from around 11 million tons in 1949 to only 12.6 million tons in 1955.[36] West German steel firms also continued to import their iron-ore from Sweden rather than from France, such that *no reciprocal dependence* or obligations could be realised. The (political) failure of the French-inspired plan was due to limited powers of the supranational 'high authority' for imposing restrictions on private, nationally-based enterprises and on the natural strengths of German steel-making; it is difficult to assess whether the ECSC was a commercial success because the 1950s boom compensated national heavy industries for any relative disadvantages created by German success. However the ECSC was largely powerless in the coal crisis of 1959 and it was left to individual national governments to sort out the mess of over-capacity and finance the massive redundancies. Furthermore, as Statz points out, the introduction of unco-ordinated national subsidies on coal in 1965 and 1966 burst open the framework of the Community Treaty.[37]

The advantages of the ECSC seem to have been less branch-specific than general, since the ECSC countries displayed greater rates of growth than other Western countries or groups (USA, Japan, EFTA) in the 1950s.[38] This in part explains the subsequent enthusiasm for the creation of a general economic community shown by respective national governments. However the Rome Treaties and the Economic Community represented a qualitatively different mode of integration compared to the sectoral 'integration' of heavy industry. As a result there was less unanimity in Germany over the EEC negotiations particularly within the ranks of German capital.

Article 3 of the Rome Treaty outlined the main policy objectives of the Economic Community:

1) a free-trade zone of all member states with 2) a common (protective) trade policy against outside countries; 3) freedom of movement for capital and labour within the EEC; common policies

on 4) transport, 5) agriculture and 6) competition; the creation of 7) instruments of crisis management and 8) the standardisation of legal statutes.[39]

Adenauer's enthusiastic espousal of this scheme was shared by the majority of his cabinet – with the notable exception of Erhard – and by a number of industrialists and bankers, but it was far from being a policy 'for Europe's sake',[40] of a 'political' rather than 'economic' nature;[41] it clearly sought to cement Germany's rapid economic recovery within a framework which would both guarantee the continuation of growth and prevent the trade isolation of the German economy which could have resulted from the growing inequalities within Europe. Far from emanating from a 'power vacuum',[42] Adenauer's foreign policy was extremely sensitive to the long-term interests of German capital in a world economic environment which did not exclusively applaud Germany's revival and increasing export penetration.[43] A central concept of this foreign policy was the 'creditworthiness' which West Germany needed to re-establish for itself at both political and economic level as a pre-condition for economic expansion within a secure Western framework. This involved above all the pacification of the French state and French capital, which regarded the European Community as a means of defence against the effects of de-colonisation and of a sectorally backward economy.[44] German capital was all too eager to jump into the market vacuums left by the colonial powers, but the German government couldn't allow this to endanger its general position within the Western economic bloc.[45] The opponents of European integration, which included Erhard and Röpke (both CDU) and the *Industriekurier* (the main mouthpiece of industrial interests), emphasised the advantages (and *morality*) of free trade and of the maintenance of naturally dynamic trading relations. 'Such regionalism (as the EEC, JL) with its bloc formations and preferences, opposes the liberal principle of the world economy.'[46] Radkau gives this view a certain plausibility by pointing out that West Germany's trade trend was moving away from Europe, notably towards the Middle East, Asia and South America.[47] Nevertheless he also stresses that non-European trade was still largely peripheral and that it affected certain capital interests but not all, and finally that 'the extensive autonomy of foreign policy from *partial interests* [my emphasis JL] undoubtedly benefited the collective interest of the economy'.[48]

The Rome Treaties on the EEC and on EURATOM were signed

on 26 March 1957, ratified by the Bundestag on 5 July of the same year and came into force on 1 January 1958 and 1 January 1959 respectively. A permanent bureaucracy was established in Brussels with fiscal resources supplied by each member state. General community policy was and continues to be determined broadly by the Council of Ministers (drawn from respective national governments) which meets regularly to discuss major issues of revenue and expenditure policy. The differences between the high-tariff countries (France and Italy) and the low-tariff countries (West Germany and the Benelux group) were resolved by agreeing external tariffs which were to be progressively modified to the average of those obtaining on 1 Jan. 1957. Internal tariffs between EEC partners were to be progressively eliminated within 12 years of the treaty. Both external and internal 'tariff disarmament' were achieved by July 1968. The result for West Germany was the general raising of its import tariffs to third countries, but a reduction of internal EEC barriers.

The question of national economic benefits are very difficult to assess, since it is not possible to construct a satisfactory model of German economic development outside the EEC.[49] What is clear is that German capital did not need the protection of the Community as much as French capital,[50] but, in view of the benefits of the DM, would not suffer from EEC membership as much as countries with stronger currencies. On balance there does not seem to be a non-contradictory logic which explains German membership or the mere creation of the EEC. It is certainly correct of Mandel and others to observe the increasing European profile of the chemical, electrical and engineering industries and of the banking and insurance sectors, as examples of the internationalisation and concentration of capital; it is correct to point out the dysfunctional variety of commercial laws, taxation systems, quality control etc. in separate European countries; it is also correct to stress the increasing importance of economies of scale for capital intensive sectors of industrial production and the relative disadvantage of some European firms in the 1950s compared to US competition. However there is no conclusive proof that 'West European capitalists . . . require their own state power in order to secure and defend their capital investments'.[51] On Mandel's own admittance the EEC is no 'real state'[52] and yet Western Europe achieved a real increase in its share of world trade between 1947 and 1965 (from 34 per cent to 40 per cent) against a fall in the US share (27 per cent to 18 per cent).[53] This increase cannot be ascribed to significant *European mergers* or co-operative agreements, but rather to the expansion of nationally based oligopolies (like Bayer, Hoechst, BASF, ICI, Royal Dutch Shell, Siemens, AEG, etc.) all of whom have considerable and growing non-European interests. The expansion up to (and beyond) 1965 has not been the result of specific European sponsored projects (ELDO, ESRO, Euratom, Airbus for example) which have attempted to resolve the problem of specific economies of scale, but by oligopolies who are able to sustain adequate economies of scale from their own operations. There is little evidence to prove Mandel's assertion regarding the impossibility of national and the indispensability of international development of, say, a nuclear energy industry.[54] (E.g. British nuclear research flourished while Euratom was floundering.) The specific identity of capital ownership seems to be less of a problem than the marketing of the final product and the sustaining of a research programme through turnover, secured loans etc. Moreover the multinational oligopolies tend to exploit the different tax laws and capital markets of separate countries as instruments of accumulation rather than complain about the lack of uniformity.

As an *interventionist body* the EEC Commission has had a marginal effect on most sectors of the European (and hence German) economy, with the exception of agriculture which has enjoyed massive and controversial subsidies as a deliberate policy of self-sufficiency. As a *customs union* it has clearly effected a shift in West Germany's trading relations – away from overseas partners towards Europe: in 1956 it conducted 26.9 per cent of its imports and 29.8 per cent of its exports with later EEC countries, whereas in 1970 these proportions had risen to 44.4 per cent and 40.2 per cent respectively. Quantitatively the share of EEC countries in world trade rose from 23.7 per cent in 1958 to 32.3 per cent in 1971, that of West Germany alone from 9.1 per cent to 12.6 per cent.[55]

The composition of West Germany's exports showed a strengthening of engineering products from 40.4 per cent in 1956 to 48.5 per cent in 1972 (as a proportion of total exports).[56]

Overall West Germany did not do badly out of EEC membership in the 1960s: it had the highest GNP growth rate of all six countries and the highest ratio of gross investments to GNP.[57] West German capital investments in EEC countries increased as a proportion of all direct foreign investments from 14 per cent in 1961 to 30 per cent in 1972, but its main investment strategy was domestically based, emphasising the dominance of goods export rather than capital export as a source of foreign earnings at this stage of its economic development (c.f. Chapter 5 below). The rising level of export dependency (see above Table 4.2), while an indicator of economic expansion and increasing national wealth, was also responsible for the increased domestic capacity which in 1966/67 contributed to the short recession.

By 1966 the trading profile of the West German economy had clearly been changed by EEC membership. There is also evidence of strong impulses from the EEC in the 1960s towards the interlocking of commercial interests between enterprises of the different member states, particularly in banking, insurance, chemicals and electricals.[58] Outside the EEC, state sponsored research in rocket systems (ELDO), space satellites (ESRO) and the development of civilian (Concorde, Airbus) and military (Tornado) aircraft projects have indicated the increased latitude for supra-national co-operation created by state awareness of technological development and competition with the USA. Interestingly European customs barriers, while reducing the relative importance of EEC-US trade, have induced a higher level of capital investments by US firms in EEC enterprises – as a means, presumably, of avoiding some of the import restrictions and of feeding off the new advances of European capital.

Up to 1966 increased capital mobility was mirrored by an increased mobility of labour – notably from the Mediterranean fringes of the EEC (Southern Italy, for example) to the industrial cities of Germany and France. The system of migrant labour, developed within Europe at the beginning of the 1960s greatly benefitted West Germany's political economy, by adding a new flexibility to the labour market at a time when full employment and the end of the westward migration of East Germans threatened to inflate labour costs (see below).

To summarise, it is difficult to judge whether the EEC has in fact provided growth impulses to West Germany,[59] which would not have otherwise emerged (more strongly perhaps) from other sources. It is however more plausible to assert that West Germany's integration into an exclusive club, which defends its wealth not just against more powerful but also against less powerful economies, has altered the political economy of world trade in a way which indirectly might threaten the growth prospects of the First World, including West Germany. The foreign economic policy of successive CDU governments predetermined the subsequent shape of West Germany's foreign economic relations, not simply by locking the country's economy into a formal bloc of developed countries but by loosening previous economic links with less developed countries. It is thus useful to take a brief look at the shape of West German policy towards 'second' and 'third' world countries.

West German Trade Policy outside the OECD

Membership of the EEC (and ECSC) determines the framework for all other foreign economic relations in terms of customs barriers and communally agreed trade preferences. However before 1958 and beyond general block membership of the West and of NATO has also determined the latitude for national economic trading relations with countries outside that bloc.

Firstly the Cold War effectively neutralised traditional expectations of expanding trade with Eastern European countries. Their pre-war share of 15 per cent of Germany's export markets sank to 2 per cent at the beginning of the 1950s. 'Interzonal' later 'Intra-German' trade (which is not included in many foreign trade statistics) fell sharply in the early 1950s and, despite subsequent growth, remained at a low level relative to normal trade.[60] The Total share of COMECON countries (including East Germany) in West Germany's export and import trade in 1953 and 1959 was 1 per cent and 3 per cent respectively. This low level of economic relations was *maintained politically* at both national and international level: the Federal Trade Ministry imposed a strict system of licensing[61] for every transaction, based on a clear distinction between normal and 'Eastern Trade'.[62] NATO pursued a specific embargo policy through its Co-ordinating Committee which, since its inception in 1949, has proscribed the export of all goods to Warsaw Pact countries deemed useful to military development. A more general restriction of Eastern Trade was created by COCOM in 1962, when it forced NATO members to limit Western credits to East European countries to 5 years.[63] In November 1962 NATO demanded a specific embargo on the delivery of wide-bore steel pipes by German firms (Mannesmann, Phoenix Rheinrohr and Hoesch) to the Soviet Union, which was dutifully imposed by the Federal Government.

This latter case was one of the few examples of an open conflict between specific capital interests and the state (before 1966) where the state annulled a signed contract after it had previously approved identical ones; Mannesmann, Hoesch and Phoenix had already delivered 660 000 tons of pipe between 1959 and September 1962. The issue highlighted the subordination of the Federal Government to US/NATO interests and the contradictions between the general defence of capitalism (by NATO) and the specific interests of certain capitals.[64] For, with the slow-down in GDP and trade growth in the early 1960s, the stable demand of East European countries began to attract an increasing number of major German firms, notably in the steel industry, but also in the chemical and electro-technical industries, which have since been involved in large plant construction work in Russia and elsewhere. This in turn led to some firms becoming partially dependent on contracts from COMECON countries for their commercial survival,[65] in contrast to the sustained, low level of the Eastern European trade of the economy in general.

In the course of the early 1960s representatives of German capital began to shift away from a tacit acceptance of Cold War embargo politics, towards a more active demand that good markets should not be sacrificed on the altar of ideology, particularly if senior NATO partners, like France and Britain, were allowing firms greater latitude in East–West trade. Prior to 1966 however there was no formal change of government policy on the issue, although it was clear that the CDU, as a mouthpiece for industrial interests, was beginning to reconsider its line towards East–West relations and to East Germany.

West Germany's trade policy with the Third World was deter-mined both by its global policy as a member of the Western bloc as well as by its national economic and perceived national–political needs. In the latter case the *Hallstein-Doctrine* exemplified the endeavours of the West German state to influence non-aligned as well as Western countries, in order to isolate East Germany politi-cally and economically; the 'doctrine' made it a condition of diplo-matic relations between West Germany and other countries that the latter refuse to recognise East Germany. Diplomatic recognition of the 'Soviet Zone of Occupation' would lead to the automatic suspen-sion of diplomatic relations with the Federal Republic, and with it the suspension of preferential trading rights, access to development aid and credit. The relative economic weakness of East Germany in the 1950s allowed the successful maintenance of this policy, but the growing influence of COMECON, especially in the Middle East, in the early 1960s neutralised the effectiveness of this threat. This contrib-uted to the fiasco in March 1965 when nearly all the Arab states broke off diplomatic relations with West Germany.[66] In the mean-time West German capital had secured important footholds in non-aligned countries. The Rome Treaty contained Articles of Associ-ation (131 to 136) which gave West German exporters preferential access to the (largely French) dependencies in Africa, in exchange for

Table 4.7   Geographical structure of West German Trade, 1961

	Imports per cent	Exports per cent
Europe	59.73	70.04
America	24.13	15.00
Asia	9.28	9.18
Africa	5.55	4.39
Australia & Oceania	1.09	1.11

Source: *Statistisches Jahrbuch der Bundesrepublik.*

low tariff imports. With the coming of independence associated status was regulated by the Yaoundé Convention in July 1963 governing 18 African states, and after British entry this was extended to 46 overseas states at the Lomé Convention of 1975. Outside the joint framework of the EEC, state trade missions in embassies and consulates, along with private trade 'missions', established seemingly modest, but important economic ties with less developed countries.[67] Measured against total trade volume, West Germany's trade with African and Asian countries was not apparently very significant, compared to its growing interdependence with OECD countries. However the quality and terms of trade reveal the vital significance of this trade to the valorisation of German capital.

The West German economy, and above all West German industry, is heavily dependent on the importation of certain raw materials to sustain the very high level of finished goods exports. Already in 1958 finished goods made up 82.2 per cent of total exports against a share of 24.7 per cent for raw materials imports. There is virtually total import-dependence on copper, tin, mercury, uranium, bauxite/aluminum and the steel purifyers manganese, chrome, nickel, molybdenum, tungsten and vanadium, and many of these are only available from African, Asian and South American countries. Figure 4.1 shows that despite an underpriced DM in the 1950s imports became cheaper and export prices were able to rise, such that the general terms of trade with the rest of the world rose by some 70 per cent between 1950 and 1972.[68] The specific rise in terms of trade with the Third World was higher. This is in part reflected in the huge trade surplus of the FRG in the 1960s with developing countries, which on average bought 12.8 per cent of West Germany's exports but provided only 8.4 per cent of its imports; Abelshauser stresses that Third World countries thereby contributed half of West Germany's total trade surplus.[69] This transfer of wealth from the Third World countries

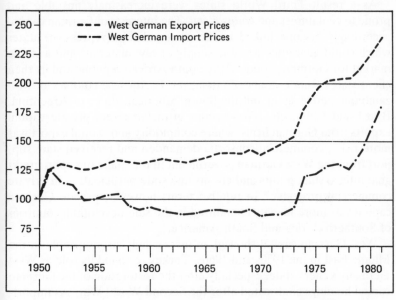

Fig. 4.1   Import and export prices, 1950–80 (DM base, 1950 = 100)

Source: Glastetter *et. al.*, *Die Wirtschaftliche Entwicklung in der Bundesrepublik*, 1950–80

epitomised the general situation in which high grade manufactured goods enjoyed a higher relative value than raw materials and semi-finished goods, and illustrated the impotence of 'development aid' to reverse the process – rather this aid has itself been described as one of a number of instruments for the enrichment of the developed world: through the IMF, the IBRD, the European Development Fund and national 'aid' programmes developing countries are made increasingly dependent upon Western financing and increasingly subordinate to foreign interference in domestic policy.[70] An important indicator of this dependence was the external debt of Third World states, which grew by an average of 14 per cent per annum in the 1960s to reach DM190 billion in 1968;[71] West German banks and the Federal Government were increasingly involved in the credit business which, long before the current debt crisis, produced severe problems for developing economies, which were rarely able to sustain interest payments, were forced to request even more costly rescheduling, and to encourage the production of cash crops and the establishment of agricultural monocultures – a situation which in most cases reinforced underdevelopment and poverty.

As a result Third World states were increasingly unstable and prone to civil unrest and *coups d'état*. The interests of German capital accordingly became linked to the more reliable (repressive) states which could guarantee a stable supply of raw materials and a stable market for German products: the South African republic and its then client states Rhodesia and Zambia, the Portuguese colonies of Mozambique and Angola and the South American states of Argentina, Brazil and Chile, etc. These states attracted direct private capital exports from German firms; where commodity and capital export was more risky, commercial consortia demanded and received state support from the West German government in the shape of export credit guarantees, state grants and credits and state participation in private commercial projects.[72] In relative terms however, private German capital was more heavily committed in the safe developing countries of Southern Africa and South America.

West German capital showed an increasingly strong profile in the Middle East in the 1950s and 1960s. Turkey resumed its role as West Germany's client state, especially after the restoration of the German capital holdings confiscated after the Second World War. As important was the general friendliness which the anti-Zionist Arab nations showed the Federal Republic – 'the only Western Great Power in the world which now as before is trusted in the whole of the Near East'.[73] The death throes of formal colonialism, in particular the Suez fiasco, brought the West Germans large contracts for industrial plant and other commodities in Egypt, Syria and Iran. This process was partly slowed by the reparations settlement with Israel (opposed by many government supporters in the Bundestag and by some industrialists with Middle East interests),[74] by later arms sales to Israel and by the 'diplomatic' conflict of 1965. Nevertheless in 1961 West German trade with the Middle East outstripped its European rivals. German exports to Turkey and Iran were higher than those of any other country, exports to Syria and Israel only second behind the USA.

In summary, West Germany's foreign economic relations were dominated by self-interest and the primacy of export trade: 'the decisive factor . . . is the interest of the national economy in sales and procurements'.[75]

DOMESTIC POLICY

The Main Features of West German Economic Growth, 1950–66

The West German economy, along with the economies of the OEEC countries, the US and Japan, grew continuously in real terms from 1950 through to 1966.[76] It differed from most of its major Western competitors by rising at a considerably faster rate per annum – for some at a 'miraculously' fast rate. Real GNP rose at an average of 8.00 per cent p.a. between 1951 and 1960, industrial production by 9.6 per cent p.a.. Real per capita national product rose by an average of 5.6 per cent p.a. between 1950 and 1965 which was over double the equivalent rate in Sweden, Britain and the USA and 1.9 per cent higher than in France, and stands out within German and European historical development.

Table 4.8   Growth rates of real per capita social product, 1870–1980
(average growth rates p.a. in per cent)

	1870–1913	1913–50	1950–65	1965–80
Germany	1.8	0.4	5.6	3.9
USA	2.2	1.7	2.0	2.3
Britain	1.3	1.3	2.3	2.0
France	1.4	0.7	3.7	4.1
Sweden	2.3	1.6	2.6	2.2

Source: Abelshauser, *Wirtschaftsgeschichte*, op. cit., p. 101.

The 'miraculous' quality of growth in this period of reconstruction has subsequently been explained in terms of a predictable development, given the combination of very favourable conditions for growth in West Germany. Western integration – in both the informal and the formal sense – was the lynch-pin of post-war expansion, the boom in world trade induced by the Korean War a major factor in stimulating West Germany's export-led recovery. The growth dynamic of West Germany's exports was far stronger than that of domestic demand, demonstrated by the virtual doubling of West Germany's export quota from 9.3 per cent in 1950 to 17.2 per cent in 1960,[77] and the near trebling of its share of world exports (from 3.5 per cent to 10.1 per cent) in the same period. Export and domestic growth were born primarily by the industrial (secondary) sector of

Table 4.9   Sectoral structure of the West German economy (incl. Saarland and Berlin after 1960) – sectoral shares of GDP, working population and labour volume (per cent)

	1950	1960	1968
1. Gross Domestic Product[a]			
Primary sector	10.3	6.3	5.3
Secondary sector	47.3	55.6	57.3
Tertiary sector	42.4	38.1	37.4
2. Working population			
Primary sector	26.0	13.8	10.4
Secondary sector	41.7	49.0	48.2
Tertiary sector	32.3	37.2	41.4
3. Labour volume			
Primary sector	26.0	12.2	9.2
Secondary sector	41.1	48.2	46.4
Tertiary sector	32.9	39.6	44.4
[a] In prices of 1954	Total hours worked		

Source: M. Welteke, M., *Theorie und Praxis der Sozialen Marktwirtschaft*, (Frankfurt, 1976).

Table 4.10   Export turnover as a proportion of total turnover in industrial companies with more than ten employees, 1950 and 1960

	1950	1960
Mining	25.9	19.6
Industrial base materials and production goods industry	10.3	15.2
Investment goods industry	13.8	25.1
Consumer goods industry	3.1	7.5

Source: *Statistisches Jahrbuch der Bundesrepublik.*

the economy. By 1961 83 per cent of all exports were finished goods (1950:64.8 per cent); of these the bulk were production goods, industrial base materials and investment goods, the latter showing the most rapid growth and the highest export quota (to turnover), as well as the highest (if fluctuating) rate of investments growth. The lower than average growth pattern of the consumer goods industry is indicative of the relative fall in the significance of private consumption compared to investments:

Table 4.11   Index of industrial production, 1950–65 (1950= 100)

	1950	1955	1960	1965
All industry	100	176	248	327
Mining	100	128	132	135
Base materials	100	176	254	348
Investment goods	100	216	323	423
Consumer goods	100	167	235	304
Public energy	100	172	245	351
Construction	100	188	260	365

Source: Federal Economics Ministry (ed.), *Leistung in Zahlen* (1973).

Table 4.12   The employment of GNP, 1950–60

	Private consumption	State quota	Investments quota	Net exports of goods and services
1950	64.2	14.4	22.6	–1.2
1951	61.1	14.7	22.3	1.9
1952	59.0	15.3	23.2	2.5
1953	60.2	14.5	21.5	3.8
1954	59.3	14.1	23.2	3.4
1955	58.0	13.3	26.3	2.4
1956	58.6	12.9	25.1	3.4
1957	58.8	12.9	24.3	4.0
1958	59.0	13.4	23.7	3.9
1959	58.1	13.6	24.9	3.4
1960	57.3	13.6	26.3	2.8

Source: *Wirtschaft und Statistik* (1960/61).

West Germany's consumption quota (per cent) was considerably lower than that of France, Britain and the USA:

	France (per cent)	USA (per cent)	Britain (per cent)	Germany (per cent)
1950	67.0	67.5	70.8	64.2
1960	63.9	64.0	65.4	57.3

this again reinforces the export-led, investment-goods based character of German expansion and indicates clear advantages in terms of domestic inflation, the latitude for private investment and the

Table 4.13   Investments growth, 1950–60 (at market prices)

	DM billion	Per cent change
1950	21.9	
1951	26.4	20.5
1952	31.5	19.3
1953	31.4	–0.3
1954	36.3	15.6
1955	47.0	29.4
1956	49.3	4.9
1957	52.0	5.4
1958	54.1	4.0
1959	61.7	14.0
1960	72.8	17.9

Source: *Wirtschaft und Statistik* (1960/61).

competitiveness of German capital over its rivals. The level of the *investment quota* and the rates of investments growth – which averaged 11.8 per cent in nominal terms from 1950 to 1960 – point to the fundamental components of growth: a rapidly expanding capital stock, increasing capital intensity and increasing labour productivity. Improved utilisation of capacity in the 1950s allowed initially high rates of capital productivity (an average rate of increase of 2.9 per cent for the period 1951–60) but the trend was clearly downwards leading to an absolute fall in the 1960s (average p.a. – 1.3 per cent) and beyond. The trend of capital productivity had a positive effect on rates of profit in the 1950s and negative effects from 1961 onwards.

The Major Determinants of Growth

The mythology of the 'Economic Miracle' implies a magic determinant to explain the otherwise inexplicable expansion process, a determinant outside the economic sphere. Accordingly the political choice of the 'social market economy' is given decisive significance by proponents of the Miracle idea. However there is now considerable evidence to support Marianne Welteke's assertion that the sustained period of high growth, with its lack of severe cyclical interruptions was the result of the competitive advantages of West German capital rather than of a coherent economic doctrine or a balanced long-term strategy of economic policy.[78] State economic policy will be dealt

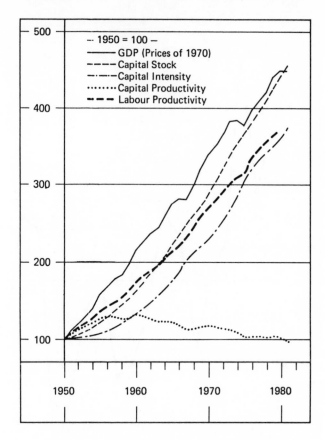

Fig. 4.2   Growth determinants, 1950–80

Source: Glastetter et al., Die wirtschaftliche Entwicklung in der Bundesrepublik Deutschland 1950–1980 (Frankfurt, 1983).

with below, but before that a survey of the major determinants of economic growth is necessary.

There are three main categories of growth determinants relating to demand, productive potential and production costs. As we have seen *global demand* was high between 1950 and 1966 because of the general process of reconstruction and the rejoining of the growth trend interrupted by two world wars and the Depression (see Figure 2.1). West Germany shared this *backlog of social demand* with other

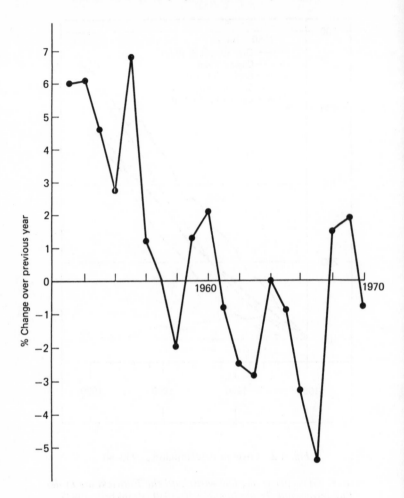

Fig. 4.3   Capital productivity, 1951–70

Source: Deutsches Institut für Wirtschaftsforschung.

countries, but in her case it was reinforced by the particularly high level of destruction of domestic property, and a combination of high technological potential and low levels of private consumption (which had been deliberately restricted in the Third Reich). World demand for all goods, but notably for capital goods, rose sharply as a result of the Korean War and, with most capitalist countries committed to relatively high levels of arms production and arms expenditure, the spare capacity of German industry, uncommitted to wasteful military production, was able to attract an increasing proportion of that increased demand. A combination of rising terms of trade (as a measure of the value equivalence of German finished goods exports and foreign raw materials imports) and a low exchange rate of the Deutschmark to all the major currencies which were involved in German finished goods sales, provided an ideal framework for the optimal development of West German industrial competitiveness.

Domestic demand was dominated by the huge shortfall in basic consumer goods and housing, and by the need to repair and expand infrastructural facilities and damaged industrial and commercial property. Housing reconstruction involved the investment of DM 64 billion between 1950 and 1957, producing 3.9 million new homes. This had significant multiplicator effects for employment and for capital goods demand: in 1958 over 2 million people were employed in the construction industry, 17 million people were rehoused in this period, creating greater general mobility of labour and by 1956 already, construction industry turnover had reached DM 23.2 billion.[79]

Behind investment goods, the building industry had the second fastest rate of growth between 1950 and 1960 (see above Table 4.11). Building reconstruction represented between 16 per cent and 18.5 per cent of domestic demand and was born predominantly by the private sector. Figure 4.4 shows the very high levels of private building activity in the 1950s (with a proportion of over 15 per cent of domestic demand) which then fell to more normal levels compared to capital equipment purchases in the 1960s and 1970s. The *productive potential* of the German economy benefitted both from the state of the productive apparatus and the quality of the expanding labour force. The considerable reserves of industrial capacity allowed a very easy absorption of increased demand by German firms. In addition the age structure of the plant was 'relatively favourable' compared to other national economies.[80] Consequently the increased utilisation of capacity between 1949 and 1955 has been calculated as having had the equivalent value of $4\frac{1}{2}$ years of additional investment at 10 per cent per annum.[81] The optimal use of capacity was above all facilitated by the huge reserves of labour represented by war returnees and refugees from both former territories and from East Germany. The reserve army of unemployed was generally highly skilled, young, mobile and obliged to accept below average conditions of labour. The annual additions to this reserve – from East Germany – maintained the general function of depressing wage levels, but reinforced

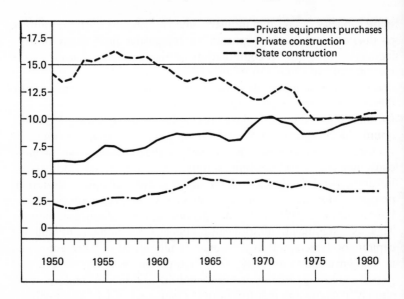

Fig. 4.4   Structure of domestic demand, 1950–80 (in prices of 1970) = 100

Source: Glastetter *et al.*, *Die wirtschaftliche Entwicklung der Bundesrepublik Deutschland 1950–1980*, (Frankfurt, 1983).

the specific advantages of age and skill. The *age structure* of refugees was strongly biased to the group of 18–25 year-olds (83.6 per cent of the total) with a corresponding high participation rate in the labour process – 58 per cent as against a national average of 48–49 per cent.[82] The *qualification levels* of the new immigrants was extremely high, leading some to ascribe decisive importance to this factor in the economic recovery: between 1952 and 1962, we are told, more than 20 000 engineers and technicians, 4500 doctors and 1000 teachers in higher education left East Germany, such that West Germany's share of technical personnel was far higher than East Germany's, even though the East German education system produced twice as many engineers per head of population as West Germany.[83a] Abelshauser asserts that this transfer of 'human capital' (as a measure of education costs) was equivalent to at least DM 30 billion in the 1950s and quantitatively far exceeded the contribution of the ERP to German reconstruction.[83b] This is reflected above all in the very low levels of state expenditure on education during the first decade of the Federal Republic's existence. This almost unique flexibility of the labour market was compounded by the *structural mobility* of the labour force as a result of the rationalisation of agriculture and industrial production processes. The overall reduction of the agricultural workforce from 5 020 000 (24.6 per cent of the total workforce) in 1950 to 3 623 000 (13.8 per cent) in 1960 and 2 876 000 (10.7 per cent) in 1965 represented a very rapid decline which helped feed the increasingly dynamic labour market. Together with structural changes within the industrial sector and towards the tertiary sector this produced a general shift towards areas of the economy with higher levels of productivity and higher rates of productivity growth, a shift to which a quantifiable structural growth effect has been ascribed, amounting to almost a sixth of national productivity increases in the 1950s.

Table 4.14   Structural effect of economic growth, 1951–63

	Growth of productivity (per cent p.a.)	Structural effect in per cent p.a.
1951	8.7	1.6
1952	7.4	1.1
1953	5.8	0.8
1954	5.0	1.1
1955	8.2	1.2
1956	4.2	1.1
1957	3.9	0.9
1958	2.8	0.6
1959	6.2	0.6
1960	7.4	0.7
1961	4.5	0.5
1962	3.3	0.1
1963	2.8	−0.1

Source: Peter Schwanse, *Beschäftigungsstruktur und Wirtschaftswachstum in der Bundesrepublik Deutschland 1950–1963* (DIW, Berlin, 1965).

The consistently high rates of productivity growth between 1950 and 1960 contributed to the minimisation of *unit costs of production* – the third category of growth determinants. Most importantly the rises in labour productivity exceeded the rises in unit labour costs.[84] Average per capita gross wages grew more slowly than in rival economies and, significantly, more slowly than business income and the increase in the capital stock. This produced a fall of 4 percentage points in the adjusted wages quota between 1950 and 1960 and a corresponding fall of wages as a proportion of production costs.

Although this produced a fall in the national consumption quota and a relative fall in consumer goods demand, it helped to minimise the pressure on domestic inflation (stimulated by high trade surpluses) and was compensated by increases in foreign (and domestic) demand for capital goods. As a national cost factor the rapid rise in West German labour productivity (compared to other countries) reflected not so much the technological enhancement of the productive apparatus (certainly not in the first decade) as the high level of capacity utilisation and the historical advantage of a sectoral economic structure in which the industrial sector – with its higher rates of productivity growth – produced a higher than average proportion of national wealth.[85]

The cost/price structure of West German goods was highly competitive – and can be seen as a result of war, occupation, good fortune and considerable sacrifices by the working population before any assistance from economic policy makers is considered. Indeed as the reflection of a response to negative, secular economic trends, the economic policies of the Adenauer/Erhard era show up the structural economic weaknesses concealed by the long boom as well as the weaknesses of political institutions in diagnosing faults and long-term problems and implementing countervailing measures.

Economic Policy and Economic Growth

The fundamental principles of Ordo-liberalism, which found political shape in the CDU's espousal of the 'social market economy', are the guaranteeing of a competitive order (anti-monopolism) and the limitation of state interference to 'global' economic policies (monetary control, competition policy, e.g.) away from policies involving the manipulation of revenue and expenditure. In this regard the reduction of the *State Quota* (the state's share of GNP) was a general aim of Ordo-liberals and reflected both a fundamental confidence in private capital to create and distribute social wealth adequately and a conviction that the state had neither the means nor the intellectual ability to plan or stimulate socio-economic progress.[86]

The failure to establish an adequate legal framework for competition – outlined in Chapter 3 above – made the maintenance of a non-interventionist stance problematic, to say the least, and the fact that the Adenauer/Erhard governments succeeded in reducing the state quota from 14.4 per cent of GNP in 1950 to 12.9 per cent in 1957, rising to only 13.6 per cent in 1960,[87a] concealed a real qualitative increase in fence-mending activities by federal and regional institutions and an ideological shift within Ordo-liberal circles towards a plausibilisation of interventionism. On the other hand the expansion of state expenditure in the 1960s and 1970s reflected not just a general trend begun in the 1950s but also the real shortcomings of Erhard's pragmatic regime.

Taxation Policy

The basic framework of taxation law and fiscal practice was inherited from the Weimar Republic and the Third Reich (the "Reich-abgabenordnung 1919) although it underwent consistent modification.[87b] The West German state authorities also inherited the specific rates of taxation imposed by the occupying powers with the Control Council Law 1946 and Law Nr 64 in June 1948. These very high rates of progressive taxation could not be altered by the German authorities without approval by the Allies both before May 1949 and during the period of the Statute of Occupation (up to 1955). This reduced the latitude of both the Economics Council and the Federal Government in pursuing their *common aim of reducing the general tax burden in favour of capital accumulation.*[88] Both bodies were thus forced to exploit the residual room for manoeuvre, notably within the Income Tax Law (EStG), and specifically by modifying para. 7 EStG relating to allowances for assessed personal income. Paragraph 7 EStG was amended several times between 1948 and 1952. In 1949 allowances for increasing the offset value of new investments were extended from farmers and other self-employed groups (para. 7a EStG 1948) to private enterprises in general.[89] In addition the 'Law on the Opening Balance in Deutschmarks and the Reassessment of Capital' (August 1949) allowed very high assessments of assets and hence great latitude for depreciation claims.[90] Furthermore the introduction of *degressive depreciation* (para. 7a EStG) provided enormous advantages for the capital formation of, above all, the consumer goods industries, by allowing 50 per cent of the re-purchasing price of new capital goods investments up to DM 100 000 to be written off in the first two years after purchase.[91] These provisions helped to compensate the high basic rates of taxation in both Income and Corporation Tax, and also the absence of an adequate capital market, by encouraging the *self-financing of investments.*

However as a policy it drew criticism from both the Allies, who perceived real dangers in the state foregoing huge amount, of taxation

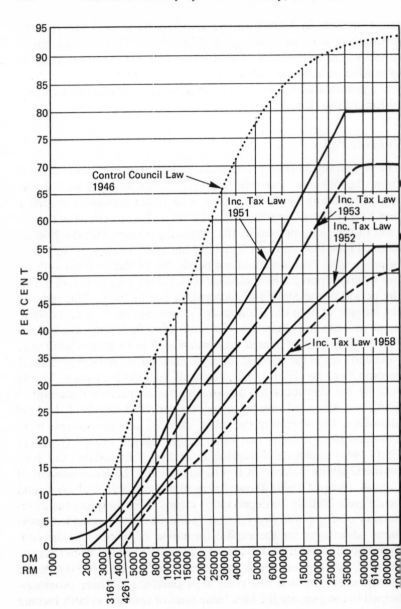

Fig. 4.5   Income tax law, 1946–58

revenue and increasing its indebtedness,[92] and from Ordo-liberals themselves, who recognised that self-financing militated against the ideologically much vaunted notion of spreading the ownership of productive wealth.[93] The level of self-financing was indeed raised from some 40 per cent (in 1927) to an average of 64 per cent (1953–60)[94], and was recognised as a cause for concern by Erhard himself, creating, as he saw it, the danger of high prices, increased capital concentration and, as a result, 'dangerous social–political demands for co- and collective ownership' which would extend 'even to bourgeois circles and parties'.[95]

The unspecific nature of such global tax allowances, as in para. 7 EStG, benefited only those firms who were capable of high enough profits to reinvest their tax-exempt income. Self-financed investments were extremely difficult in the energy sector, in the Iron and Coal industry, in water services and in the railways because of the persistance of price controls, and high-interest loans were out of the question as an alternative source of finance. Despite central government grants of DM 1.3 billion in 1949 and 1950,[96a] there was a real danger of production bottlenecks in these branches of the economy which were so vital to the manufacturing sector. This danger was most clearly exposed by the Korea-Boom.

In order to increase the capacity of energy, coal and water production and the freight capacity of the railways, the government introduced its 'Investment Aid Law' in December 1951, which involved a *mandatory loan* from manufacturing industry to the hard-pressed sectors of DM 1 billion, and *special depreciation allowances* of DM 3.2 billion. The levy on manufacturing industry, which had clearly benefited from the fixed prices of energy, water and transport services, was executed by the state finance offices, transferred to a special 'Industrial Credit Bank' which then channeled funds to the appropriate firms in exchange for fixed (low-) interest bonds which were presented to the creditors. The DM 1 billion, though providing only 7 per cent of the capital needs of the recipient enterprises, were supplemented by extensive additions to the tax allowances already available under para. 7 EStG: For example, through para. 36 of the Inv. Aid Law special depreciation allowances were possible for the 3 years 1952–54, whereby firms could write off up to 50 per cent of the appropriation and production costs of moveable assets and up to 30 per cent of the purchase costs of immovable assets.

The law was so successful that investments in energy, iron and coal industries doubled in the first two years of its operations[96b] Significantly, however, subsequent production increases lagged behind the increased capacity afforded by the law.[97] Within five years of the Act's enforcement surplus capacity became a severe problem, especially for the coal industry,[98] which was beleaguered on the one side by cheaper American coal and by the increasing competitiveness of oil for energy production on the other. The coal crisis could only be resolved by renewed government intervention – with higher duties on imported coal, a tax on heating oil and with state grants to coal owners to pay off miners made redundant by pit closures.[99] The Investment Aid Law did not simply involve a significant intervention by the government to adjust market forces – 'a spectacular case of investment planning'[100] – but predetermined further costly state intervention by failing to achieve a balanced increase in (coal) capacity.[101]

The acute general problem of self-financing remained – the Inv. Aid Law merely served to extend the facility of self-financing to other branches. The government suspended the special allowances under para. 7a EStG for a short time in 1951 and reduced tax rates instead in 1951 and 1953, raising general allowances as well. In 1951 the top rate for income tax was reduced from 95 per cent to 80 per cent, in 1953 from 80 per cent to 70 per cent, when corporation tax was also lowered from 60 per cent to 40 per cent. In 1958 the top rate of income tax was reduced further to 53 per cent which compared very favourably to the then top rates in Britain (88 per cent), USA (88 per cent) and France (71.5 per cent).[102] Such reductions did not however halt either the rise in the self-financing quota of new investments nor its correlate, the increasing concentration of personal and corporate wealth, nor is it clear how they could have been expected to have had such an effect. Erhard's theoretical linking of excessive self-financing with an 'excessively high progressive burden on higher incomes'[103] seems to have been severely flawed, since none of the measures adopted prevented the peak self-financing quota of 75 per cent in 1959.[104] This includes the specific *Law Concerning the Promotion of the Capital Market* from September 1952, the intention of which was to increase the flow of private savings into the capital market and thus spread the ownership of productive capital. It allowed income from fixed-interest securities to be wholly or partially exempt from tax, resembling the earlier 'Social Mortgage Bonds' which were used to stimulate housebuilding. The Capital Market Law had some success as an instrument of capital formation but none as an instrument of redistributing capital ownership more equitably.[105] The 'redistributive purpose' of the Act can be interpreted as humbug, since, as

Borchardt points out, the law contravened the 'accepted social principle' of taxing unearned income higher than earned income.[106] The primacy of capital formation overrode any rhetorical commitment to redistribution. In 1952 the perceived fall in the rate of economic growth moved the government to re-introduce degressive depreciation allowances, only a year after the suspension of similar concessions.

Wage-earners clearly did not benefit from the state foregoing some DM 2 billion in taxation yearly from 1951 to 1954, nor apparently from the 1953 law concerning 'Wealth Formation' for low income earners. Rather the taxation burden on those paying Wages Tax[107] has increased exponentially since the beginning of the 1950s, and the relative burden on business income has decreased.[108] Indirect taxation has decreased as a proportion of total revenue, with Turnover Tax – by far the largest contributor to state funds in 1950 – falling into second place behind Wages Tax. The Cumulative Turnover Tax, which taxed each act of exchange from production to retail stage at a rate of 3 per cent (1946) and then 4 per cent (1950) persisted throughout the Adenauer/Erhard era despite its negative effects on concentration (see above Chapter 3) and on consumer spending power (given that the levy could be passed on in higher prices). It was only replaced in 1968 by a one stage Value Added Tax (10 per cent/5 per cent on 1 January 68, 11 per cent/5 per cent from 1 July 68). It is significant that the tax burden of the wage-dependent through the two main mass taxes (Wages Tax and Turnover Tax) has increased absolutely and relatively to that of the self-employed, the corporations and the recipients of unearned income (from dividends, interest, rent etc.) and there seems little doubt that this was part of a *deliberate policy* by the Federal Government and Ministry of Finance.

This policy was characterised by the specific decisions to subsidise investment by foregoing tax revenue, as demonstrated above, but just as strongly by *non-decisions* relating to the *progressivity of income tax*. In contrast to the repeated reductions in top income tax rates (95 per cent in 1951 to 53 per cent in 1958) there was only one significant change at the lower end (in 1957) which raised the beginning of tax liability to 1630 DM. The 1958 reform adjusted the progressive curve downwards but maintained the starting point, which was again unaffected by the adjustments of 1965. The function of this inactivity by the state has been the so-called 'cold-progression' of taxation, whereby with economic growth an ever increasing proportion of wage earners' incomes becomes taxable. By the same token high income earners escape from the progressive scale after DM

750 000 with a constant rate of 53 per cent – i.e. they are not equal victims of cold progression. Equally, Corporation Tax (along with Wealth Tax) is levied at a constant rate – not subject to progression – a rate moreover which was reduced during the 1950s, in contrast to the effective raising of wage tax liability.

The taxation policy of the period 1949–66 was, on the one hand, in tune with the primacy given to capital formation in the CDU Manifesto of 1949[109] and with the warnings of a slow growth in the standard of living.[110] However, by contributing to a 'considerable modification of capital flows' away from that which a free market would have achieved,[111] the state functioned in an interventionist manner, albeit reducing its potential constructive influence on capital formation,[112] which effected the opposite of the CDU's policy goal of spreading productive wealth more widely.[113] Its effect on income and wealth distribution again placed in question the moderating ('social') influence of the state in the 'social market economy', as will be shown below (see pp. 126ff).

Revenue Development, 1949–66

The primacy of promoting private capital formation gave rise to some significant developments on the revenue side. The decentralised fiscal structure has from the outset been subject to a complex system of tax distribution within which the Federal Government has exclusive use of certain revenues (customs, tobacco and spirits duties, fuel oil taxes, capital transfer tax and others), the Länder exclusive use of others (wealth tax, road tax, beer tax, gambling levies, etc.) and the local authorities exclusive use of rates and 'bagatelle taxes'; the Federal Government and the Länder have shared use of Income Taxes (wages tax, assessed income tax, corporation tax) and turnover tax, although up until the Tax Reform of 1968/69 the Bund had exclusive use of turnover tax. Thus the only major tax revenue at the joint disposal of both Bund and Länder in the Adenauer/Erhard period was represented by taxation from incomes.

Revenues from individual types of tax and duty varied considerably, such that Federal taxes in general grew more slowly between 1951 and 1966 (245 per cent) compared to the exclusive taxes of the Länder (+556 per cent). In a period of trade liberalisation there was far less flexibility in customs and excise duties (the revenue from which rose by a mere 253 per cent in this period) than in taxes based on economic growth. Federal revenue growth from its own taxes was sustained by the rapid expansion of road transport and corresponding oil tax income (+1635 per cent between 1951 and 1966) which partly compensated for the below average growth of customs (+235 per cent), duties on tobacco (+107 per cent), coffee (+119 per cent), spirits (+231 per cent) and even of Turnover Tax (+267 per cent).

Income taxes grew by an average of 494 per cent between 1951 and 1966 – Wages Tax by 581 per cent, Assessed income tax by 598 per cent and corporation tax by 238 per cent.

Table 4.15   Development of revenue from individual taxes, 1951–66

Tax		Per cent change of yield, 1951–66	Per cent share of total revenues, 1951	Per cent share of total revenues, 1966
Wages tax		+581	12.9	19.6
Assessed income tax		+598	10.4	16.5
Corporation tax		+238	10.6	7.9
Turnover tax		+267	31.4	25.8
Mineral oil tax		+1635	2.1	8.2
Customs duties	Federal duties	+235	3.8	2.8
Tobacco duty		+107	11.0	5.1
Coffee tax		+119	1.9	0.9
Sugar duty		−73	1.9	0.1
Spirits duty		+231	2.4	1.8
Beer tax	Land duties	+273	1.2	1.0
Motor vehicles Licences		+597	1.8	2.9

Sources: Bundesbank Monthly Reports, 1967 *passim*; own calculations.

The result of this differential development of revenues was the need to adjust the distribution of revenues between federal and regional levels – in accordance with para. 106 of the Basic Law. The *process of equalisation* was begun in 1951 with the establishment of shared revenue from income taxes with regular amendments of the ratios (in 1952, 1953, 1955, 1958, 1963, 1964). Even within these adjustments there was a very irregular pattern of revenue growth for both Bund and Länder which indicated the lack of a co-ordinated revenue plan between the two levels of tax legislators and a certain amount of fiscal self-interest. As the main supplicant for a larger share of jointly administered funds, the federal government would appear to have benefited least well from revenue distribution with

Table 4.16 State revenue development, 1950–66 (Bund and Länder)

Year	Bund revenue (DM billion)	Per cent change	Per cent of total revenues	Länder revenue DM Billion	Per cent change	Per cent of total revenues	Federal taxes as per cent of t.r.	Länder taxes as per cent of t.r.	Income taxes as per cent of t.r.	Bund share of inc. Taxes
1950	9 593		59.5	6 510		40.4	59.5	7.0	33.3	
1951	14 616	52.3	67.5	7 053	8.3	32.5	60.0	5.5	34.4	27%
1952	18 737	28.1	69.3	8 261	17.1	30.5	55.9	5.2	38.7	37%
1953	20 444	9.1	69.1	9 112	10.3	30.9	54.1	6.0	39.7	38%
1954	21 297	4.1	69.1	9 495	4.2	30.9	54.6	7.0	38.2	38%
1955	23 795	11.7	69.6	10 379	9.3	30.4	57.2	6.9	35.7	33.3%
1956	26 103	9.6	67.9	12 312	18.6	32.1	55.6	7.4	36.9	33.3%
1957	26 963	3.2	65.8	13 960	13.3	34.2	52.7	7.7	39.4	33.3%
1958	28 179	4.5	65.7	14 702	5.3	34.3	51.9	8.1	39.8	35%
1959	31 567	12.0	65.7	16 478	12.0	34.3	51.7	8.4	39.8	35%
1960	36 594	15.9	64.2	20 396	23.7	35.8	49.2	7.9	42.8	35%
1961	41 700	13.9	62.9	24 533	20.2	37.1	47.2	7.8	44.8	35%
1962	45 532	9.1	62.1	27 726	13.0	37.8	46.1	8.1	45.6	35%
1963	49 409	8.5	63.3	28 542	2.9	36.7	45.7	7.8	46.3	35%
1964	54 545	10.3	63.8	30 947	8.4	36.2	45.7	8.0	46.1	35%
1965	59 029	8.2	64.5	32 366	4.5	35.5	47.0	8.0	44.9	35%
1966	62 225	5.4	64.1	34 869	7.7	35.9	46.3	8.0	45.5	35%

Sources: Bundesbank Monthly Reports; own calculations.

revenue growth of 326 per cent between 1951 and 1966 compared to Länder revenue growth of 394 per cent.

The trend of revenue growth in this period – to the disadvantage of the federal authorities and to the apparent advantage of the Länder – has continued to the present day, such that in 1983 the Bund received 58.3 per cent, the Länder 41.7 per cent of their combined revenue. While this trend did not manifest itself in any marked need to increase federal borrowing in the early period – because of constant growth up to 1966, the distribution ratios (albeit amended regularly) contributed considerably to the pressures on the federal government to increase its indebtedness to compensate for revenue shortfalls in the period of interrupted growth 1966–84 (see below Chapter 5). More significantly the constant need to re-negotiate the revenue ratios of income tax and later turnover tax gave the Länder and the Bundesrat considerable influence over federal revenues and thus indirectly over federal expenditure.

From this it is clear that a state which chose to ease the burden on corporate and private capital income was all the more unwilling to

Table 4.17   Indebtedness of Bund and Länder, 1950–66

	Bund Indebtedness (DM million)	Bund debt as per cent of revenues	Länder indebtedness (DM million)	Länder debt as per cent
1950	7 289	76	12 843	197
1951	8 220	56	13 294	188
1952	8 897	47	13 717	166
1953	16 725	82	14 563	159
1954	17 893	84	15 018	158
1955	17 868	75	15 522	149
1956	17 614	67	15 741	128
1957	19 722	73	13 963	100
1958	20 076	70	14 707	100
1959	20 985	66	14 919	90
1960	22 571	62	14 694	72
1961	25 950	62	13 903	57
1962	27 255	60	13 402	48
1963	30 136	61	13 329	47
1964	31 337	57	14 290	43
1965	33 042	56	17 401	53
1966	35 606	57	20 327	58
1983	341 444	157	212 026	102

Sources: Bundesbank Monthly Reports *passim*; own calculations.

forego the advantages of cold progression in income tax, particularly since these advantages were in part calculable. It is also clear that a system, where the revenue growth of federal and regional authorities varies so much, is not particularly well suited to the planned deployment of fiscal resources à la Keynes.

State Policy and Income and Wealth Distribution

Changes in the distribution of income are an expression of changes in the political economy of a country as a whole, along with developments in the distribution of wealth. They are not mono-causal in origin and cannot thus be solely ascribed to the influence of the state. The state in a capitalist society mediates the power relations in a number of important respects, guaranteeing the framework of private ownership of productive property and of private acts of exchange, as well as attempting to soften the impact of negative social and economic trends on the economic order through (largely marginal) measures of monetary, fiscal and social policy. The major determinants of changes in the distribution of income in West Germany up to 1966 were clearly related to the workings of national and international markets. Nevertheless the role of the state is significant both in terms of the pledge by the ruling party (CDU) to effect a more equitable spread of income and wealth and in terms of its response to identifiable secular trends.

Income distribution is traditionally assessed according to a number of categories. There is a fundamental differentiation of *income from labour* (wages and salaries) and *income from capital* (entrepreneurial activity, investments, savings and rents). For the capitalist state and for bourgeois economists the differentiation is a heuristic convenience in that for them capital and labour make equally important contributions to wealth creation but income from the two activities is accrued in a superficially different manner, the one regularly according to timed inputs of labour, the other irregularly according to trade volume and the margins between turnover and costs. Accordingly tax law treats the two forms of income differently, the one taxed weekly/ monthly at source, the other (in the main) taxed retrospectively by assessment. For socialist economists, on the other hand, the equation of labour and capital as parallel contributors to wealth creation is theoretically flawed, since it is only through labour, according to them, that capital is created as a value (qua artefact) or given a value (qua raw material): capital is thus the mere aggregate of labour.

These two opposed perspectives on the same differentiation tend to colour the modes of determining differences in income distribution – in particular they determine the nature and degree of differentiation. Official statistics and bourgeois analyses concentrate, in the main, on the proportion of national income (net social product at factor costs) accruing to capital income and to labour income. The resulting *gross income* trend indicates a rising wages quota as a proportion of national income and a diminishing capital quota.

However, *as an indicator of actual income distribution the gross wages quota is worthless*, since it ignores the increase in the labour force as a proportion of the working population and the corresponding fall in the number of independent businessmen – i.e. it does not illustrate the development of gross income per head; equally it ignores differences in the development of *net income*. Table 4.18 shows the effect of changes in the class structure on the generalised impression given by global gross income figures. Between 1950 and 1967 the number of self-employed (including family members employed in the small family business) fell from 6.4 million to 5.1 million, or by 20.3 per cent. The number of employed (wage dependent) workers rose by 7.5 million from 13.7 million to 21.2 million or by 54.7 per cent. The gross wages quota (see above) rose only 8.6 percentage points, the share of self-employed income of national income fell only by a corresponding amount. Thus the relative *per capita share* of self-employed income to national income rose by 31 per cent from 129 per cent of the mean in 1950 to 169 per cent of the mean in 1967, while the relative per capita share of wage income fell from 85 per cent to 83 per cent of the mean.

Table 4.18   Gross per capita income (average), 1950 and 1967

		DM	Per cent
1950	Mean (*nat. income* working pop.)	3,760	100
	Average per capita gross income (self-employed)	4,864	129
	Average per capita gross income (wage-dependent)	3,216	85
1967	Mean	13,768	100
	Average per capita gross income (self-employed)	23,288	169
	Average per capita gross income (wage-dependent)	11,477	83

Sources: *Statistisches Jahrbuch*; own calculations.

The ratio of average per capita gross wage income to average per capita self-employed income fell from 66 per cent (1950) to 49.2 per cent (1967).

If one considers net average per capita income, the advantages of the self-employed are even more striking, since the deductions from gross wages and salaries (including employers' contributions to social insurance funds) rose from an average of 25.5 per cent between 1950 and 1958 to 28.8 per cent (1959–67) while deductions from self-employed income averaged 20.3 per cent and 22.8 per cent respectively.[114]

These figures (as averages for the general categories of capital and labour) are still misleading in that (as averages) they understate the extremes of income and (as categories) they each include widely different occupations. In the category of labour are included both white collar workers and civil servants as well as wage labourers; in the category of capital are included a large number of small farmers, artisans and shopkeepers. A minor refinement of the statistics demonstrates that the low average income of farmers depresses the income averages in the independent group and that the high average earnings of civil servants and white collar workers exaggerates the average wage income. Figures for 1962/63[115] show that the net average household income of farmers was below that of white collar workers and civil servants and considerably less than that of other businessmen (98.4 per cent of the equivalent household of four persons of white collar workers and civil servants and 68.2 per cent of the equivalent household income of other businessmen). The worker household in 1962/63 had net income earnings of 68.5 per cent of the other groups in the category labour and 47.4 per cent of the average 'independent' household.[116] If the category capital is further refined to exclude small producers and small businessmen, a more realistic picture of actual income relations emerges. Kurt Lungwitz presented

Table 4.19   Net income development, 1950–68 (1950=100)

	Net income from labour	Net income from small business	Net profit from capital
1950	100	100	100
1960	200.3	209.0	350.0
1968	342.3	368.0	678.3

Source: K. Lungwitz *Die Verteilung und Umverteilung des westdeutschen Nationaleinkommens*, 9 (DWI, Berichte, 1970).

Table 4.20   Average gross weekly income (DM) of industrial workers, 1950–65

	1950	1955	1960	1965
All industrial workers	61	87	122	189
Male workers	68	98	134	205
Female workers	40	57	82	138

Source: *Statistisches Jahrbuch* 1957 *passim.*

(unelaborated) net income figures for the categories labour, small business and capitalist property which, after adjustments for the change in the working population, shows a disproportionate advantage for capitalist profits over the income of the two other categories. Net profits from capital are shown to have risen at nearly double the rate of net income from labour, by 578 per cent over 242 per cent from 1950–68. These figures can be differentiated even further by breaking down the category of wage labour into skill groups and into male/female comparisons. The latter comparison reveals the significantly lower rates of pay for female employment between 1950 and 1967, which clearly had a depressing effect on general labour costs. The ratio of gross wages for women per week to gross wages for men improved only marginally from 58.8 per cent in 1950 to 61.1 per cent in 1960 and 64.1 per cent in 1967.

Comparative income statistics still do not reveal the enormous latitude of independent business people for passing off private consumption as commercial costs – in the form of company cars, subsidised travel, meals, telephone expenses etc. – which is not shared by the normal West German taxpayer. These advantages – if they were adequately quantifiable – would widen the distribution gap yet further in favour of the self-employed.

The redistribution of income from wage labour to capital between 1950 and 1967 was concealed by the general rise in real income, by the gradual achievement of full employment and by constant official appeals to moderation in wage claims, which implied an almost immoderate level of mass consumption and a correspondingly immoderate wages quota.

The false impression of equal shares in the Economic Miracle also concealed the *shift in the distribution of wealth*, which was a natural consequence of the inequitable development of incomes distribution and the very high investment quota (as a correlate of the low consumption quota). The Currency Reform of 1948 had already altered the distribution of wealth in the Western zones by effectively devaluing money-based savings by 90 per cent (RM 10 were exchanged for DM 1) while the value of real assets remained constant in relation to the new DM, i.e. increased in relation to RM holdings. This reduced the wealth of households with money savings and fixed interest securities (workers, pensioners etc.) and strengthened the position of those with capital assets (self-employed, farmers, industrialists, etc.). After 1949, as Jörg Huffschmid points out,[117] income and wealth distribution in West Germany involves a threefold disadvantage for the mass of wage earners: their incomes are considerably lower than those of white collar workers, civil servants and the self-employed; their low income means a more limited ability to save, i.e. accumulate money-based wealth; the lower amounts of savings produce not just an absolutely but also relatively smaller yield than larger sums. The result of this 'natural law' for the period 1950–1965 is a considerable reduction in the share of pensioners and the employed (including white collar staff) of the increased stock of social wealth in West Germany, against the self-employed and private enterprises, whose relative position was maintained, and the state, which increased its share from 14.5 per cent of real wealth in 1950 to 33.6 per cent in 1965.

Table 4.21   Structure of real wealth in the Federal Republic, 1950–65

	Share of national wealth (per cent)		
	1950	*1960*	*1965*
Workers (blue & white collar)	34.7	15.6	17.2
Pensioners	5.1	2.5	2.6
Self-employed & private enterprises	45.7	49.3	46.6
State	14.5	32.6	33.6

Source: Gleitze, B., *Sozialkapital und Sozialfonds als Mittel der Vermögens-politik* (Cologne, 1968).

If one excludes corporate bodies (private enterprises, state institutions) the accumulation of personal wealth can be seen to mirror the inequalities of the distribution of income, but in a more exaggerated manner, confirming the cumulative disadvantages cited above:

These averages conceal the exceptional accumulations of wealth which accrued to a small number of very wealthy households. Between 1960 and 1966 the number of households with a total wealth of more than DM 1 million rose from 14 000 to 300 000. In 1966 0.14

Table 4.22   Average per capita wealth formation, 1950–63

	DM
Blue-collar worker	2 100
White-collar worker	4 800
Civil servant	6 800
Farmer	3 400
Self-employed (excl. farmers)	22 000

Source: J. Huffschmid, *Die Politik des Kapitals,* op. cit. p. 30.

per cent of private households owned 13.6 per cent of total wealth, just 2 per cent owned 32 per cent of wealth. There was a minimal change of total wealth accumulation with a slightly broader spread at the top and with modest accumulations accruing to top managers and top civil servants, but most significantly the policy principles of the CDU and its 'wealth formation' legislation did not fulfil their prom-ised results. Neither the general laws designed to bolster the capital market – the 1952 'Capital Market Law'[118] and the 1959 'Law on Savings Premiums' – nor the specific law on 'Wealth Formation' for wage earners of 1961 (revised in 1965)[119] produced a property owning working class which could be said to control a relatively larger share of social wealth.[120]

The structure of total real wealth distribution is however less significant than the structure of the distribution of *productive wealth*. The former clearly reflects relations of social power, but the owner-ship of the means of creating (further) social wealth – i.e. the ownership of the productive apparatus of the West German economy – reflects these power relations more exactly and more strongly. According to Siebke, in 1960 1.7 per cent of households in West Germany owned 70 per cent of all productive wealth (against 34 per cent of total wealth). This share had risen to 74 per cent by 1966.[121] If the *effective relations of power* between big and small capital are also taken into consideration (see above Chapter 3), the concentration of productive wealth was extremely high and the trend up to the end of the Erhard era in 1966 was towards ever greater concentration, in contrast to total wealth distribution which showed a marginal spreading of wealth between 1960 and 1965.

The relationship between concentrated economic power and democratic politics was a contentious issue at the inception of the Federal Republic and brought forth pledges to control the spread and abuse of monopolies. All the indications point not simply to govern-mental toleration of increasingly inequitable relations of economic wealth but to a consistent encouragement of that process – through policies designed to maximise levels of investment and exports, to minimise wage rises and consumption and to cultivate international competitiveness through national and international mergers. The legacy of the Erhard era, while demonstrating the restored dominance of German industry in Europe, contained a number of features which clearly defined the subsequent development of the economy and its subsequent and future structural and cyclical problems. Wealth and income distribution was one of these problems.

Monetary Policy, 1949–66

The official purpose of West German monetary policy is to achieve the optimal stability of the nation's currency (para. 3 Law on the Bundesbank, 26 July 1957). This means the control of domestic inflation and the maintenance of a stable international rate of exchange for the Deutschmark as the framework for the stable growth of the domestic economy. In the period 1948 to 1966 this aim – judged by accepted modern standards – seems to have been achieved very successfully. In the first two cycles up to 1958 the average yearly rate of inflation (for GDP) was 2.6 per cent, and in the second two cycles (1958–66) just 3.2 per cent. The rate of exchange was adjusted right at the outset (on 28 September 1949) when the Deutschmark was devalued against the dollar by 20.6 per cent along with the pound sterling and set at the 1933 value of DM 4.2 to $1. This rate was maintained for 12 years until 4 March 1961, when the Deutschmark was revalued by 4.6 per cent to a higher rate of DM 4.0 to the dollar. Thus between 1950 and 1966 there was below average inflation and an enviable stability of the Deutschmark as a foreign currency. Accordingly the international strength of the German economy – measured by it foreign currency reserves – was ascribed to the success of 'monetary, credit and fiscal policies which were able to maintain stable domestic price levels in a system of fixed exchange rates and thus strengthened considerably the competitive position of German industry in world markets'.[122]

Such praise was extravagant and in part misplaced. Clearly the Federal Bank (Bank deutscher Länder up to 1957) had not abused its power like the Reichsbank between 1914 and 1923 and between 1933 and 1945. On the other hand, as the primary agent of monetary and credit policy, the central bank could still not claim all or most of the credit for the stability of the West German currency. Market conditions made it comparatively easy to service the money supply without the risk of domestic or international devaluation: at home the labour market kept wage costs and consumption levels under control; internationally West Germany's terms of trade were very favourable (and even rose in the 1950s) despite a low exchange rate with the dollar, because of the relative glut of (foreign) raw materials and the strong demand for West German finished goods. Thus the potential inflationary effects of consistent balance of payments surpluses were largely neutralised by a falling consumption quota and a rising export quota. Government borrowing was modest, the state's share of GNP even fell during the 1950s. Bank liquidity, general capital markets and state coffers were fed increasingly well by the sustained boom. The central bank had little to do but tinker around on the sidelines with its control mechanisms, in the firm knowledge that its autonomy freed it from government orders and from electoral legitimation.

That said, the central bank was increasingly criticised by opposition parties and trade unions and also by governmental bodies for its very inactivity. In 1957 already, the 'Academic Sub-Committee of the Economics Ministry' stressed the long-term foreign-political and domestic dangers of the increasing 'accumulation of gold and currency reserves in the Bank deutscher Länder' and recommended an immediate revaluation of the DM to avoid the trade war which threatened to end West Germany's honeymoon with the Bretton Woods System.[123] This advice was ignored. Instead the issue was postponed by minor discount rate reductions totalling 1.75 per cent in progressions from September 1957 to January 1959 (Discount rate: 4.5 per cent to 2.75 per cent; Lombard rate: 5.5 per cent to 3.75 per cent). In 1959 the Federal Government also endeavoured to relieve pressure on the Deutschmark by accelerated repayment of war reparations[124] and by increasing its foreign arms procurements by DM 2.27 billion over 1958.[125] However, gold and currency reserves were only slightly dented in 1959 and more significantly the surplus continued to increase (by DM 5.3 billion in 1959 and DM 5.2 billion in 1960).

As a result, gold and currency reserves rose by over DM 8 billion in 1960 alone to stand at a new record level of DM 32.8 billion. One reason for the surge in capital transfers to Germany may have been the Bundesbank raising Discount and Lombard rates at the end of 1959 (by 2.25 per cent to June 1960). These measures were designed to counteract the overheating of the economy, which was growing at an accelerated rate (see Figure 4.6) and increasing the money supply through exports and credit demand, but with domestic inflation at

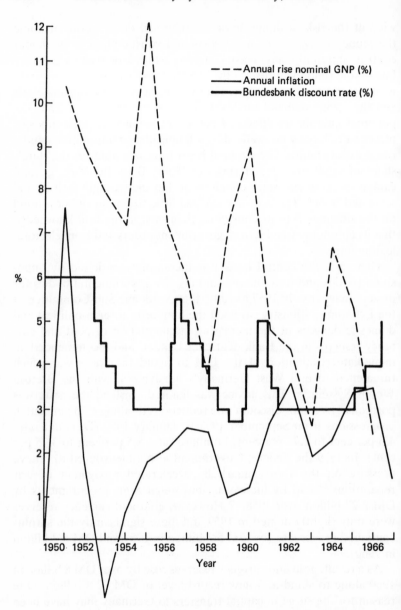

Fig. 4.6   The development of GNP, prices and discount rates, 1950–67
Sources: *Statistisches Jahrbuch*; Bundesbank *monthly reports*.

very low levels (1959: 1 per cent, 1960: 1.2 per cent), the increase in domestic interest rates served only to attract more "hot money" from abroad because of both the high rate of real interest (difference between nominal interest rates and the rate of inflation) and the expectation of a revaluation of the DM at some time in the near future.[126] The raising of minimum reserve ratios and the lowering of rediscount quotas by the Bundesbank clearly affected bank liquidity, but liquid reserves were at such a high level that the cumulative effect of the brief period of credit restrictions was seemingly minimal.

The Bundesbank's policies in 1959 and 1960 were thus largely dysfunctional. Currency reserves rose inexorably and interest rates appear to have contributed to the rise in inflation in 1961 and 1962 (see Figure 4.6). Because of this self-evident failure, Erhard became increasingly convinced of the need for a revaluation. In November 1960 the Central Committee of the Bundesbank still refused to consider the idea and reverted to lower interest rates; Karl Blessing, the Bundesbank president, even threatened to resign, should a revaluation be forced on him.[127] Nevertheless Erhard achieved an unspectacular compromise in March 1961 which resulted in the 4.76 per cent revaluation. The compromise reflected the extreme pressure exerted by industry to maintain the considerable competitive advantages of an underpriced Deutschmark and prevent any revaluation; the campaign against revaluation in the early months of 1961 was described by Röpke (CDU) as almost 'terroristic'[128] and yet despite the modest rise, the BDI still froze its monthly contribution of DM 100 000 to CDU funds in protest.[129a] Ehrenberg argues very plausibly that the revaluation issue was postponed and then fudged by both Federal Government and Federal Bank, because of their acknowledgement of the primacy of capital interests.[129b] Capital representatives seemed unconcerned about the long-term international implications of accumulating trade surpluses, and were only aware of the short-term price and cost advantages of a cheap Deutschmark: apart from the effects on wage costs of a low consumption quota, the mild inflation produced by payments surpluses reduced further the real value of wage awards, reinforcing the effects of productivity on unit costs.[130]

The effects of the revaluation were modest but significant. The purchasing power of domestic wages against foreign goods was raised, contributing towards the narrowing of the trade surplus gap and towards the real improvement of living standards. This coincided with the achievement of full employment and the end of mass emigration from East Germany, and all three factors were reflected in the 2 per cent rise in the adjusted wages quota between 1960 and 1962. The terms of trade rose slightly but stabilised for the rest of the 1960s after 1962. The revaluation marks the end of the period of extensive accumulation at the expense of foreign competitors, customers and the domestic labour force, and the beginning of a period of intensive capital growth.

In 1961 the Bundesbank removed its severe credit restrictions (Discount and Lombard rates, minimum reserves and rediscount quotas) and went into virtual hibernation for over two years, not bothering to respond to a further rise in inflation. However suddenly in 1964, the spectre of further capital inflows was seen to threaten further inflation and induced a new period of restrictive policy, initially with rises in the minimum reserves and a reduction in rediscount quotas. At the same time the Federal Government declared its intention to impose a *Withholding Tax* on interest payable to foreigners on German fixed interest securities which came into force in March 1965 and was accompanied by staged rises in discount rates. This restrictive response to potential inflation was quite inappropriate, since, with international interest rates rising and the Federal Government spending over DM 24 billion on arms imports between 1961 and 1966 (a measure linked to balance of payments considerations) the gold and currency reserves remained consistently below the peak of 1960 and there were small balance of payments deficits which, according to the OECD, were 'more than sufficient to offset the increase in capital inflows'.[131] Furthermore the new restrictive phase coincided with a downturn in the business cycle. *Monetary policy thus functioned procyclically* by depressing domestic business activity still further. In contrast to the period 1959 to 1961, the squeeze hit the banks when their liquidity ratios were considerably lower, such that they could not absorb the pressure from both the demand and the supply side with the ease of four years earlier (liquidity ratios 1959: over 18 per cent, 1964: below 12 per cent, 1966: below 6 per cent). Domestic demand was beginning to fall at the end of 1964, when rediscount quotas were lowered and was falling through 1965 and 1966, while the squeeze was tightened. The result was that the central bank compounded the secular trend of the economy and reinforced the effects of the recession which set in in the winter of 1966. The causes and effects of the recession will be examined in detail below. It is sufficient here to point out that it marked the end of a period of uninterrupted growth in the German economy, in which the Bundesbank (Bank deutscher Länder) had few serious problems to solve. However in the few cases where a response was appropriate the Bundesbank demonstrated that it lacked sufficient foresight and the instruments to control macro-economic developments in a positive way. Long before the official espousal of monetarism, the contradictoriness of a national monetary policy was exposed, where the weaknesses of domestic demand allowed a relative increase in trade surpluses but induced a response which at best was *only appropriate to domestically produced over-heating* not to the vagaries of the world capital markets. The evidence thus shows that restrictive monetary policy in the two major squeeze phases of this period was largely dysfunctional.

State Expenditure Policy, 1950–66

This section is concerned with the specific deployment of fiscal resources by the West German state as a means of influencing national economic affairs, in contrast to the indirect influence of taxation or monetary policy dealt with above. Although many of the central government's taxation policies amounted to hidden subsidies, they cannot be considered as a part of expenditure policy as such.

Economists use a variety of general indicators for 'state' expenditure which vary according to the specific academic or ideological purpose of the analysis.[132] The most valuable indicator for the period 1950 to 1966 is the 'Expenditure of the Area Authorities' which excludes the social insurance funds but includes all other specific social transfers and thus allows a reasonable survey of state expenditure as a programme of reallocating social wealth.

According to this indicator the share of West Germany's GNP deployed by the state remained fairly constant from 1950 to 1966, averaging 31.2 per cent from 1950 to 1959 and 31.8 per cent from 1961 to 1966.[133] Figure 4.7 shows the annual growth of GNP and state expenditure, whereby the expenditure curve shadows the GNP curve more or less pro-cyclically throughout the period. This pro-cyclical pattern seems to reflect the general rejection of Keynesian anti-cyclical interventionism on the part of successive government leaders, as well as the specific desire to engineer economic recovery as quickly as possible. The exceptional task of post-war restoration, making good the massive discrepancy between national output and productive potential, made a linear policy of spending as soon as the revenue became available most plausible, at least until the beginning of the 60's. This was particularly so, because the Allies (under the

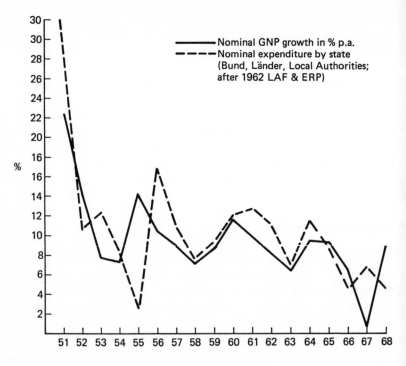

Fig. 4.7   State expenditure and growth cycles, 1950–68

Occupation Statute obliged the West German state to pursue a policy of balanced budgets without recourse to deficit spending.[134] As it was, GNP growth was so high that West Germany's modest taxation levels allowed sufficient revenue to finance an expanding expenditure programme. The recovery itself, however, reinforced the longer term pro-cyclical pattern of expenditure policy by deluding many CDU politicians into believing that the phenomenon of cyclical recessions had been banished for ever, thereby making Keynesian demand management and forward planning redundant. In practical policy making the Adenauer/Erhard era displayed a 'planning-phobia',[135] if not an 'intervention-phobia',[136] which persisted as dogma to outlive the period where the state had the luxury of not intervening systematically.

However the absence of a planned strategy cannot simply be ascribed to a 'planning-phobia' but also to the absence of a unitary fiscal structure which could have helped the comprehensive deployment of resources. *The federal fiscal constitution imposed on the West*

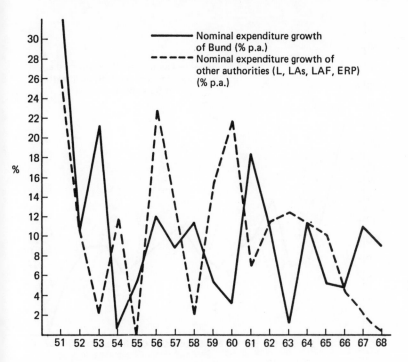

Fig. 4.8   Comparison of central government expenditure and expenditure of other area authorities, 1950–68

German state by the Americans made the co-ordinated use of tax revenue by central, regional and local authorities much less likely than in a centralised fiscal system. There was no marked rivalry between central and regional authorities in this period, even though, for example, the migration of refugees put greater financial burdens on states like Schleswig-Holstein. General rising prosperity allowed real expansion at federal and regional level. However, if one breaks down 'state expenditure' into a simple division between central government and the other authorities (Länder, Local Authorities, Equalisation Fund and ERP-Fund) a curiously volatile pattern of expenditure emerges, which does not mirror the GNP growth cycles in the same way as their combined expenditure.

Figure 4.8 shows the irregular pattern of expenditure growth of central and other authorities, demonstrating both the irregular flow of particular tax revenues to particular authorities and the general tendency to spend those monies when they became available. However,

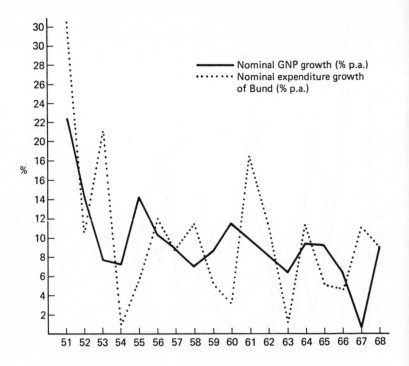

Fig. 4.9   Central government expenditure and growth cycles

apart from Fritz-Schäffers attempt to accumulate reserves in the mid-1950s' boom for later arms expenditure (the so-called 'Julius-Tower'), there is clear evidence of an attempt by the Bund to contain the growth of the economy in line with the Federal Bank's restrictive monetary policy in the two (exchange rate) crises 1959–61 and 1963–66. However Figures 4.8 and 4.9 show that this potentially anti-cyclical thrust of central government expenditure (including a real reduction in 1963) was neutralised by correspondingly strong pro-cyclical expenditures of the other authorities.

There are perfectly good reasons for these anomalies, in large part resulting from the *severe demographic fluctuations* due both to migration and the effects of two world wars and the depression. However the differing patterns of expenditure clearly demonstrate the general differences in expenditure priorities of central and regional authorities and the failure to co-ordinate long-term expenditure policies.

Concealed behind the expenditure patterns of the Bund and other

authorities is the relative reduction of the federal budget as a proportion of total expenditure (1950: 51.5 per cent, 1966: 46.9 per
cent). In the 1950s the average annual share of the Bund was 54.1 per
cent, from 1960–66 the average fell to 48.4 per cent and in general the
trend has continued downwards.[137] This indicates a further weakening of central fiscal control (intended in the constitutional arrangement) and contradicts the contentions of an increasing centralisation
of political control. The growing 'particularism' of state expenditure
indirectly strengthened the power of the large private enterprises –
with their increasing accumulations of capital as a lever for influencing policy in the partial apparatuses of the state. Conversely it
weakens any 'control' that the electorate might have over state
policy, because an *increasing proportion of state revenue is expended
in areas outside the remit of the central and particular area authorities*.

If one moves from global expenditure patterns in West Germany to
specific branches of expenditure, noteworthy developments emerge.
The two areas which reflect the exceptional demands of post-war
recovery are social security and housing construction. Refugee im-
migration, war damage and war pensions posed the major problems.

The population of the Western zones was already 7.1 million
higher in 1946 than before the war, 2.5 million more arrived between
1946 and 1950 and a further 3.6 million left East Germany between
1950 and 1962 for the West.[138] This effectively made the West
German state responsible for the social welfare of some 13.2 million
additional people on top of its own previous population. Beside the
general system of social insurance for accidents, invalidity, unemployment, sickness and old age, the area state authorities provided
additional grants towards the pension funds (Bund), social benefit
(Bund), child benefit (Bund) and a wide range of welfare provisions
for war victims (Bund & Länder). Pensions for war widows, war
orphans and for the parents of war dead were available, also for
invalids from war service or prisoner of war camps and their families.
The initial benefits from the War Victims Law ('Bundesversorgungs-
gesetz', 20 December 1950) were very modest, because of both a
limited allocation of resources and the large numbers of eligible
'victims'. Equally *unemployment benefit* and *old age pensions* were
set at low levels in relation to previous earnings and were thus
exposed initially to the influence of inflation. It was only in 1957 that
pensions became indexed to average earnings (while maintaining
occupational differentials). This affected the central government
grants to the insurance funds but at a time when the burden of social

Table 4.23   Expenditure of State Area Authorities, 1950–66 (DM million)

Fiscal year	Total exp.	Law and order	Defence	Education	Science	Soc. Sec.	Health	Food agric., etc	Civil Eng.	Housing constr.
1950	28 527	596	4 265	1 673	408	6 356	947	974	934	1 584
1951	38 282	958	7 904	2 194	524	5 426	1 238	1 422	1 113	2 038
1952	42 452	1 041	7 866	2 544	599	9 719	1 359	1 492	1 320	2 660
1953	47 706	1 160	5 529	3 014	714	12 024	1 465	1 064	1 577	2 911
1954	51 855	1 232	5 905	3 320	779	12 068	1 606	1 347	1 745	3 353
1955	53 228	1 315	6 078	3 547	571	12 937	1 734	1 555	2 413	3 177
1956	62 226	1 414	7 259	4 148	1 077	13 950	2 037	2 258	2 844	3 695
1957	69 174	1 575	7 483	4 485	1 228	15 154	2 275	3 484	2 643	3 927
1958	74 535	1 754	8 747	4 962	1 566	16 171	2 528	3 170	3 758	4 021
1959	81 562	1 766	9 519	5 339	1 772	16 544	2 700	3 263	4 260	4 684
1960s)	28 553	1 477	8 460	4 463	1 542	12 973	2 348	3 474	3 964	3 885
1961	103 123	2 125	13 174	6 628	2 966	18 639	3 515	4 535	5 673	4 420
1962	114 772	2 306	17 094	7 274	3 010	20 539	4 055	4 641	7 004	5 077
1963	122 765	2 598	19 433	8 238	3 474	20 581	4 484	5 073	8 359	5 235
1964	136 903	2 735	19 008	9 438	4 371	24 290	5 104	5 389	9 119	5 560
1965	147 782	3 005	19 234	10 802	5 131	27 238	5 662	5 775	9 708	5 576
1966	154 739	3 264	19 809	11 735	5 538	27 859	5 174	5 400	10 071	5 138

1950 Federal Territory without Berlin; up to and including 1959 without Saarland. Thus includes Area Authorities plus the LAF (after 1962 includes ERP fund).
1960 = 9 months (change round from financial to calendar year).
Source: Statistiches Jahrbuch.

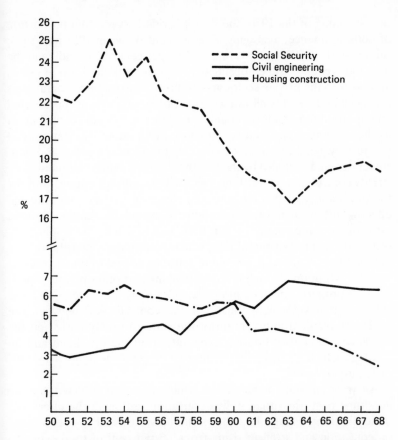

Fig. 4.10   State expenditure on social security, civil engineering and housing construction as a per cent of total expenditures (excluding the social insurance funds), 1950–68

benefits had been steadily reduced as a result of the improvements in the labour market (unemployment in 1950: 8.2 per cent, 1955: 2.7 per cent, 1960: 0.6 per cent) and the general increase in household earnings. Welfare provisions for war victims continued throughout the period however, and in 1969 still accounted for over 18 per cent of social expenditure by the area state authorities. Figure 4.10 shows the overall drop in the share of social to total expenditure from the peak of 25.2 per cent in 1953 to 18.5 per cent in 1968, despite the effects of pensions indexing.

The housing provision similarly shows a marked decline from 6.5 per cent of the combined budgets in 1954 to 2.9 per cent in 1968. At the beginning of the 1950s the state provided a very high proportion of housing finance, averaging 42.2 per cent between 1951 and 1953; this proportion fell to an average of 29.7 per cent of all funding in the next four years.[139] State housing expenditure took the form of grants and loans to the private sector and of direct construction programmes for social housing; tax allowances on housing investment represented an important indirect form of aid. The state's substantial contribution to the housing repair and construction programme was determined not just by need and the weakness of the capital market and consumer demand, but also by the fact that housing rents continued to be strictly controlled up until June 1960, with significant implications for the profitability of private housing investment. After 1960 and the effective lifting of most rental controls, speculative capital flooded into the housing market – for both building and development – setting off a spiral of rental rises which greatly exceeded the rate of inflation (See *Fig*. 4.11). The coincidence of an end to rental controls and the exceptionally high levels of banking and other private liquidity gave property speculation in West Germany a unique boost. The subsequent development illustrates the contradiction between the necessary planned intervention of the state to satisfy basic housing needs and to control housing exploitation on the one hand and an ideology which eschewed such intervention and demanded its ultimate suspension.[140]

An area of state expenditure which was also affected by the abnormal post-war situation was education, although the effect was quite different. Figure 4.12 shows the upward trend of expenditure on education and science, rising from 7.3 per cent of total expenditure in 1950 to 11.2 per cent in 1966. What the figure does not show is the low level of education expenditure compared to other countries with an equally developed economic apparatus. Measured as a percentage of GNP and particularly as a percentage of total state expenditure the West German state compared unfavourably with most European countries in its allocation for teaching, research and development. By 1963 the USA spent 4.8 per cent of its GNP on Education and Science (17.5 per cent of State Expenditure), Holland 5.7 per cent (24.2 per cent of SE), Sweden 6.7 per cent (21.3 per cent of SE) and West Germany 3.1 per cent of GNP (9 per cent of SE). By 1967 the gap had widened still further, such that the share of expenditure on education and science as a percentage of TSE was, at 11.2 per cent, barely more than half the proportion of Holland, Sweden and France and 50 per cent less than Upper Volta and Haiti![141]

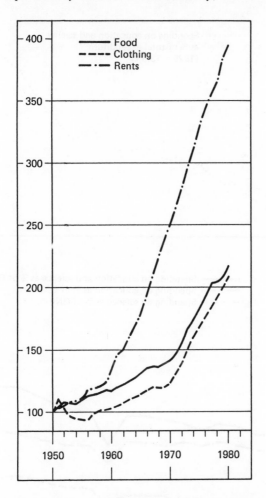

Fig. 4.11   Price development of rents, clothing and food, 1950–80
(1950 = 100)
Source: Glastetter *et al.*, *Wirtschaftliche Entwicklung.*

This apparent neglect of the educational system – as a vital external factor of production – was due in large part to the ongoing boom of the 1950s and early 1960s combined with a vast reserve of qualified workers, represented by the thousands of highly skilled refugees from former territories and from East Germany that continued to flood onto the labour market until 1961. Together, the boom and the skill reserves reduced demands on the education service as the source

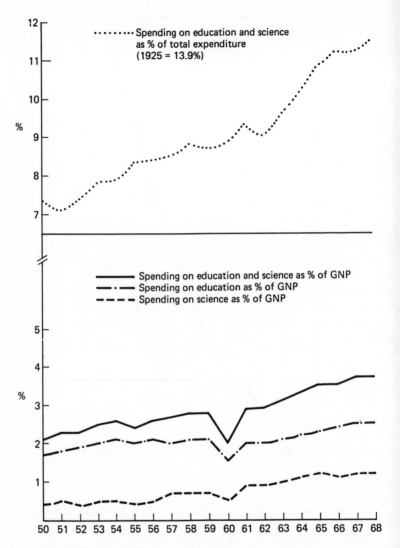

Fig. 4.12   State expenditure on education and science (a) as a per cent of total state expenditure and (b) as a per cent of GNP, 1950–68

Sources: Statistisches Jahrbuch, 1969; own calculations.

both of trained workpeople and innovative research, because industry and commerce was able to expand extensively into reserves of capacity and 'human capital'. This produced a complacency at government level about demands on the educational system which were observed by contemporary commentators as being extremely short-sighted, creating a 'technological lag', which would require considerable changes to avoid a rapid decline in German competitiveness.[142] In fact limited state commitment to school and further education and to scientific research (with the exception of arms research) produced a situation in the 1960s when a shortage of trained scientists and engineers coincided with the sudden, though clearly forseeable, appearance of the post-war bulge at universities, with the result that the facilities could not cope. This represented a structural economic problem which, along with cyclical weaknesses, was bequeathed to the state administrations after 1966. Tackling both produced in turn further problems for West Germany's political economy in the 1970s.

Another area of the economic infrastructure, where the state has direct influence over planning and investment is that of *transport and communications*. Both represent vital external factors of production, the price of which directly affects the cost levels and profit margins of private enterprises. The area authorities are involved in the building and maintenance of roads, canals, bridges, harbours and airports, the Bund owns the Federal Railways, the Federal Postal Service and the overwhelming majority of shares in Lufthansa. The regional and local authorities have direct or indirect control over a large proportion of local passenger transport and radio and television networks.

Apart from the acute problems of reconstructing the transport and communications network after the war – which dominated policy making in the early 1950s – the period up to 1966 was characterised by a number of structural changes in both areas. Above all the expansion of private road transport ended the monopoly of the railways in passenger and freight services. Despite controls on rail fares and freight charges up to 1961, and an absolute rise in freight and passenger traffic up to 1964 and 1962 respectively, the relative proportion of total transport turnover enjoyed by the Federal Railways fell consistently throughout the period with corresponding effects on revenue and manpower. The cumulative losses of the Railways reached DM7.2 billion by 1966, despite generous grants from the central government after 1957 to sustain the railways' pension scheme and other non-commercial obligations. Without state subsidies to distort the 'operating results', the cumulative debt of the Bundesbahn would have reached some DM30 billion DM by 1965; even so its reduced debt totalled 14.5 billion.[143] The increasing levels

of subsidy and debt reflect the constitutional status of the Bundesbahn as a service which by statute has to be maintained without
primary regard to profitability. The (huge) public losses of the
German railways imply certain cost savings for private commercial
users of railway services and hence another indirect contribution by
the state to the reproduction and accumulation of private capital. It
appears anomalous that the state authorities, otherwise reluctant to
use the instruments of fiscal interventionism and deficit spending,
should have tolerated the mounting deficits of the railways with such
equanimity. The Federal Bank, on the other hand, was highly critical
of what it regarded as a squandering of resources.[144] However, there
seems to be little doubt that the Bund pursued a deliberate policy of
subsidy in order to minimise the direct external costs of production
for private capital.

While the competitiveness of railways was receding behind a
screen of state subsidy and mounting debt, postal and telecommuni-
cations moved into a much more favourable period, both because it
was able to maintain its effective monopoly in this area, but also
because it was at the forefront of the communications 'revolution'
which has dominated the post-war period. The turnover of the
Federal Postal Service rose consistently throughout the period to
reach over DM10 billion in 1966; it employed an increasing number
of staff and overtook the railways (with a declining payroll) as the
largest employer in West Germany. Again in contrast to the railways,
the postal service produced consistent profits – with the exception of
1953/54 – although cumulative contributions to the Federal Government budget of DM5.7 billion (by 1966) are presented as costs in the
official annual results. In contrast to federal subsidies which 'improved the annual results' of the railways, the FPS is required to hand
over 6 per cent of their operating revenue to the Federal Government; the cumulative total of these annual payments to 1966 was
nearly as much as the cumulative subsidy of the Bund to the railways
(DM5.7 billion against DM6.9 billion). The cumulative profit of the
FPS was thus set at DM500 million, as opposed to a real figure of
5618 million. The cross-subsidising of state-owned enterprises is thus
reasonably evident. The rationality of state policy in these two areas
of communications infrastructure remained that of minimising – in
the short term at least – industry's external costs. Even though the
performance of the FPS 'rose more strongly than the national product', 'charges in the postal service proper were not sufficiently adjusted to growing costs. . . . The chances offered by a raising of rates

Table 4.24   Results of the profit and loss account of Federal Railways and Federal Posts

Millions of DM

Business Year	Profit (+) Loss (–) according to official annual results	Federal payments improving annual results	Profit (+) Loss (–) after deduction of column 3	Business year	Profit (+) Loss (–) according to official annual results	Payment to Federal government	Profit (+) Loss (–) including Column 7
	1	2	3	4	5	6	7	8
2nd half								
1948	– 82.4	—	– 82.4	1948/49	—	—	—
1949	+ 30.4	—	+ 30.4	1949/50	+181.3	140.0	+321.3
1950	– 154.0	—	– 154.0	1950/51	+249.4	143.3	+392.7
1951	+ 153.4	—	+ 153.4	1951/52	+ 57.4	156.4	+213.8
1952	– 103.5	—	– 103.5	1952/53	– 51.0	173.1	+122.1
1953	– 447.8	—	– 447.8	1953/54	–220.7	186.4	– 34.3
1954	– 462.7	—	– 462.7	1954	+135.7	160.4	+296.1
1955	– 158.2	—	– 158.2	1955	+158.8	238.7	+397.5
1956	– 481.1	—	– 481.1	1956	+ 34.4	258.2	+292.6
1957	– 678.3	200.0	– 878.3	1957	–131.8	275.9	+144.1
1958	– 576.7	280.0	– 878.3	1958	–116.4	299.6	+183.2
1959	– 356.8	257.7	– 614.5	1959	+ 38.6	324.8	+363.4
1960	– 13.5	388.5	– 402.0	1960	+ 70.6	362.3	+432.8
1961	– 29.8	755.2	– 785.0	1961	+142.5	388.3	+245.8
1962	– 110.2	948.9	–1 059.0	1962	–382.0	422.3	+ 40.3
1963	– 409.4	852.4	–1 261.8	1963	–250.8	477.7	+226.9
1964	– 970.4	883.7	–1 854.1	1964	– 19.0	500.9	+481.9
1965	–1 278.0	1 147.0	–2 425.0	1965	– 45.0	590.0	+645.0
1966	–1 106.0	1 597.0	–2 703.0	1966	–285.0	668.0	+953.0
Total	–7 235.0	6 964.0	–14 197.4	Total	+500.0	5 766.0	+5 678.3

Source: Bundesbank *Monthly Reports* (Mar. 1966 and Apr. 1971).

were thus not fully exploited'.[145] FPS revenue would have been far higher under conditions of normal commercial practice, but so would the costs of the private user of the services.

The transfer of FPS revenues to the railways could be justified because of the higher levels of gross investments required to maintain railway services in this period. Up to 1966 gross investments by the FR amounted to DM34.9 billion, compared to DM22.6 billion by the FPS. Even with the additional funding for the FR and the FPS contribution to government funds, the self-financing ratio of investments was only 26 per cent for the railways compared to 38 per cent for the postal services. The channelling of funds to assist the investment programme of the FR clearly reduced their borrowing requirement while increasing the borrowing requirement of the FPS to a 'tolerable' level. However, it can be argued that state policy on rail transport did not go beyond what was in effect a holding operation, which lacked the speculative element of, say, French rail policy – spending more in the short term to save more in the long term.[146]

Thus while subsidised infrastructural costs remained the major element of rail policy, there was little attempt to produce a co-ordinated transport policy. Rather the liberalisation of the Transport Laws in 1961 – with the 'Road Haulage Law', the 'General Railways Law' and the 'Inland Shipping Law' – compounded the need for increased drip-feed subsidies, larger debts and short-term rationalisation in the railway sector. While serving the interests of the motor vehicle and road-haulage lobby, the 'planning-phobia' of the Adenauer/Erhard era clearly proved to be dysfunctional when general transport costs rose after 1973.

The final major area of state expenditure to be considered here is *agriculture*. The structural position of agriculture within capitalism is unique, in its heavy dependence on geophysical factors (soil, climate, terrain, etc.), since these pre-determine and limit real and potential levels of productivity and hence indirectly both the labour/capital input per unit of production and the ownership and size of farmholdings. Thus in contrast to industry and commerce, relations of exchange are a secondary (if vitally important) factor behind geophysical conditions. As a result of this and the fact that it serves to supply basic human needs, agriculture in Germany has been subject to particular and intense interest by the state, particularly since the agricultural disasters of the mid-nineteenth century and the explosion of the urban population. The primary importance of food supplies for an increasingly non-agricultural society has made state protection of domestic agricultural production and farm incomes a permanent feature of expenditure and general social subsidy. Apart from enjoying the general advantages of a state transport infrastructure, German agriculture has been protected by high customs tariffs on imported cereals and animal produce since 1878. This benefited particularly the cereals producers – mainly aristocratic big land-owners – and to a lesser extent the small livestock farmers who still had to sustain added fodder costs. Up to the 1920s protectionism produced a contradictory result of maintaining agricultural production, particularly on marginal land, but also maintaining inefficient methods and inefficient structures of ownership – the latter charac-terised by the polarity of huge estates on the one hand and the mass of peasant small-holdings on the other. The 'Reich Law on Farm Inheritance' ('Reicherbhofsgesetz') of 1933 produced a severe ration-alisation of small holdings at the expense of many peasant supporters of the Nazi party. Despite this and the strictly controlled, cartellised market for agricultural products, the major contradiction of German agriculture persisted beyond 1945 – namely between its generally small scale commodity production and the advanced stage of devel-opment of productive forces within agriculture and within the wider economy.

The basic thrust of agricultural policy has remained surprisingly constant this century: maximise domestic production, minimise im-ports and stabilise prices and farm incomes. While abandoning the expansionist purpose of autarky and dismantling the Nazi cartellised markets, the post-war governments persisted with a policy of protec-tionism and indirect subsidies. This was in part determined by the general nature of agriculture within the national economy – but more importantly by the large increase in the population, the severe pressure on the balance of payments and the need to sustain agricul-tural employment and resettle refugee farmers. Although West German agriculture contributed only 11.3 per cent of GDP in 1950, it sustained 23.2 per cent of the working population (or 5.1 million people) – a considerable and largely conservative part of the electo-rate. The application of ORDO-liberal principles to West German agriculture would have been economically and politically disastrous for the CDU. Their electoral programme for 1949 thus specifically withdrew agricultural policy from the general policy guidelines on the economy and established principles of market regulation and long-term planning which defied the official ideology, while evoking the symbol of the independent farmer as the ideal representative of the new spirit of honest enterprise and toil![147]

In the 1950s national policy stopped short of introducing quota systems and minimum prices but used an assortment of means to achieve maximum output as well as the gradual rationalisation of agricultural production:

(a) from the outset farmers were given generous tax allowances to fund the purchase of building equipment, materials and live-stock;

(b) resettlement grants were made available to refugee farmers;

(c) the 'Agriculture Law' of September 1955 formalised the policy of rationalisation and introduced a series of 'Green Plans' which involved a system of grants for combining smallholdings, estab-lishing co-operatives for sales and procurement, draining land, supplying water and electricity, building roads, clearing waste-land, etc. In addition cheap credit was made available to im-prove farm liquidity, and wholesale fertiliser prices were subsidised;

(d) domestic agricultural produce was protected by high national customs barriers up to 1960 and gradually replaced by common EEC customs duties up to 1968.

Total state expenditure on agriculture and the related areas of forestry and fisheries was considerable, rising from an average of 3.6 per cent of the combined expenditure of the Area Authorities in the 1950s to 3.9 per cent between 1960 and 1967.[148] This figure still conceals the real extent of social subsidy, because it neither reflects the cost of tax allowances nor does it reflect the effect of customs duties on domestic prices: with world market prices for certain products often running at less than 60 per cent of domestic prices, the indirect cost of agricultural support can be assumed to have been considerable. If one then also adds the annual contributions to the EEC after 1960 as effective agricultural expenditure, a more realistic level of total social subsidy could be calculated.

The system of indirect planning in West Germany and later in the EEC clearly contributed to a slow but steady rationalisation of production and landholdings and to an increase in European self-sufficiency. Nevertheless the process was urged on and reinforced by secular developments in the general economy, whereby income levels and job opportunities in industry and commerce sucked away a large number of low income farmers and agricultural workers.

Average farm incomes remained low for this period (see above pp. 128ff) reflecting not simply the relative backwardness of German agriculture in general – compared to Holland and Great Britain – but also the *specific weakness of small farmers in relation to monopoly suppliers* (of agricultural machinery, feed, fertilisers, etc.) *and to monopolised customers* (food industry), all of which have exploited the particular advantages of a sector whose economic survival the state guarantees. The increasing proportion of small producers which have been drawn into permanent supply contracts with the oligopolies of the food industry shows both the 'modernisation' of agriculture and its relative backwardness. The state/EEC support system must, in my view, be seen in part as a function of this contradiction (which it perpetuates) rather than the main cause of the growing vertical concentration of food production, as Siebels and Lenke contend.[149] Both the expenditure programmes of successive CDU governments and their maintenance of non-competition in the agricultural sector, confirm both the limits of their ideology and their recognition of the monopolistic tendency of the economy as a whole. What the CDU's agricultural policy did not do was to resolve the dilemma of agriculture (subsidy/import limitation versus 'efficiency'/ free trade) which remained one of the major contradictions of European capitalism in the 1970s and 1980s.

Table 4.25   Development of agricultural workforce and agricultural production, 1950–69

	Agricultural working Population (million)	As per cent of total W.P.	Share of agriculture in GDP
1950	5.1	23.2	11.3
1960	3.6	14.0	6.6
1965	2.9	11.1	5.1
1969	2.5	9.6	4.3

Source: *EEC Yearbook of Agricultural Statistics* (1972).

State Labour Policy, 1950–66

Labour, as the primary factor of production, made a vital contribution to the economic recovery of the 1950s. The minimisation of labour costs (through wage 'restraint' and productivity rises) facilitated an investment/export-led boom which marked the subsequent development of West Germany's political economy. Much of this can be ascribed to the dynamics of the labour market (with its constant reserves of labour) combined with the impact of national defeat and the limited expectations of the general population. However, beyond the rhetorical exhortations to work hard for modest rewards,[150] the CDU governments assisted the process in two important areas: the formalisation of industrial relations and the establishment of a system of migrant labour.

Between 1951 and 1955 the Adenauer governments enacted a series of laws governing the representation of the labour force in their places of employment: the 'Co-determination Law in the Coal, Iron and Steel Industries' (1951), the 'Works Constitution Law'(1952) and the 'Law on the Representation of Personnel' (1955). The three laws were ostensibly the realisation of the electoral pledge of the CDU for co-determination in industrial affairs.[151] One common feature of the first two (industrial/commercial) laws[152] is that representation is *based in the employing company* – in contrast to *industry-based trade union representation*. Neither law breaks the primacy of company interests: although the 1951 'Co-determination Law' for heavy industry was forced through by the two major trade unions (IG-Metall, IG-Bergbau) against the will of both employers and initially of the government, and although it contained provisions for parity representation of the workforce on the supervisory boards of major heavy industrial companies, it was limited in its effect (on asserting the interest of labour) (a) by the obligation for all supervisory board members to consider company viability above all other things (viz. the Shareholding Law 1937, revised 1965), (b) by a 'neutral' arbiter on the board, and (c) by limitations on communications between worker representatives in both supervisory and managerial boards[153] and the workforce. The expectations of both the supporters of the 51 Co-determination Law – 'a revolutionary act'[154] – and its conservative opponents – 'a state political revolution'[155], an 'unconstitutional' offence[156] against the 'divine right of property' [sic!][157] – were not realised. Rather the enlightened conservatism of politicians like Gerhard Schröder (Cabinet minister from 1953 to 1969) and the scepticism of left-wing opponents proved correct. The predicted 'social peace' (Schröder)[158] in a heavy industrial sector hitherto riven with class antagonisms reigned throughout the period 1951 to 1966, despite massive reductions of the mining labour force, the 'equal obligations' of owners and workers facilitating considerable increases in productivity.[159] Equally the 1951 Law confirmed and reinforced the property rights of owners, a number of whom had been convicted of crimes against humanity and all of whom had for some time been under the threat of complete expropriation. For the KPD the greatest danger to workers interests lay in class collaboration which implied 'responsibility for the securing of the capitalist economy'[160] and which would render the hope of real power-sharing into a 'farce – or what would be worse – a confidence trick'.[161]

There were fewer illusions about the 'Works Constitution Law' (Betr. V.G.) of July 1952 and the 'Law on Personnel Representation' (P.V.G.) (1955). While the 1951 Law can be described as 'a concession by the ruling class to workers and to the unions',[162] the two later laws were vigorously opposed by the unions and compared by some to Nazi labour law.[163] The Betr. V.G. introduced a system of works councils elected by the workforce of individual firms which were independent of trade union influence and which were charged primarily with maintaining industrial peace (§ 49) and limited to questions of working conditions in negotiations with the firm's management; works council delegates to the supervisory board of joint stock companies were powerless to assert workers' interests, since they held only one third of the seats on the board and were in any case bound to conditions of loyalty to company interests.

There seems little doubt that the formalisation of industrial relations by the state fulfilled a double function of limiting the powers of organised labour and strengthening the ideological illusion of 'social partnership'. There are no empirical grounds to assert that labour law directly reduced labour militancy; there seems little doubt, however, that, as statutory requirements, the institutions of participation absorb a considerable amount of organisational energy and time, develop their own interest perspectives (distinct from trade union perspectives) and by implication would have reinforced the natural paralysing effects of a labour market, where, for the most part, the supply of labour was greater than demand.

Apart from subsidies to maintain employment in structurally weak sectors like agriculture, the railways and later the coal industry, the labour market was left very much to its own devices in the 1950s, in accordance with the official doctrine of non-interference. Plans for an active policy of job-creation in 1950 were made unnecessary for the government because of the Korea boom and the rapid subsequent absorption of the reserves of labour in the period of uninterrupted

Table 4.26 Employment in West Germany, 1954–67

	Total working population (1000s)	W.P. as per cent of total population	Employed workforce (1000s)	Foreign workers (1000s)	Foreign workers per cent change p.a.	Foreign labour quota (per cent)	Vacancies 1000s	Registered unemployed (1000s)	Rate of unemployment (per cent)
1954	21 995	47.7	15 968	70		0.4	137	1,221	7.1
1955	22 830	48.3	16 840	77	+ 9.6	0.5	200	928	5.2
1956	23 435	48.6	17 483	95	+24.1	0.5	219	761	4.2
1957	23 940	48.8	17 992	105	+ 9.7	0.6	217	662	3.5
1958	24 124	48.6	18 188	123	+18.0	0.7	216	683	3.6
1959	24 381	48.1	18 531	152	+22.8	0.8	280	476	2.5
1960	26 240	47.8	20 252	279	+73.1	1.4	465	271	1.3
1961	26 591	47.7	20 730	491	+81.6	2.4	552	181	0.9
1962	26 783	47.3	21 053	631	+28.6	3.0	574	155	0.7
1963	26 880	47.0	21 303	773	+22.6	3.6	555	186	0.9
1964	26 979	46.6	21 547	904	+16.9	4.2	609	169	0.8
1965	27 153	46.3	21 841	1 121	+24.0	5.1	649	147	0.7
1966	27 082	45.7	21 870	1 240	+10.6	5.7	540	161	0.7
1967	26 292	44.7	21 180	1 014	−18.1	4.8	302	459	2.1

Sources: Wirtschaft und Statistik; own calculations.

growth; by 1960 the number of jobless had fallen below the number of vacancies – an accepted indicator for full employment. This, however, coincided with a number of other developments which made a more active labour market policy necessary: the flow of immigrants from East Germany ended abruptly with the frontier closures and the Berlin Wall of 1961; the employment quota of the indigenous population began to fall rapidly after 1960 as a result of the non-replacement of those retiring, due to the lower birth rate during the Second World War and the increasing demand for higher education; this latter development was fuelled by low state investment in post-school training in the 1950s (see above); the cumulative result of these developments was a much slower rise and then an absolute fall in the West German working population. This was perceived as a threat to the growth of the West German economy and led, as is well known to the introduction of an *extensive system of migrant labour*. The proportion of foreign workers to the total working population rose from below 1 per cent up to 1959 to 5.7 per cent (1.2 million) in 1966. The increase is unremarkable inasmuch as it clearly compensated for the increasing shortfall of domestic labour and coincided with the increases in job vacancies – i.e. with the needs of the private economy. What is significant in the context of government policy is the set of organisational and legal principles adopted by the state to administer the system.

There was in fact a considerable controversy among economists concerning the introduction of a system of migrant/immigrant labour. The government clearly rejected the view of those who claimed that the introduction of migrant workers would hinder improvement of labour productivity and hence slow economic growth,[164] and subscribed rather to the common view that it would add a vital element of flexibility to the labour market;[165] this flexibility was seen to be able to contribute, firstly, to an *improved sectoral mobility* of labour, allowing the transfer of German labour from 'dying' industries to newer, more advanced branches of industry and the service sector; secondly, to an *improved regional mobility* of labour, balancing out the effects of settled immobile German workers and filling out regional gaps in the labour market; and, thirdly, migrant labour was expected to allow a *counter-balance to cyclical fluctuations* in growth – as a 'conjunctural buffer'.[166] Absolutely central to the system was the principle of controlled deployment of the additional imported labour, and successive governments contributed to the application of this principle in two important ways: in 1959, when labour migration began to accelerate, the regulations governing residence permits for foreign workers were amended to make one year the standard period for permits, with the statutory requirement to reapply for residence every year, if a worker wished to stay. Only after five years residence or marriage to a German could renewal be extended on a three-year basis.[167] With these limitations, extended residence in West Germany was to be discouraged and the state was to be given an instrument for controlling the inflow of labour, so that a flexible system of *rotation* could be established, maintaining a high turnover of unskilled labour and a corresponding lever on sectoral and regional demands.

The second contribution of the state towards the establishment of a system of migrant labour was the co-ordination of the recruitment of prospective workers in Mediterranean countries, through embassies, consulates and legations, and the subsequent police and health screening of the newly arrived migrant workers. In certain instances bilateral agreements were made between the West German and other states (e.g. Turkey) to facilitate the rotating transfer of labour. Finally the German judiciary was in general a willing instrument in the optimal realisation of the system of rotation.[168]

The controversy about the efficacy of this system for the national economy continued through and beyond the 1960s – in general quite separately from any consideration of its international economic and specific social effects. What is clear from a cursory analysis of labour market trends is that in the early stages of its implementation the system of migrant labour contributed considerable flexibility to the control of labour – in sectoral, regional and demonstrably, in 1966/67, in cyclical terms.

Merx illustrates the positive sectoral function of migrant labour:

(a) in the expansion of the workforce in labour-intensive branches (motor vehicles, electrotechnical industry);
(b) in the replacement of German workers in engineering and other manufacturing sectors with a general expanding workforce;
(c) in the replacement of German workers in structurally weaker sectors with a gradually diminishing workforce (steel-forming, glass, woodworking, etc.); and
(d) the partial replacement of German workers in rapidly shrinking industries (textiles, iron and steel, timber shipbuilding etc.).[169]

This process facilitated the upward mobility of German labour into better paid jobs, for example in the service sector, encouraged the partial withdrawal of married women from full-time into part-time employment and compensated for the discrepancy between the generations of the German workforce.

The regional effects are less clear, but nevertheless significant. In the 1960s regional levels of employment showed far less wide divergencies than, say, in Britain or Italy; regional divergences in the participation rate of the German population were in part compensated by corresponding rises in the migrant labour population (namely Saarland, North Rhine Westphalia)[170] – equally the proximity of the South German states of Bavaria and Baden Württemberg to Italy and Yugoslavia made these states more attractive to migrating labour and hence less susceptible to high unemployment in later periods, as well as economically more stable.[171]

The cyclical efficacy of the system of migrant labour will be examined in greater detail below in relation to the three recessions since the mid-1960s. It is sufficient here to point merely to Table 4.25 which shows an abrupt decline of foreign workers between 1966 and 1967 which helped to reduce the effect of 800 000 lost jobs, limit the rise in registered unemployed to some 300 000 and hence reduce the material cost of state support to the jobless and their families.

The limitations of this dubious instrument of social engineering and anti-cyclical policy were only to emerge after the end of the Adenauer/Erhard era. It is important to stress however that, by establishing this inhuman, divisive and short-sighted system the CDU-state chose the convenient path of least resistance which made few intellectual demands on the economic planners, requiring only the virtues of legislative and bureaucratic indifference to basic human rights (namely The Foreigners Law, 1965) and the compliance of weaker states such as Italy, Spain and Turkey.

Interventionism and the End of the Erhard Era

The picture which emerges from an examination of economic policy under Erhard (Economics Minister 1949–63, Chancellor 1963–66) is a confusing one. Intellectually Erhard and his fellow ORDO-liberals, eschewed state interference because of a firmly rooted belief in the efficacy of anonymous markets as a motor of economic development and because of their expectation that the corporatist and cartell-based tradition in Germany could be dissolved and replaced by open markets and free competition. Chapter 3 demonstrated the illusoriness of the 'Social Market' theory and the failure of monopoly control. The survey of economic policy in Chapter 4 shows that the state was cushioned politically by the rapid recovery of the private economy but was obliged both in the early stages to spend considerable sums on reconstruction and in the later stages to attempt to implement counter-cyclical measures – particularly in the case of the Federal Bank, but also in the case of the Federal Government.

In general, however, expenditure grew pro-cyclically and it was this that provoked direct or indirect criticism from within state institutions and within the CDU (quite apart from the SPD opposition which was increasingly committed to Keynesianism). Most important among the observations was the recognition that 'rapidly increased concentration' prevented sufficient market elasticity (Bundesbank, 1958);[172] in 1959 the Bundesbank, however, still expressed surprise that prices did not fall when production costs were reduced.[173] Müller-Armack, one of the main architects of the SME-theory, bemoaned the lack of effective help for small capital, the excessive privileges for large firms and the failure to develop even the most modest anti-cyclical policy.[174] While the Academic Sub-Committee of the Federal Economics Ministry had demanded (in 1956 and 1957) a more active policy by the state to control market fluctuations,[175] the Bundesbank in November 1959 demanded the adoption by the state of an anti-cyclical posture: 'The Central Bank Council appeals particularly to all those offices responsible for the preparation of public fiscal policy to behave anti-cyclically as far as is possible when formulating the budget for the next budgetary year and thus to support (or if possible to relieve) the credit policy of the Federal Bank.'[176] In 1961 the Academic Sub-Committee of the Economics Ministry demanded an extension of the state's armoury of counter-cyclical instruments in the form of legislation which was finally adopted officially in 1964. The 1964 report specifically cited the altered 'conditions and presuppositions for future economic growth' (Section 3). In the previous year the Federal Government had already appointed a 'Council of (Economic) Experts' (Sachverständigenrat), comprising five independent economics professors, which was charged with producing an annual report on the West German economy, including forecasts and recommendations. This represented an important recognition by the central authorities of the need for a degree of conjunctural planning. Unsurprisingly the first report by the 'Council of Experts' (SVR) for 1965/66 stressed the need for a 'rational economic policy' as a precondition for creating greater structural flexibility in the West German economy (§ 219).

In the wake of the currency crises and in the face of the evidence of growth and structural weaknesses in the economy, the ideological consensus within the state and the CDU/CSU party leaderships had changed to endorse a more pragmatic policy on interventionism. This new pragmatism involved a tacit shift away from anti-monopolism as official policy in the direction of a specific policy of national (and in part European) monopolism (see below). Just as important, however, it was accompanied by an initiative within the CDU (with the full support of Erhard) to redefine the legitimacy of the state and the social order under the heading of the 'Formed Society' (a vague translation of the vague concept 'formierte Gesellschaft'). The notion was given great prominence at the Düsseldorf party conference in March 1965 and in the rest of the run-up to the September Federal Elections. The general gist of this mysterious new policy aim was the advancement of a national consensus which would acknowledge the sanctity of the CDU-state and end the pluralistic rivalry of interest groups by committing all members of society to a common weal – albeit within the framework of unaltered property relations. This new national consensus would serve to raise the standing of the Federal Republic as a world power and as a model for developing countries.[177]

There would have been nothing surprising about this new concept of the 'formed society' with a new collective will, had not the CDU firstly developed from a fundamentally anti-collectivist posture and then secondly, drawn specific parallels between the early abortive attempt to create such a society (in the Third Reich) and its own new initiative [sic].[178] The echoes of 'Gleichschaltung' were all too strong, for not only was a new ideal presented of collective endeavour under the charismatic leadership of the entrepreneur, but a ruthless eye was cast on those workers who did not feed off this charisma and particularly on intellectuals who hindered the general acceptance of economic ideals: 'The intellectual proceeds from the rational, but the sphere of the economy is in large measure irrational. . . . The rule of the intellectuals, their frequently calamitous rule, can only be confronted if we, in our modern world, restore the strength to pursue ideals.'[179]

In rejecting pluralism and individualism, Erhard seemed to acknowledge the corporate tradition which had re-established itself despite his initial fierce opposition to the 'unhealthy solidarity' of businessmen[180] and the campaigning of the ORDO-liberal stalwarts in the CDU in 1951. The new ideological activity within the CDU was not just a reflection of electoral opportunism, not just another attempt to refine 'one-nation' politics, but the expression of an *ideological crisis which corresponded to the developing crisis of the national economy.* The abrupt rehabilitation of Keynes in 1967 was in fact pre-figured in the peacemeal modifications of state policy in the late 1950s and more particularly in the early 1960s. The general thrust of central government initiatives on anti-cyclical policy was towards dampening excessive growth and inflationary pressures, but implicit at least in these new outlines (namely the 1965 'Law on Securing the Budget') were reflationary possibilities as well.

Between 1949 and 1966 the economy of West Germany had advanced to a state where it dominated the European continent. The contribution of the state to this development did not amount to the masterly management of a sick economy ascribed to Erhard's leadership. Rather state budgetary policy relied on a mixture of tax inducements, piecemeal support for structurally weaker sectors, the luxury of constantly increasing revenues to finance its armaments programme and on good fortune, which allowed it to postpone infrastructural programmes. However with decreasing rates of growth and expanded budgetary commitments the state in 1966 was objectively confronted with a far broader range of responsibilities than in 1949, if it was to maintain its commitment to growth. Above all the responsibility for accelerating the improvement of the productive forces – through research, education and training programmes – was becoming ever greater, compounded by demographic factors and by state dilatoriness, but greater nevertheless.

What this chapter has shown, however, is that it was extremely difficult to create a cohesive approach to national economic policy when the sovereign partial apparatuses of the state pursued their own partial interests. And yet, until 1966 all the negative indicators were obscured by the general growth of national product and real incomes, allowing Theodor Blank to proclaim the demise of economic crises and the development of full employment as a "permanent condition".[181]

Notes

1. T. Vogelsang, *Das geteilte Deutschland*, op. cit., p. 152.
2. Official Communiqué on the Potsdam Conference, Section III, para. 3.
3. Badstübner/Thomas, *Restauration und Spaltung*, op. cit., p. 411.
4. Rudolf Augstein claimed – not implausibly – that the West German

state itself had been created in order 'to put a German army into the field against the Soviets', 'Waffen statt Politik' in: *Bilanz der Bundesrepublik* (Cologne, 1961,) p. 48.

5. K. A. Adenauer, *Erinnerungen 1945–53* (Stuttgart, 1965) p. 385.
6. Adenauer had already discussed plans to rearm with General Speidel in December 1948, see Badstübner/Thomas, *Restauration und Spaltung*, op. cit., p. 411. There followed a series of denials by the CDU before and after the foundation of the West German state of any intention to rearm.
7. Gerhard Brandt, *Rüstung und Wirtschaft in der Bundesrepublik* (Witten-Berlin, 1966), p. 84.
8. Thus Christian Krull, *Wirtschaft und Rüstung* (Frankfurt, 1955) p. 5. The attitude of industry to rearmament is a very contentious issue, viz. Fritz Vilmar, *Rüstung und Abrüstung* (Hamburg, 1973) 97ff; there is some evidence that certain firms maintained a considerable interest in arms manufacture (e.g. with secret research). However, it seems wholly untenable to postulate the early re-emergence of a revanchist military–industrial–political oligarchy which conspired with the USA to rearm West Germany, as Neelsen suggests, *Wirtschaftsgeschichte der BRD*, op. cit., 105ff.
9. H. D. Klingemann stresses the negative influence of siphoning off 872 000 members of the workforce for military or military-related work (by 1968), 'Volkwirtschaftliche Konsequenzen der Rüstung in der Bundesrepublik' in *Beiträge zur Militärsoziologie* (Sonderheft 12, 1968) p. 244.
10. Figures from Alfred Mechtersheimer, 'Der militärisch-industrielle Komplex in den USA und in der Bundesrepublik Deutschland', in *apuzg*, B28/1971, p. 21.
11. Cf. Manfred Lesch, *Die Rolle der Offiziere in der deutschen Wirtschaft nach dem Ende des Zweiten Weltkrieges*, (Berlin, 1970); Wolfgang Zapf, *Beiträge zur Analyse der deutschen Oberschichte* (Munich, 1965); Franz Kurowski, *Deutsche Offiziere in Staat, Wirtschaft und Wissenschaft* (Herford und Bonn, 1967); Mechtersheimer, 'Der militärisch-industrielle Komplex', op. cit., pp. 26ff.
12. Viz Hallgarten/Radkau, *Deutsche Industrie und Politik*, op. cit., p. 486.
13. Mechtersheimer, 'Der militärisch-industrielle Komplex', op. cit., p. 14.
14. BDI-Bericht 1954/55, p. 195, cited in Vilmar, op. cit., p. 101.
15. Hallgarten/Radkau, *Deutsche Industrie und Politik*, op. cit., p. 488.
16. BDI-report 1958/59, p. 252, cited in Vilmar, op. cit., p. 104.
17. CEPES, *Wirtschaftspolitische Grundsatzfragen beim Aufbau einer Rüstungswirtschaft in der Bundesrepublik Deutschland* (Frankfurt, 1957) p. 12.
18. F.-J. Strauss; quoted in Kurt Johannson, *Vom Starfighter zum Phantom* (Frankfurt, 1969), pp. 60f.
19. Mechtersheimer, 'Der militärisch-industrielle Komplex', op. cit., p. 14.
20. Ibid., p. 15.
21. Vilmar, *Rüstung und Abrüstung*, op. cit., p. 113.
22. Ibid., p. 112.
23. Ibid., p. 116.

24. Ibid., pp. 189ff; Neelsen, *Wirtschaftsgeschichte der BRD*, op. cit., p. 147.
25. Vilmar, *Rüstung und Abrüstung*, op. cit., p. 96.
26. Abelshauser, Wirtschaftsgeschichte, op. cit., p. 147.
27. Thus E. Mandel, *Die EWG und die Konkurrenz Europa-Amerika* (Frankfurt, 1968) p. 10; Cf. also Albert Statz, 'Zur Geschichte der west-europäischen Integration bis zur Gründung der EWG' in F. Deppe (ed.), *Europäische Wirtschaftsgemeinschaft* (Hamburg, 1975) p. 113.
28 Thus Abelshauser, *Wirtschaftsgeschichte*, op. cit., p. 154.
29. Ibid., p. 153.
30. See Hallgarten/Radkau, *Deutsche Industrie und Politik*, op. cit., p. 468.
31. Such views are echoed in Vogelsang, *Das geteilte Deutschland*, op. cit., pp. 151f and W. Besson, *Die Außenpolitik der Bundesrepublik* (Munich, 1970).
32. Hallgarten/Radkau, *Deutsche Industrie und Politik*, op. cit., p. 447.
33. Statz, *Zur Geschichte der westeuropäischen Integration*, op. cit., p. 135.
34. Thus Jean Monnet, (the architect of the Schuman-Plan): 'Germany is going to develop rapidly, we cannot prevent its rearmament' quoted in Badstübner/Thomas, *Restauration und Spaltung*, op. cit., p. 402.
35. Statz, 'Zur Geschichte der westeuropäischen Integration', op. cit., p. 131.
36. Thus Badstübner/Thomas, *Restauration und Spaltung*, op. cit., p. 409.
37. Statz, 'Zur Geschichte der westeuropäischen Integration', op. cit., p. 150.
38. Ibid., p. 161fn.
39. See F. Deppe, 'Zur ökonomischen und politischen Struktur des Integrationsprozesses' in F. Deppe (ed.), *Die EWG*, op. cit., p. 176.
40. Vogelsang, *Das geteilte Deutschland*, op. cit., p. 152.
41. Besson, *Außenpolitik*, op. cit., pp. 187ff.
42. A. Baring, *Außenpolitik in Adenauers Kanzlerdemokratie, vol. II* (Munich, 1971) p. 286.
43. See Adenauer's Gürzenich speech (at the BDI Conference in May), quoted in Hallgarten/Radkau, *Deutsche Industrie und Politik*, op. cit., pp. 469.
44. See Mandel, *Die EWG*, op. cit., p. 46 and Statz, 'Zur Geschichte . . . ', op. cit., p. 170.
45. See Hallgarten/Radkau, *Deutsche Industrie und Politik*, op. cit., pp. 469ff.
46. Thus W. Röpke, 'Gemeinsamer Markt und Freihandelszone', in *ORDO*, 1958, vol. 10, p. 38.
47. Hallgarten/Radkau, *Deutsche Industrie und Politik*, pp. 480f.
48. Ibid., p. 481.
49. See Abelshauser, *Wirtschaftsgeschichte*, op. cit., p. 158.
50. Mandel, *Die EWG*, op. cit., p. 46.
51. Ibid., p. 21.
52. Ibid., p. 47.
53. Ibid., p. 12.

54. Ibid., pp. 53f.
55. Deppe, 'Zur ökonomischen und politischen Struktur des Integrations-prozesses', op. cit., p. 188.
56. Import and export of selected commodities 1956–72 as per cent of total

	Foodstuffs & tobacco		Mineral fuels		Raw materials		Machines & vehicles		Chemical products & finished goods	
	I	E	I	E	I	E	I	E	I	E
1956	28.5	2.4	10.8	7.8	31.5	3.5	5.0	40.4	24.2	45.7
1964	20.6	2.1	9.2	4.8	19.5	3.0	12.0	46.5	38.8	43.6
1972	15.1	3.9	9.7	3.0	12.2	2.8	20.2	48.5	42.6	41.8

Total Imports = 100, Total Exports = 100.
Source: F. Deppe (ed.), *Die EWG*, op. cit.

57. Deppe, ibid., pp. 222 & 226.
58. For details see Mandel, *Die EWG*, op. cit., pp. 35–9.
59. Cf. Abelshauser, *Wirtschaftgeschichte*, p. 159.
60. Ibid., p. 29.
61. See Außenwirtschaftsgesetz, para. 23.
62. See Röpke's warnings of the dangers of regarding 'Eastern Trade as mere business' and his insistence that such trade should be conducted according to 'political' considerations. In: *Freie Welt und Totalitarismus* (Bremen, 1957), p. 20.
63. Claudia von Braunmühl, 'Ist die "Ostpolitik" Ostpolitik' in Rittberger/Jahn (eds), *Die Ostpolitik der BRD* (Opladen, 1974) p. 21.
64. By 1973 Mannesmann's exports were 30 per cent dependent on Russian orders, those of Gutehoffnungshütte 15 per cent, Thyssen 10 per cent and Demag 8 per cent, ibid., p. 22.
65. See Kurt P. Tudyka, 'Gesellschaftliche Interessen und auswärtige Beziehungen. Das Röhrenembargo' in H. J. Varain (ed.), *Interessenverbände in Deutschland* (Cologne, 1973).
66. See Besson, *Außenpolitik*; op. cit., pp. 352ff.
67. Radkau draws attention to the economic diplomacy of Alfried Krupp in the 1950s, Hallgarten/Radkau, *Deutsche Industrie und Politik*, op. cit., pp. 466f.
68. See W. Glastetter/R. Paulert/V. Spörel, *Die Wirtschaftliche Entwicklung in der Bundesrepublik Deutschland 1950–1980* (Frankfurt, 1983) p. 489.
69. Abelshauser, *Wirtschaftsgeschichte*, op. cit., p. 160.
70. See Teresa Hayter, *Aid as Imperialism* (London, 1971).
71. See *Der Imperialismus der BRD* (Berlin, 1973) p. 445.
72. Neelsen, *Wirtschaftsgeschichte*, op. cit., p. 149.
73. Thus Abdel Megid Amin, 'Deutsche Orientpolitik heute' in: *Außenpolitik* 5/1954, vol. 1, p. 33.

74. Hallgarten/Radkau, *Deutsche Industrie und Politik*, op. cit., p. 471.
75. 'Formen und Wege der Entwicklungshilfe' in *Wirtschaftsdienst*, Nr. 1/1959, p. 21.
76. Many of the OECD countries enjoyed real growth right up until the 1974 recession. West Germany's growth rates were only exceeded by Japan in the 1950s.
77. Export quota as a proportion of Net Domestic Product, viz. Abelshauser, *Wirtschaftsgeschichte*, op. cit., p. 148.
78. Welteke, *Theorie und Praxis*, op. cit., p. 41.
79. Housing Construction, 1950–57

Completed	*1950*	*1951*	*1952*	*1953*	*1954*	*1955*	*1956*	*1957*
dwellings	*360*	*410*	*443*	*518*	*543*	*542*	*559*	*529*
(1000s)								
Funding bill								
(total) DM	3.8	4.7	6.3	7.8	9.0	10.1	10.9	11.5
Capital mkt	1.6	1.4	1.6	2.5	3.9	4.9	5.0	4.8
Public funds	1.7	2.2	2.7	2.8	3.0	2.8	3.2	3.3
Other funds	0.5	1.1	2.0	2.5	2.1	2.4	2.7	3.4

Source: *Tatsachen über Deutschland* (Bonn, 1960).

80. Thus Welteke, *Theorie und Praxis*, op. cit., p. 47.
81. See A. Shonfield, *Modern Capitalism* (London, 1965), p. 274.
82. Abelshauser, *Wirtschaftsgeschichte*, op. cit., p. 95.
83a Ibid., p. 96.
83b Ibid., p. 96.
84. Peter Czada, *Wirtschaft – Aktuelle Probleme des Wachstums und der Konjunktur* (Berlin, 1980) p. 66.
85. See Glastetter *et al.*, *Die wirtschaftliche Entwicklung*, op. cit., p. 161.
86. See the critique of the planned economy in the Düsseldorf Principles, reprinted in Huster *et al.*, *Determinanten*, op. cit., p. 431.
87a See H. Ehrenberg, *Die Erhard-Saga* (Stuttgart, 1965), pp. 30/31.
87b Ibid.
88. Welteke, *Theorie und Praxis*, op. cit., pp. 71f.
89. 1. Law on Provisional Re-organisation of Taxes, 20 Apr. 1949, WiGB1, 1949, p. 69, and 2. New Version of EStG 1949, WiGB1 1949, p. 266.
90. Abelshauser, *Wirtschaftsgechichte*, op. cit., p. 73.
91. Ibid., p. 74.
92. See Abelshauser, ibid., pp. 75f and Welteke, *Theorie und Praxis*, op. cit., p. 72.
93. Welteke cites Müller-Armack, who in 1951 had observed the negative consequences of self- financing for distribution and consumption, ibid., p. 71.
94. Figures for joint-stock companies only.
95. Erhard in *Sonderhefte zum Bericht über die wirtschaftliche Lage der Bundesrepublik Deutschland*, vol. 3 (Bonn, 1957) p. 3.
96a Knut Borchardt in Stolper/Häuser/Borchardt, *Die deutsche Wirtschaft seit 1870*, op. cit., p. 290.

96b Ibid.

97. Welteke, *Theorie und Praxis*, op. cit., p. 75.

98. Gross investments in coal increased by 46 per cent between 1955 and 1961, gross assets by 67 per cent but capacity utilisation fell by 10 per cent, Welteke, ibid., p. 75.

99. See above chapter 3.

100. Abelshauser, *Wirtschaftsgeschichte*, op. cit., pp. 75f.

101. It can be argued that the precipitate closing of pits at the beginning of the 1960s increased the long-term costs of energy, by allowing too heavy a dependence on oil, which as early as 1973 proved extremely expensive and the long-term availability of which was known to be shorter than domestic coal reserves.

102. See Ehrenberg, *Die Erhard-Saga*, op. cit., p. 80.

103. Erhard in a radio broadcast from 21 Mar. 1962, quoted in Ehrenberg, ibid., p. 80.

104. Welteke, *Theorie und Praxis*, op. cit., p. 71.

105. There is clearly the possibility that such tax exemption schemes were used by tax lawyers to reduce still further the tax burden of wealthy clients.

106. Borchardt, *Deutsche Wirtschaft*, op. cit., p. 289.

107. Wages Tax is equivalent to the British PAYE system and distinct from Assessed Income Tax which is paid retrospectively at the end of the financial year by the self-employed.

108. See H. H. Hartwich, 'Entwicklung zum Lohnsteuerstaat?' in *Gegenwartskunde* 1/78, pp. 57ff.

109. See Düsseldorf Principles, op. cit., p. 438.

110. Ibid., p. 436.

111. Thus Borchardt, *Deutsche Wirtschaft*, op. cit., p. 290.

112. See Abelshauser, *Wirtschaftsgeschichte*, op. cit., p. 72.

113. Thus the Düsseldorf Principles, op. cit., p. 437.

114. Glastetter *et al.*, *Die wirtschaftliche Entwicklung*, op. cit., pp. 313 & 326.

115. Source: Huffschmid, *Die Politik des Kapitals*, op. cit., p. 16.

116. These figures do not show calculations per capita but *per household* – which would also tend to flatter the worker's income.

117. Huffschmid, *Politik des Kapitals*, op. cit., p. 28.

118. See above p. 120.

119. Gesetz zur Förderung der Vermögensbildung – Bundesgesetzblatt I 909. This legislation exempted specified amounts of savings from taxation and social insurance liability. These exemptions would have done little more than compensate payers of Wages Tax for the failure to adjust tax bands and the subsequent effects of 'cold progression'.

120. Huffschmid, *Politik des Kapitals* (op. cit., p. 29) cites figures for 1965, according to which the employed and pensioners expended 63.4 per cent and 54.4 per cent of their savings on 'household investments' respectively, which reduced their effective share of real wealth from 17.2 per cent to 8.9 per cent.

121. J. Siebke, *Die Vermögensbildung der privaten Haushalte in der Bundesrepublik Deutschland*, quoted in U. Jaeggi, *Kapital und Arbeit* (Frankfurt, 1969) p. 69.

122. Report of the Academic-Sub-Committee of the Fed. Min. of Economics, 30 Apr. 1957, quoted in Ehrenberg, op. cit., p. 51.
123. Paras 17–24, quoted at length in ibid., pp. 53ff.
124. Abelshauser, *Wirtschaftsgeschichte*, op. cit., p. 157.
125. Vilmar, *Rüstung und Abrüstung*, op. cit., p. 103.
126. US investments in West Germany in 1960 rose from $795 to $1006 million and by approximately $300 million in subsequent years. See Hallgarten/Radkau, *Deutsche Industrie und Politik*, op. cit. The foreign assets of the Bundesbank rose by a total of DM10 billion in 1960, *see* OECD, *Monetary Policy in West Germany* (Paris, 1973).
127. Thus Ehrenberg, *Die Erhard-Saga*, op. cit., p. 60.
128. Röpke quoted in Hallgarten/Radkau, *Deutsche Industrie und Politik*, op. cit., p. 505.
129a Thus Jaeggi, *Kapital und Arbeit*, op. cit., p. 116.
129b Ehrenberg, *Die Erhard-Saga*, 49ff, in particular p. 68.
130. Ibid., p. 68.
131. OECD, *Monetary Policy*, op. cit., p. 48.
132. Of the variety of bases for calculating the 'state quota' the most common are 'state consumption', 'public utilization', 'expenditure of the Area Authorities' and 'Total Expenditure of the State'. *State Consumption* is generally taken to signify all expenditure by Bund, Länder und Local authorities on administrative services and including defence but excluding interest payments, transfer payments (social expenditure – direct or through social insurance – the Equalisation Fund and wealth transfers) and excluding gross investments. (There is some confusion about the inclusion of Social Insurance in this rubric – *see* Glastetter *et al.*, *Die wirtschaftliche Entwicklung*, op. cit., pp. 259 & 260, where it is both excluded and included). *Expenditure of the Area Authorities* signifies all expenditure by state bodies, excluding social insurance institutions, but including government grants to these funds, other transfers and investments as well as the expenditure of the Equalisation Fund and the ERP-Fund. *Total Expenditure of the State* comprises all expenditure of state bodies including that of the social insurance funds. This latter indicator is often misused by conservative critics of state policy to describe the overweaning profile of a state creeping, as it were, towards socialism (*see* K. Biedenkopf/M. Miegel, *Die programmierte Krise*, Bonn, 1979), postulating a 'state quota' as the ratio of total expenditure to GNP (1970 = 40 per cent, 1983 = 50.8 per cent). However by including the Net Social Insurance Funds (exclusive of government grants) as part of social resources accumulated by and for the state, these proponents of a state 'roll-back' neglect to point out that the Net Social Insurance Funds represent the collective savings of the present and former working population which, with the exception of unemployment and accident insurance, revert to most of the contributors in proportion to their working income and to current income levels. *State consumption* is a useful indicator of the ultimate employment of consumed social wealth, since it takes account of all state transfers to private households and, by excluding the state's additions

to 'social wealth' in terms of real investments, presents a 'state quota' in marked contrast to the roll-back ideologues – 1970: 15.8 per cent, 1983: 20 per cent.

Nevertheless, Area Authorities Expenditure allows a consideration of the specific re-allocation of social resources and is therefore taken here as the main indicator. Other attempts to qualify Total Expenditure by comparing it to productive potential in order to calculate the state quota (thus Abelshauser, *Wirtschaftsgeschichte*, op. cit., p. 88) are not very valuable for our purposes.

133. The calculations here and in the remainder of the chapter are based on a compilation of data from the 1975 Annual Report of the SVR, the Monthly Reports of the Bank deutscher Länder and after 1958 of the Bundesbank. The series is complicated by the changeover in 1960 from the tax year (Apr. to Mar.) to the calendar year as the statistical base, such that figures for 1960 only relate to the 9-months Apr. to Dec. 1960 and by the re-inclusion of the Saarland after its extended period of Allied control which ended in 1959.

134. Abelshauser notes the fierce response of McCloy to West German budget policy at the beginning of the 1950s with its generous tax concessions and high borrowing requirements, *Wirtschaftsgeschichte*, op. cit., pp. 76f.

135. Thus Welteke, *Theorie und Praxis*, op. cit., p. 88.

136. Thus Gerold Ambrosius, *Der Staat als Unternehmer* (Göttingen, 1984) p. 108.

137. Viz. Glastetter *et al.*, *Die wirtschaftliche Entwicklung*, op. cit., p. 259.

138. Abelshauser, *Wirtschaftsgeschichte*, op. cit., p. 95.

139. See above p. 113. Borchardt calculates that the tax concessions granted by the state authorities increased the real contribution of the state to housing finance to some 50 per cent in the 1950s (*Die deutsche Wirtschaft*, op. cit., p. 315).

140. It is not so much the culpability of the state in ever attempting a planned housing policy that was at fault (as Heinz Lampert suggests, *Die Wirtschafts- und Sozialordnung der BRD*, Bonn, 1976, p. 273) but the abrupt abandonment of controls at such a crucial time, when there was a lot of money sloshing around the economy.

141. *See* UNESCO *Statistical Yearbook* (1969).

142. *See* Welteke, *Theorie und Praxis*, op. cit., p. 65.

143. *Bundesbank Monthly Report*, Mar. 1966.

144. Viz. a series of articles on the finances of the Bundesbank and the Bundespost, Mar. 1966, Apr. 1971, Aug. 1974, July 1977, Aug. 1980 and Aug. 1983 in the *Bundesbank Monthly Reports*.

145. *Bundesbank Monthly Report*, Mar. 1966; postal charges were effectively pegged until 1963.

146. Electrification investments could have been pushed forward, as well as long-term plans for the rationalisation of the rail network, speeding up transit North-South, Northwest-Southeast, Northeast-Southeast through line-straightening, additional track laying etc.

147. *See* The Düsseldorf Principles, op. cit., pp. 442ff.

148. See Table 4.23, p. 142 above.
149. F. Siebels and H. Lenke, 'Kapitalisitsche Vergesellschaftung der Land-wirtschaft und "Gemeinsamer Agrarmarkt" in der EWG' in F. Deppe (ed.). *Die EWG*, op. cit., p. 353.
150. See *Düsseldorf Principles*, op. cit., pp. 436f and Erhard's radio and television broadcast, quoted at length in Ehrenberg, *Die Erhard-Saga*, pp. 75ff.
151. See *Düsseldorf Principles*, op. cit., p. 445 and the *Ahlen Programme 1947*, ibid., pp. 425ff.
152. The Law on the Representation of Personnel concerns employees in public service.
153. The 'labour director' on the managerial board (Vorstand) was elected effectively by the workforce but subject to the same restrictions.
154. Thus W. Pahl, 'Mitbestimmung in der Montanindustrie' in *Gewerk-schaftliche Monatshefte*' no. 5 (1951) p. 255.
155. Thus Seelos (Bavarian Party), Verhandlungen des deutschen Bunde-stages, First legislative period 1949, stenographic reports, vol. 6, 117th Sitting, 14 (Feb. 1951) p. 4452.
156. Thus Euler (FDP), Verhandlungen, op. cit., 132nd Sitting, ibid., p. 5086.
157. Thus Ott (BHE-DG), op. cit., 117th Sitting, ibid., p. 4453.
158. Thus Schröder, 132nd Sitting, ibid., 5073/74.
159. Ibid.
160. Thus Harig (KPD), ibid., pp. 5071f.
161. Thus Agartz (KPD), 117th Sitting, ibid., p. 4459.
162. Thus F. Deppe, *Kritik der Mitbestimmung* (Frankfurt, 1972).
163. Thus Otto Brenner, quoted in F. Deppe, ibid., p. 123.
164. See e.g. Carl Föhl, 'Stabilisierung und Wachstum bei Einsatz von Gastarbeitern', in: *Kyklos*, vol 20, (1970) pp. 119ff; Uwe Harms, 'Wirtschaftliche Aspekte des Gastarbeiterproblems', in: *Hamburger Jahrbuch*, 1966, pp. 277ff.
165. See Rosenmöller, 'Volkswirtschaftliche Aspekte der Ausländerbeschäfti-gung', *Bundesarbeitsblatt* (1970).
166. For a summary of the discussion concerning their 'buffer function' see Volker Merx, *Ausländerbeschäftigung und Flexibilität des Arbeitsmarktes der Bundesrepublik* (Cologne, 1972) pp. 22f.
167. Law on Labour Mediation and Unemployment Insurance, Bundesgesetz-blatt, Part I, p. 689 – 9th Procedural Statue.
168. See F. Franz, 'Die Rechtstellung der ausländischen Arbeitnehmer in der Bundesrepublik Deutschland' in F. Klee (ed.), *Gastarbeiter* (Frankfurt, 1972) pp. 36ff.
169. Merx, Ausländerbeschäftigung, op. cit., pp. 39ff.
170. Ibid., pp. 83ff.
171. This was only partly neutralised by the huge influx of Turks after 1968 and the EEC ruling on unconditional residence for EEC citizens in all EEC countries.
172. *Bundesbank Geschäftsbericht* (1958) p. 28.
173. *Bundesbank Geschäftsbericht* (1959) pp. 17ff.

174. Alfred Müller-Armack, *Wirtschaftsordnung und Wirtschaftspolitik* (Freiburg, 1966) pp. 227 & 213f.
175. Quoted at length in Ehrenberg, *Die Erhard-Saga*, pp. 50ff.
176. *Bundesbank Monthly Report* (Nov. 1959).
177. Ludwig Erhard, 'Programm für Deutschland', Speech at the 13th Party Conference of the CDU, Düsseldorf, 31 Mar. 1965. Cf. also L. Erhard, 'Der Weg in die Formierte Gesellschaft', *Bulletin of the Federal Government* (28 July 1965).
178. Cf. *Gesellschaftspolitische Kommentare*, no. 10 (1965), Report by Leo Schütze und Werner Riek, quoted in R. Opitz, 'Der große Plan der CDU: "Die Formierte Gesellschaft" ' in *Blätter für deutsche und internationale Politik*, no. 9 (1965).
179. From a speech by Albrecht Pirkert at the Economic Conference of the CDU, 1965, quoted from press releases.
180. Erhard, quoted in: *Handelsblatt* (20th Aug. 1948).
181. Theodor Blank at the Düsseldorf Party Conference of the CDU, Mar. 1965, quoted in Welteke, *Theorie und Praxis*, op. cit., p. 125.

5 State and Crisis Management, 1966–85

THE RECESSION OF 1966/67

The year 1966 marked a distinct turning point in the political economy of West Germany. It is possible to overdo talk of 'watershed', but clearly the recession of 1966/67 represented more than an economic hiccough. Up to 1966 state institutions had been showing signs of nerves and irritation at the political failures of others, but in general their concern was about the inflationary dangers of over-stretched state budgets. Thus they sailed mostly unawares into the winter of 1966/67 and the unexpected calamity of no growth and 800 000 job losses. As recessions go, it was a relatively mild affair, but against the background of 18 years of uninterrupted growth, it was a considerable shock, particularly to the credibility of the state, whose legitimacy was founded on the expectation of economic stability and constant growth. Not surprisingly therefore it coincided with the end of the 'Erhard-Era', the formation of a 'grand' coalition between Christian and Social Democrats and the brief experiment with Keynesian demand management under Karl Schiller.

The second Erhard cabinet (a coalition of CDU/CSU and FDP) which was formed after the September elections 1965, fell apart in October 1966, not because of the imminent recession, but because of disagreement over the extent of further budget cuts, which the Federal Bank was demanding. The withdrawal of the FDP ministers and the sudden downturn of the economy then forced the CDU/CSU to abandon Erhard and make overtures to the SPD, and then to form the coalition cabinet under Kiesinger (CDU) with Brandt (SPD) as foreign minister, Strauss (CSU) as Finance Minister and Karl Schiller (SPD) as Economics Minister. The coalition was officially endorsed by the Bundestag on December 1st 1966 and rapidly introduced a programme of fiscal reforms and anti-cyclical (reflationary) measures to restore the flagging economy.

The Causes of the Recession

In its annual report for 1967/68[1] the 'Council of Economic Experts' (from now on SVR) laid the bulk of the blame for the real fall in GNP on the state bodies responsible for economic policy: up until the end of 1966 economic policy had been restrictive and deflationary, defying the signs of a weakening economic climate, which had been evident since the 'spring of 1966'. Above all the credit squeeze of the Federal Bank had 'forced state investors to postpone numerous projects, even though falling private investment activity would have demanded the opposite' (para. 6); indeed the Länder and the local authorities had 'continued to adjust their expenditure, especially investment expenditure, to their falling revenues way into 1967' (para. 7).

By thus emphasising the pro-cyclical stance of state authorities in its diagnosis, the SVR was able conveniently to recommend a co-ordinated anti-cyclical cure for the economy's ills (para. 232). The SVR's diagnosis was only half-correct however. Undoubtedly the raising of central bank discount rates through 1965 and 1966 and the reduction of planned state expenditure by about two and a half billion Deutschmarks in 1966 compounded the weaknesses of the private economy and possibly even tipped GNP below zero growth, but the weaknesses were already in evidence. Quite apart from the running problem of trade surpluses, pressure on exchange rates and the perceived problem of increasing state borrowing (made worse by electoral tax cuts in 1965),[2] the deceleration of growth since the 1950s boom had begun to destabilise certain features of domestic markets; average annual growth of real GNP was 9.4 per cent between 1951 and 1955, 6.6 per cent between 1956 and 1960 and 4.9 per cent between 1961 and 1965. 1959 would seem to be a key year, since it marked both the achievement of *full employment* and the point at which *capital productivity begins its slow decline* after rising throughout the 1950s. Even with the compensatory influence of migrant workers, the labour market began to favour the sellers rather than the buyers of labour power: thus gross wages rose faster than GNP between 1960 and 1966 or by 75.8 per cent compared to 62.6 per cent. In order, in part, to relieve the pressure on unit labour costs, investment was intensified with the result that the capital stock also grew faster than GDP, causing the marginal capital coefficient to rise. Both factors had a depressive effect on the rate of profit. From 1960 the trend of capacity utilisation was downwards and in 1963 the deviation from the normal level of utilisation (adduced by the SVR at 97.25) was almost 1.5 per cent below.[3] More significantly capacity utilisation in the manufacturing sector was falling consistently from the beginning of the 1960s to the outbreak of the recession, despite a

Table 5.1 Real growth of GNP and Capital Stock compared with development of capital productivity, the (unadjusted) gross wages quota and the Capital Coefficient in West Germany, 1960–66

Year	GNP (real growth in per cent p.a.)	Capital Stock (real growth in per cent p.a.)	Capital productivity change (per cent p.a.)	Gross wages quota (per cent of national income)	Capital Coefficient[a]
1960	+9.0	+6.2	+2.1	60.4	3.06
1961	+4.9	+6.5	−0.8	62.7	3.06
1962	+4.4	+6.6	−2.5	64.1	3.07
1963	+3.0	+6.4	−2.9	65.1	3.11
1964	+6.6	+6.5	0.0	64.8	3.17
1965	+5.5	+6.6	−0.9	65.6	3.20
1966	+2.5	+6.3	−3.3	66.6	3.22

[a] Capital Stock
———————
Prod. Potential

Sources: Statistisches Jahrbuch; K. G. Zinn, *Der Niedergang des Profits* (Cologne, 1978); own calculations.

rise in net production,[4] reflecting the influence of the additional capacity added through very high manufacturing investment in this period.

In contrast to the SVR, Mandel and others[5] stress the importance of this surplus capacity, of 'over-accumulation' as the primary cause of the 1966/67 recession, quite simply because the productive potential increasingly exceeded potential demand. Despite higher levels of domestic consumption, domestic demand could still not match the producers' expectations of sales (and profits) and it was only an increase in export sales which in part neutralised the real decline in domestic demand in 1966. This had the effect of increasing the trade and payments surplus, and creating large accumulations of currency reserves without domestic investment or import outlets, which in turn put pressure on the money supply and hence invited the ill-considered monetary squeeze by the Federal Bank.

The pre-recession sectoral inequalities between a) the manufacturing sector (high investment/lower utilisation) and the investment goods sector (needing high sales *and* utilisation) and b) firms with a high foreign turnover (engineering, vehicles, chemical, electro-technical) and those with minimal foreign sales (construction) produced predictable results in the recessionary period.

Between 1965 and 1966 manufacturing demand did not fall but it did not rise sufficiently to halt the decline in utilisation, so that at an early stage (Spring 1965) manufacturing investment was curtailed, which produced an accelerating decline in engineering orders through 1965 and 1966 and, coupled with cutbacks in state investment, a rapid reduction in building activity from early 1966.[6] The multiplicator effects were marked: a decline in utilisation from 93 per cent to 82 per cent in the investment goods sector between 1964 and 1967 and from 87 per cent to 78 per cent in manufacturing between 1966 and February 1967, which together with seasonal factors raised unemployment levels to 673 000 by the end of February 1967. The enforced or voluntary withdrawal of 300 000 migrant workers and many thousands of women from the labour market helped to keep unemployment from reaching the million mark, but the number of workers on short time rose from just over 1000 in 1965 to 142 694 in 1967. Investments fell by 9 per cent in real terms, profits fell sharply and bankruptcies leapt to 4337 in 1967.

State Policy in the Recession

The government response to the crisis corresponded to the semi-
official diagnosis of the SVR, i.e. it ignored the fundamental and
increasing vulnerability of capital realisation and confined itself to
rectifying the political flaws of the past, by applying (for West
Germany) new instruments of macro-economic control within the
framework of a crisis coalition government.

The 'Law on the Furtherance of the Stability and Growth of the
Economy' (Stability Law 1967) created the formal framework for
redressing these political flaws:

1. To counteract the *institutional* weakness of a federal fiscal system
   combined with an independent central bank, the Law obliged all
   the state area authorities (central regional and local governments)
   to regulate their revenue and expenditure in a manner which was
   'appropriate to the economic cycle' (Stab. Ges. § 5–8, §§ 14 + 16).
   This required the alteration of Article 109 of the Basic Law, which
   had previously established the fiscal sovereignty of regional and
   local authorities. The new Article 109 made central legislation
   possible to match central and regional budgets to the requirements
   of an anti-cyclical policy (Clause 3). Accordingly a new state
   forum, the Conjunctural Council, was set up (Stab. Ges. §18) in
   order to co-ordinate policy and expenditure plans. One further
   institutional reform involved the creation of a tripartite discussion
   forum between agencies of the state (central and regional governments and the Federal Bank), employers organisations and trade
   unions (§3), which was dubbed 'Concerted Action'.
2. The *instrumental framework* for these institutional reforms was to
   be established by the preparation of 'Orientation Data' by the
   Federal Government which would facilitate discussions between
   the various parties within the Conjunctural Council and 'Concerted Action' and help to produce agreement on medium-term
   economic goals (§3). The state would thus also be able to establish
   five-year plans for their respective budgets (§§9–11).
3. The *resources* for a co-ordinated anti-cyclical policy would be
   made available within the framework of the medium-term financial strategy by the use of *increased state borrowing* in periods of
   cyclical weakness and the establishment of 'conjunctural reserves'
   in periods of high growth (§15), the creation of which the federal
   government could insist on.

4. The goal of stable growth would thus be achieved by both the planned deployment of state investments to stimulate or restrict economic activity and the planned variation of levels of taxation to stimulate/depress private demand and balance state budgets in the long term – with changes of up to 10 per cent (up or down) in Income Tax rates (§§26–8). Furthermore price stability would be facilitated by agreement within 'Concerted Action' to control incomes.

The successful short-term functioning of this new system of 'global steering' (Schiller) therefore depended not simply on the technically efficient deployment of resources by the state but on the consensual behaviour of all sections of the state apparatus together with the main representatives of labour and capital. If one merely applies the global criteria of the 'magic square' – price stability, full employment, healthy trade balance and steady real economic growth (§1) – Schiller's new Keynesianism was a model success:

Table 5.2   The 'Magic Square', 1968 and 1969

	1968	1969
Cost of living rise in per cent	+1.6	+1.9
Real economic growth (GNP) in per cent	+7.3	+8.2
(Investments)	+10.5	+22.6
Registered unemployed in 1000s	323	179
Balance of payments +/– in DM billion	+10.9	+ 6.2

Sources: Statistisches Jahrbuch; *Bundesbank Monthly Reports.*

The inherent practical and theoretical problems of 'global steering' revealed themselves over a longer period of time – but in fact sooner rather than later – and will become clear after a brief examination of the concrete measures taken to manage the German economy out of recession.

* * *

There were two major expenditure programmes designed to stimulate private investments, the first drafted and funded by the central government alone, the second constructed by all three levels of the state administration in conjunction with private enterprises. The first

Contingency Budget of the Bund, amounting to additional expenditure on investments of approximately DM2.5 billion, was announced as early as 13 December 1966 in the Coalition Government's Declaration and became law on 14 April 1967, even before the Stability Law had been passed. Approval for increased state borrowing to finance the programme was given by the Federal Bank in February. The expenditure was aimed at implementing ('long overdue')[7] infrastructural investments, notably in the railways, the postal service and in the road network.

Table 5.3   First Investment Programme of the Federal Government, April 1967

Area of expenditure	Expenditure in DM million	Per cent of total
Federal Railways	743.7	29.8
Trunk roads	534.0	21.4
Federal Postal Service	488.1	19.5
Defence	203.5	8.2
Social housing	149.3	6.0
Food, agriculture, forestry	200.0	8.0
Science and research	73.00	2.9
Waterways	48.7	1.9
Building construction	20.01	0.8
Student hostel	20.00	0.8
Total	2 498.3	100.0

Source: Bundesdrucksache, V/3630.

In addition to these direct expenditures, the government offered *special depreciation allowances* on investments in machinery (10 per cent) and buildings (5 per cent). The resources for financing the cost of direct expenditure and of foregoing tax revenue were found through the issue of government stock (bonds of up to four years duration).

It is perhaps too much to assert that the First Programme had an 'insignificant' effect on the trade cycle,[8] since the multiplier effects of this, admittedly modest, stimulus would have added another DM1.8 billion in additional demand, according to Czada.[9] Nevertheless it effectively only restored the budget cuts of 1966 and more significantly was in part neutralised by the continuing expenditure cuts of the regional and local authorities in the first half of 1967.

The *Second Investment Programme* was implemented after the Stability Law and thus represented more truly the co-ordinated approach demanded by Keynesian politics. It was approved by the Federal Cabinet and by the regional and local authorities in the 'Conjunctural Council' on 13 July 1967, after the Federal Bank had (grudgingly) agreed to further deficit spending in June, and was subsequently welcomed by the employers and trade unions in the July meeting of 'Concerted Action'. It was a more ambitious programme of investment, totalling some DM10 billion, of which the state provided nearly DM5.3 (Federal government: DM2.8 billion, regional governments: DM2.0 billion and the local authorities: DM0.5 billion). These amounts complemented nearly 5.6 billions of private capital attracted by interest relief of DM48.4 million.[10]

Of the investment from this Second Programme 90 per cent went into the building sector,[11] which had by far the highest level of registered unemployed (133 939 in 1967).[12] Including the effect of credit relief, direct demand was increased by some DM12.5 billion which, with the triggering of multiplicator effects, produced *a total additional stimulus of some DM21 billion*[13] or nearly five times greater than the First Investment Programme.

Just as significant, though, for the rapid recovery which set in in 1968 and 1969 were the agreements reached within the 'Concerted Action' meetings. These 'non-binding' discussions between state bodies, employers and trade unions took place at regular intervals, beginning in February 1967. As a kind of crisis forum, the group considered above all the reflationary measures of the central government and then of all the area authorities on the basis of the 'orientation data', relating to given and forecast economic trends, supplied by the Federal Economics ministry. The government projections laid particular stress upon the key role of income growth levels, whereby business income should be given priority as a motor of investment. In the face of high unemployment, social–democratic participation in government and a broad national consensus on the need for 'concerted' policies, the trade union representatives agreed to recommend the projected levels of income growth to their constituent bodies as a basis for subsequent wage negotiations: for 1967 net wages and salaries were to rise by 2.4 per cent, net income for shareholders and the self-employed by 5.3 per cent and undistributed profits by 22 per cent.[14] One vital factor involved in the trade unions' self-restraint was the assurance by Karl Schiller that, once the economy had been set right by an investment-led recovery, the temporary disadvantage of wage and salary earners would be rectified on the basis of 'social symmetry' through fiscal and general economic measures.[15] Quite apart from the oddly inappropriate nature of the concept in relation to West Germany's economy and class structure, it was never strictly defined by Schiller as the restoration of any *status quo ante* in income distribution, as the trade unions understood it.[16] Rather, Schiller subsequently adopted the employers' interpretation of social symmetry, namely that 'multi-lateral agreements should result in an increase of real income for all'.[17]

The social symmetry assurance turned out to be a confidence trick, albeit a very successful one: the individual trade unions accepted the recommendation to moderate wage claims and, just as important, agreed to a new eighteen-month term for wage contracts. The *income* agreement turned out to be just as much a confidence trick as the catchword 'symmetry', since wages and salaries were pre-determined contractually, whereas business incomes were dependent on general market conditions which were not definable in advance. As a result of real growth of GNP far exceeding the projections, private income from business activity and undistributed profits rose far more strongly than the already generous projections.

Table 5.4   Incomes and growth, 1967–69

	1967	1968	1969
GNP projected nominal rise in per cent		(+6.2)	(+7.0)
actual nominal rise in per cent		+9.0	+12.1
Net wages & salaries (DM billion)	177.3	186.9	206.1
(per cent change over previous year)	–0.4	+5.4	+10.3
Net wages per employee (average in DM)	8,371	8,762	9,402
(per cent change over previous year)	+2.0	+4.0	+7.0
Productivity per labour hour	+8.1	+8.6	+7.1
(Industry) per cent change			
Net Income from business (DM billion)	99.0	116.8	121.8
(per cent change over previous year)	–0.5	+18.0	+4.3
Net per capita income (self-	32,814	39,646	41,612
employed, average in DM)			
(per cent change over previous year)		+20.0	+4.9

Sources: *Statistisches Jahrbuch; Wirtschaft und Statistik* (Lange Reihen); own calculations.

The trade unions were thus confronted with a far greater re-distribution of income than they had bargained for. The gross wages quota[18] fell by 1.8 per cent from 66.6 per cent in 1967 to 64.8 per cent in 1968, the net wages quota[19] by 2.7 per cent from 64.2 per cent in 1967 to 61.5 per cent in 1968. All the denials by Schiller that 'Concerted Action' was no more than wages control[20] were made to sound very hollow. There is little doubt that in the subsequent 'Concerted Action' discussions on social policy and competition the representatives of the state and the employers did not demonstrate the same kind of amenability as the trade unions had shown on wages, and these predictably produced no agreements. Finally the wild-cat strikes of September 1969 and the internal debates within the trade union movement revealed the disillusionment of workers in tripartism and over hopes for a new era of participation by the labour movement in macro-economic affairs. After 1969 'Concerted Action' was an increasingly ineffective forum and in July 1977 the unions finally withdrew.[21]

In the long term 'Concerted Action' was far less of a success than the British NEDC, upon which it was modelled, but in the short term it produced a voluntary wages policy which helped to fuel the invest-ment-led boom. The direct savings from the wage bill (assuming a constant wages quota from 1966) were some 9.8 Billion Marks between 1967 and 1969.[22] Undistributed profits rose by 95 per cent between 1966 and 1968, and briefly the decline in capital productivity was halted, rising by 1.5 per cent in 1968 and 1.9 per cent in 1969.[23] The disproportionately high rises in distributed and undistributed business income were a clear material and psychological boost to the 'investment climate' in 1968 and 1969 on top of direct state invest-ment. However, the *de facto* end to 'Concerted Action' with the wild cat strikes and the end of the Grand Coalition in October of the same year signalled the end of national consensus politics and suggested the fragility of the whole Keynesian experiment.

THE CONTRADICTIONS OF DEMAND MANAGEMENT AND ITS APPLICATION, 1967–72

The decline of the image of Keynesianism and its leading proponent, Karl Schiller, was as rapid as its rise. Up to the spring of 1969 the conservative economic correspondents of West Germany's conserva-tive media were astonishingly positive in their appraisal of Schiller's technocratic leadership. However, in the electoral year 1969 Schiller began to receive increasingly bad press. Despite very low inflation the press critics, as if on cue, zoomed in on the inflationary dangers of the state's expenditure programme in an attempt to define the limits between moderate CDU economic policy and the immoderate 'creeping socialism' of the SPD. Academic ordo-liberals declared 'global steering' to be 'unconstitutional', 'totalitarian' and 'over-rationalistic'.[24] In both cases the critics were guilty of considerable humbug, because they proceeded from assumptions about the self-regulatory powers of the market which were demonstrably inappropriate. 1966/67 had shown clearly that West Germany's economy had lost that self-regulating facility because of the continued monopolisation of markets, increased capital concentration and increasing capital intensity. In order to sustain a proportionately larger capital apparatus, growth in output, productivity and research, West German industry and commerce needed the power to resist price cuts – a power afforded by monopolised forms of control – but increasingly they needed the assistance of the state to reduce costs, either through the increased funding of education, training, research, transport and local services (as external costs of production) or through the control of wage costs by formal institutions such as 'Concerted Action' and by informal 'moral persuasion'. More importantly perhaps, capital collectively could not reproduce itself fast enough, given the constraints of diminishing marginal gains from additional investment, to avoid crises of over-production/over-capacity.

It is this framework which Schiller accepted as the point of departure for his policy of 'global steering': capital concentration is a fact of life which cannot be reversed, 'the competitive model of independent economic units simple Biedermeier'; Schiller, rather, agreed with the view that 'the big units, the concerns . . . are the actual pacemakers of progress'. All one needs is the 'constant corrective of state competition policy' and a 'growth-conscious medium-term economic policy'.[25] However, the primacy of the oligopoly is not just left unchallenged, but is built into the medium term planning process, as Huffschmid has pointed out: 'global-steering . . . is a theoretical concept which can only be realised in an economy, in which capital is predominantly concentrated and centralised'.[26] Given the central role accorded by Schiller (and others) to investments and the limitation of state activity to global (macro-) economic measures rather than a 'planified' directing of private investments,[27] the forward planners in the Economics Ministry were wholly 'dependent on the co-operation of the powerful groups in a highly concentrated economy' and were obliged 'to involve these groups, because of their predominance, in the drafting of the plans'.[28] Global planning would not be possible 'in an atomised competitive economy', because of the impossibility of adducing future investment programmes adequately.[29] Schiller himself talked of 'giving oligopolies and organised groups access to macro-decisions'[30] and, by excluding small businessmen from policy discussions,[31] he effectively subordinated his policy of national demand management to the investment plans of large oligopolies, whose *primary interests, however, are not national but private wealth, not national but private viability.* All other things being equal, the reliance of the state on global data and consistent behaviour from private concerns was more than the 'calculated risk' required to stimulate the 'chain of disequilibriums' [sic] that is the nature of dynamic growth.[32] It represented the acceptance of the state's function of nursemaid to big capital, coupled with a general indifference to the maintenance of competition, and as such it revived the strong tradition in Germany of corporatist co-operation between the state and economic interests[33] which had not resurfaced so strongly after 1948.

Schiller's pragmatic and technocratic approach, which epitomised the trend in the SPD since Bad Godesberg in 1959, was thus fundamentally flawed in its acceptance of the reliability of monopoly capital as such. It was, however, equally flawed by a number of generalised *ceteris paribus* assumptions about micro-economics, national economic policy and politico-economic institutions: for example:

(a) *investments* are in general taken as a unitary phenomenon which has equally beneficial results for growth, incomes and employment. All the state needs to do, according to this assumption, is, in the absence of sufficient private investment, to top up the economic engine to produce the required levels of growth, etc. However, numerous surveys have shown that since the end of the 1950s (and the period of extensive expansion) investments have served to *intensify production* as much as to extend capacity.

The function of rationalisation is to increase productivity and lower unit wage costs and hence reduce the long-term demand for labour either relatively, in the event of constant strong growth, or absolutely in the case of weak growth and recessionary periods. This process was already evident in the 1960s with the constant rise in capital intensity (ratio of capital stock to labour force): between 1961 and 1968 capital stock increased by

Table 5.5   Investment aims in industry, 1970–83 (results of limited poll sample – IFO)

	1970	1975	1978	1981	1983
Extension of capacity	55%	28%	17%	34%	18%
Rationalisation of capacity	34%	46%	47%	41%	55%
Replacement of capacity	11%	26%	36%	25%	27%

Sources: IFO-Institut (Munïch); various polls.

62.6 per cent, GNP by 38.1 per cent, but the working population fell from 26.2 million in 1960 to 25.9 million in 1968. This trend of capital stock growth and employment decline has continued into the 1980s. A reduced labour force implies a relative reduction in domestic demand and hence an increased reliance on foreign markets. Investment trends could be further differentiated according to sector and in relation to relative rates of return.[34] What is however clear from this cursory glance is that micro-economic decisions (upon which 'global steering' depends) do not conform to the theoretical model of the 'magic square', in particular the equivalence of stable growth and stable employment. The non-correlation is demonstrated by the consistent underestimation of unemployment in the annual Economic Report of the Federal Government since 1972, despite corresponding underestimations of growth.[35]

(b) A major flawed assumption about national economic policy related to the *flexibility and thus effectiveness of state expenditure*. The budgetary plan – embodied in the Stability Law – of creating a pattern of surplus-deficit-surplus to counteract the cycle of boom-recession-boom, ignored the predominant commitment of state expenditure to *non-cyclical* areas in defence, education, research, environmental protection, agriculture, etc. The major component of anti-cyclical policy – namely, state investments – was never more than 17.8 per cent of total state expenditure (excluding the social insurance funds) in 1964, and even then, of those investments the majority would have represented constant (non-cyclical) commitments rather than particular, manipulable stimuli to growth. What stands out in fact is the

Table 5.6 Expenditure of State Authorities (excluding social insurance funds) on investments and personnel as a proportion of total expenditure 1950–72 (per cent)

Year	Investments	Personnel
1950	6.7	24.9
1955	9.7	23.1
1960	12.2	24.6
1961	12.7	24.8
1962	14.5	24.7
1963	15.9	25.3
1964	17.8	25.3
1965	16.5	26.7
1966	15.9	28.3
1967	13.2	27.9
1968	14.0	28.5
1969	14.5	29.3
1970	16.4	30.2
1971	15.3	31.0
1972	14.3	31.9

Sources: K. Biedenkopf, and M. Miegel. *Die programmierte Krise*, (Bonn, 1979).

decline of investments as a proportion of state expenditure and the rise of personnel costs since 1964 (see Table 5.6), which implies, at least, a reduced flexibility of the state to respond to cyclical fluctuations in line with the 'Stability Law' (§§ 5–8, 14, 16). This reduced flexibility corresponds to increased general expenditure commitments for the state as an economic fire brigade and therefore contains the real danger of a (cyclically unrelated) constant increase in state indebtedness and ultimately of a real fiscal crisis.

(c) The third in this chain of vital assumptions by Schiller and other 'global steering' theorists concerns the ability and willingness of all sections of the state apparatus to co-ordinate and implement policy. As was shown in Chapter 4, the *revenue* of central, regional and local authorities fluctuated in the 1950s and early 1960s, despite the mechanisms for rectifying anomalies, and their *expenditure* patterns varied according both to revenue and to particular commitments (housing, education, defence, etc.). The *nature of their expenditure* varied considerably; whereas central government in 1966 spent only 15.4 per cent of its budget on investments and 15.3 per cent on personnel, the regional governments spent 26.3 per cent and 36.3 per cent and the local authorities 40.1 per cent and 25.0 per cent respectively. The absolute expansion of educational and social facilities by regional and local authorities in the 1950s and 1960s involved considerable investment in schools, hospitals and recreational facilities. This programme was accelerated in the late 1960s, not just by the anti-cyclical budgets of 1967 and 1968, but also because of significant demographic trends and by the state's constitutional obligations. However, these investments also meant a considerable *increase in subsequent current expenditure* because of the need to maintain the increased stock of facilities. The expenditure implications of co-ordinated investment programmes for regional and particularly local authorities were therefore far wider than might be assumed from the perspective of central government, despite the high levels of initial central funding for these programmes. The investment expenditure of the Bund was generally lower than at the other levels and in specific cases offered a real (Bundespost) or potential (Railways) return on capital.[36] Schools, kindergartens universities and roads entail high subsequent costs and do not (generally) produce revenue for the authorities responsible for them.[37]

The mechanistic view of anti-cyclical state investment as a pump-priming boost, limited in time, is thus naive; the real scope for flexible state investment is far narrower than might be assumed, and within the unequal distribution of state investment responsibilities between central, regional and local authorities there must be a *natural tendency on the part of the lower levels of the state, particularly after the early 1970s, to resist the pressure to use investments as a counter-cyclical weapon and rather to consolidate budgets procyclically.* By itself the nature of local and regional government in West Germany made long-term co-ordination quite unlikely, before any consideration is made of the differing political colourings of the eleven Länder and some 15 000 local authorities.

The problems of policy co-ordination are made far worse by the *independence of the Bundesbank* – dubbed by some 'a second government'[38] – as the agent of monetary policy, for in a situation other than a classical trade cycle (i.e. where there are no structural, demographic, regional, electoral, budgetary or international problems) the federal bank would always pursue its primary goal of

currency stabilisation. In the general disequilibrium which characterised the German economy after 1968, the loyalty of the Federal
Bank, as well as the regional and local state bodies was exposed to
considerable pressures. The theoretical assumptions of 'global steering' were shown to be flawed in relation to the nature and function of
private and state investment and specifically in terms of the constitutional constraints of an independent central bank and a federal
fiscal structure.

* * *

West Germany's experiment with Keynesianism was very brief. It
clearly did not survive the second recession in 1975 and its demise can
be dated either to Schiller's resignation in 1972 or even to 1969, the
year of the break-up of the Grand Coalition and the wage revolt of
the September strikes.

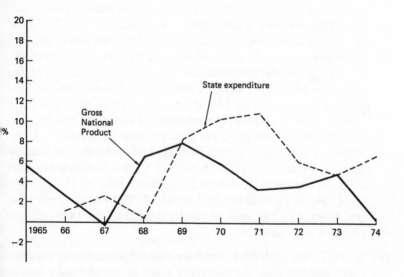

Fig. 5.1 Real growth p.a. of GNP and state expenditure (without social
insurance funds), 1966–74 (per cent)

If one applies the primary criterion of 'the appropriateness of
budgetary policy to the business cycle' (§§ 5–8, 14 and 16 Stability
Law), then it is clear from Fig. 5.1 that between 1966 and 1968 total

state expenditure was anti-cyclical in nature: in 1967 when GNP fell by 0.2 per cent in real terms state expenditure increased by 2.6 per cent over 1966; conversely in 1968 real state expenditure grew by only 0.5 per cent, while real GNP growth shot up by 6.5 per cent. Between 1969 and 1973, however, expenditure returned to its pro-cyclical pattern, so that despite rates of real growth which never fell below 3.3 per cent (1971) and which averaged 5.1 per cent over the five years, state expenditure grew conspicuously in real terms – at an average of 7.9 per cent.[39] There were various reasons for this, which had little to do with any subversive aim of the Social Democrats to 'raise the state quota' regardless.[40] What happened in 1969, 1970 and 1971 when real spending by the state rose by 8.0 per cent, 10.3 per cent and 10.9 per cent respectively, was a function of *demographic pressures* (particularly in education), *the contradictions of demand management, structural economic factors and of the boom itself*:

(a) The backlog of reforms in education became very apparent between 1965 and 1968 when the number of school leavers with university entrance qualifications rose from 51 747 to 77 032 and the numbers of university students rose from 308 000 to 363 000, reflecting not just the effect of the post-war rise in the birth rate but also the higher participation rate of school leavers in higher education (especially among women). The Länder and the local authorities were obliged by articles 35, 36 and 39 of the Basic Law to provide appropriate educational facilities, and the statutes of German universities in principle granted access to all with Abitur. Thus, quite separate from cyclical demands, total expenditure on education would have had to rise considerably after 1965. In the event education expenditure rose by 183 per cent from 1965 to 1973 (in nominal terms), GNP by only 99 per cent, and from 10.1 per cent of total expenditure to 14.5 per cent (1961: 8.6 per cent).

(b) In 1967, the objective need to expand educational facilities corresponded with the perceived need to expand state investment to counteract the recession; an accelerated building programme (which included a large proportion of educational buildings) seemed to meet the bill. Although the central government's First Investment Programme of April 1967 only included DM20 million for the building of student hostels and DM72.9 million for science and research, the Second (joint) Programme included nearly DM2 billion earmarked for communal projects,

Table 5.7   Nominal State expenditure on education, science and research and construction, 1961–73

Year	Education (DM billion)	(Per cent of total state expenditure)	Science & research (DM billion) (per cent)	Construction (DM billion) (per cent)	
1961	8.1	(8.6%)	1.3	10.5	(11.0%)
1965	14.2	(10.1%)	1.5	18.7	(13.3%)
1966	15.4	(10.5%)	1.8	18.9	(12.9%)
1967	16.3	(10.4%)	2.1	18.3	(11.7%)
1968	17.4	(10.9%)	2.2	18.6	(11.7%)
1969	20.3	(11.6%)	2.4	21.2	(12.1%)
1970	24.7	(12.6%)	2.8	25.7	(13.1%)
1971	31.2	(13.8%)	3.5	30.3	(13.4%)
1972	35.6	(14.1%)	4.0	31.9	(12.7%)
1973	40.4	(14.5%)	4.5	32.9	(11.8%)

Source: *Statistisches Jahrbuch*; own calculations.

which in turn included school building and modernisation. However, it is clear from a break-down of expenditure that many of the projects planned under the 'Second Programme for Special Conjunctural and Structural Measures 1967/68' did not in fact come on line until 1969, i.e. after the cyclical recovery of 1968 and during a year of very high real growth (7.9 per cent): the expenditure of the regional and local authorities in fact fell in real terms in 1967 and 1968 (by 0.3 per cent and 3.5 per cent respectively – see Fig. 5.2), housebuilding activity (also earmarked in the Second Investment Programme) fell from 1966 to 1969, and general building activity also fell in real terms (see above). The delay – caused by predictable problems of drafting, developing, submitting planning applications, etc. – produced *an enormous pro-cyclical surge of regional and local investment expenditure in 1969, 1970 and 1971*, with real increases of total expenditure of 12.4 per cent, 32.3 per cent and 19.7 per cent, which had the effect of contributing to the overheating of the economy evident in the rise in the rate of inflation (1969: 1.9 per cent, 1970: 3.4 per cent, 1971: 5.3 per cent, 1972: 6.9 per cent). Disregarding the important structural function of building expenditure (which made up some 90 per cent of the Second Investment Programme), the 2 to 3 year delay in its implementation demonstrated how unwieldy it was as an instrument of

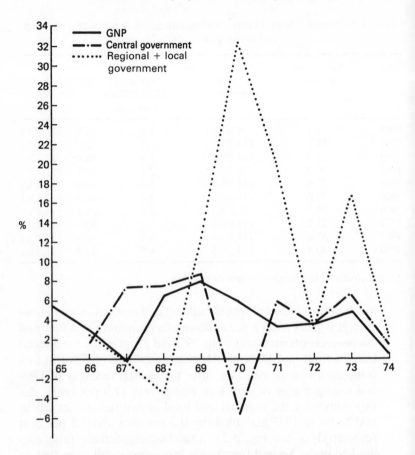

Fig. 5.2 'Global steering' in practice: real growth of GNP, central government expenditure and expenditure by regional & local authorities, 1966–74 (per cent p.a.)

anti-cyclical policy and how the effectiveness of investments in stimulating economic development was itself (in part) dysfunctional.

(c) By 1969 the revenue of all the state authorities had increased to a degree which allowed an expansion of expenditure without much additional borrowing. The borrowing requirement of the local authorities fell noticeably in 1967 and 1968 and only rose slightly in 1969, so that their net borrowing in the two years prior to the recession (1965 and 1966) was higher than in the three years 1967 to 1969, as was that of the regional authorities, whose borrowing

Table 5.8   State borrowing requirement, 1965–73 (DM billion)

Year	Total	Interest payments	Central government	Regional governments	Local governments
1965	9.3	(3.2)	1.7	3.1	4.5
1966	9.2	(4.1)	2.6	2.9	3.7
1967	14.3	(5.2)	7.9	3.9	2.5
1968	8.0	(5.4)	3.7	2.1	2.2
1969	0.2	(5.9)	−1.8	−0.5	2.5
1970	7.5	(6.6)	1.9	2.0	3.6
1971	15.8	(7.4)	1.5	5.2	7.6
1972	18.6	(8.5)	6.5	4.0	8.1
1973	12.5	(10.2)	6.1	2.5	3.9

Source: Deutsche Bundesbank *Monthly Reports*.

requirement fell in 1969, despite an expanded budget. *Only the central authorities demonstrated a strict anti-cyclical deficit policy* (à la §§5–8 Stability Law), increasing its borrowing requirement by DM7.9 billion in 1967 and by DM3.7 billion in 1968, but reducing it by DM1.8 billion in 1969.

In 1969 therefore revenue was high and borrowing was low, but in addition the capital markets showed huge domestic liquid reserves, in part as a result of the inflow of speculative money from abroad which was (correctly) anticipating a revaluation of the Deutschmark.[41] The *restrictive monetary policy* of the Federal Bank which was quickly introduced from April 1969 onwards to combat the danger of inflation, failed to dampen investment activity and investment borrowing and *only succeeded in attracting even more foreign money* because of the higher real interest rates. It can thus be argued that *both the fiscal policy of the state authorities and the monetary policy of the Federal Bank had an inflationary effect* in this period: expensive credit for private firms could be offset both by the general expectation of higher profits in a boom period and in certain cases by passing these costs on to the committed customer – in the case of the building industry to the local and regional authorities. The disproportionately high rises in building prices (+27 per cent in the two years 1970-71 compared to a cost of living rise of 8.8 per cent in the same period) can be put down to some shrewd profiteering by building firms that had suffered hardest in the recession and to the real strength of demand, reinforced by the prestige projects for the 1972 Olympics. But these huge price rises also contributed to budget overshoots by the state in general and to increased borrowing after 1970 (see above, Table 5.8). Together with high discount rates (which fell only briefly to 3 per cent in 1972) the state investment programmes meant that it was impossible to consolidate state finances in line with an anti-cyclical policy and in accordance with the main principles of the Stability Law. This is demonstrated both by the high levels of borrowing from 1971 to 1973 as well as in the fact that interest payments in 1973 (at DM10.2 billion) were approaching the level of the net borrowing requirement of DM12.5 billion.

The fiscal arrangements of the Second Investment Programme involved grants by the central and regional authorities as an initial boost towards local building projects which the local authorities would however have to sustain in the longer term, and it is clear that the proportionately higher borrowing requirement of the local authorities (as a ratio of total expenditure) in 1971 and 1972 was evidence of the inequitable implications of their commitment to the apparently cheap deal of the Investment Programme,[42] and their political commitment to sustaining and improving education, housing and local services. Keynesianism worked least well for the local authorities, despite the fiscal reform measures which came into effect in 1970.[43]

The overall development of state expenditure between 1966 and 1973 indicates the limited success of 'global steering' and its ultimate ineffectiveness. The negative development was however clearly observed and after 1969 there was a flurry of activity at various levels to restore the threatened stability and to depress the boom:

In March and May 1969, in January and May 1970 measures were agreed at Bund and Land level to use increased tax revenue to create conjunctural reserves totalling DM7.8 billion;

Discount and Lombard rates were raised to record post-war levels (7.5 per cent and 9.5 per cent respectively in March 1970), which were lowered only briefly in 1971 and 1972;

After opposition from German exporters, the Mark was finally revalued by 9.3 per cent in October 1969 to a new parity of DM3.66 to one dollar; after further pressure from hot money there were further revaluations of 13.6 per cent in December 1971 and 11.1 per cent in February 1973 before the Deutschmark was finally 'floated' in March 1973 along with other European currencies.

Other short-term measures to encourage imports and slow the rise of exports were put into force from December 1968 to March 1970 under the heading of 'Law on Foreign Economic Stability', which was reintroduced in modified form in January 1972; repayable extraordinary tax levies were made in 1970 and 1971 in the order of 10 per cent of total tax liabilities for Wages, Income and Corporation Tax, and in July 1973 a non-repayable levy on 800 000 high earners was made under the label of a 'Stability Surcharge'; in the same package investments were discouraged by an 11 per cent investment tax limited to two years, by the suspension of degressive and other depreciation allowances.

Up to 1973 none of these numerous measures appeared to have any positive stabilising effect particularly on inflation which, even before the first 'oil-price-shock' reached 6.9 per cent in 1973. Above all investments, the lynch-pin of Schiller's demand management, fluctuated even more dramatically during the period of 'global steering' than before, in response to renewed signs of overcapacity, lower returns and expensive domestic credit. (High levels of interest were also clearly in part responsible for the increasing levels of bankruptcy after 1969.)

Table 5.9   Gross investments and capacity utilisation. 1967–73

	1967	1968	1969	1970	1971	1972	1973
Gross investments annual real growth in per cent	−9.0	+10.5	+22.6	+16.7	+4.8	−0.1	+2.0
Capacity utilisation (Ifo-Munich) in per cent	78	84	90	92	89	86	88

Source: M. Welteke, *Theorie und Praxis der Sozialen Marktwirtschaft* (Frankfurt, 1976).

Even before Schiller's resignation, state anti-cyclical policy was in a bit of a mess. In the absence of both effective exchange controls and co-ordinated planned investment, the state's economic strategists were overwhelmed by the irregularities of monopolised markets and by the contradictions of state investment programmes. By 1974 and the onset of the second recession, any hope of reproducing the unanimity of 1967 had evaporated.

The Significance of Schiller's Resignation

Karl Schiller resigned as 'double minister' of Economics and Finance on 7 July 1972. In the media his departure was portrayed as the only solution to the 'Schiller-Crisis', as the inevitable step of an increasingly isolated member of the Federal government, who had alienated his supporters within the SPD as well as the special (middle-class) 'Schiller voters' with his 'high-handed' and 'obstinate' behaviour.[44] There certainly were clashes within the cabinet which had led to the earlier resignation of the Finance Minister Alex Möller (SPD) and also between Schiller and the Bundesbank president Klasen, but these were essentially personalised reflections of the fundamental contradictions in West Germany's political economy, contradictions which were not resolved by Schiller's departure. Nevertheless his resignation did mark the final passing of the co-ordinated technocratic attempt to reconcile West Germany's monopolised economy with its federal fiscal structure and independent central bank, in order both to manage cyclical and structural problems *and* realise the Social Democrats' (the Social-Liberal) reform programme. Despite the November 1972 election victory for the SPD and the electorate's apparent vote of confidence in the government's economic management, *the primary role for the management of the economy had passed over to the Federal Bank.* All the heated discussions within the cabinet about expenditure plans and the permissable limits of state borrowing compounded the *fundamental ignorance of the state regarding future market trends* and hence the increasing difficulty of fine-tuning à la Keynes. This ignorance, demonstrated by the inadequacy of the government's 'orientation data' (see above), allowed the maintenance of a variety of dogmatic views on expenditure within the cabinet, which, however, palled into insignificance in the face of world economic developments. The dollar and the pound crises had produced a renewed inflow of 'vagabond capital'[45] into West Germany which threatened to accelerate inflationary trends far more significantly than the state debt. The cure proposed by the Social Democrat Schiller was to maintain a free market for capital but to reduce the attractiveness of cheap foreign credit by raising the interest-free minimum deposit on foreign loans from 40 per cent to 50 per cent[46]. The president of the conservative Federal Bank, on the other hand, proposed exchange controls measures (!) which would, among other things, require the licensing of all foreign purchases of German securities.[47] The effectiveness of neither of the policies was empirically testable, but a decision had to be taken and, since the guiding principle, according to Arndt (of the DIW), was that '50 per cent of all decisions are wrong, so let us decide',[48] a decision was made: to support Klasen against Schiller. This had significant implications:

1. it gave the impression of affirming the more strongly interventionist wing of the SPD and their view of the fallibility of the market, against a 'free-marketeer' who had succumbed to CDU pressure to limit social spending – this was electorally expedient, if nothing else;
2. equally expedient in the run-up to the election was the appearance of unity between Federal Government and Federal Bank; the alternative to the collective abandonment of Schiller would have been a front against the Federal Bank and could have appeared as a threat to monetary stability; Klasen was thus less dispensable than Schiller in the short term;[49]
3. the transition to exchange controls, administered by the Federal Bank, however, placed state borrowing from abroad under the supervisory control of the guardians of monetary stability and thus limited its room for manoeuvre fundamentally;
4. what appeared as strong-united government was thus a mixture of electoral opportunism and politico-economic weakness.

The new primacy of the Federal Bank was confirmed by the joint floating of European currencies in March 1973, since it increased the influence of interest rate manipulation and liquidity policies.[50] The autonomy of the Federal Bank was further emphasised by its public announcement in December 1974 of a specific target for money supply growth in 1975 (of 8.0 per cent), thus severely limiting the latitude for the *real* expansion of state expenditure required to counteract the impending recession. The withdrawal of effective support by the Federal Bank for counter-cyclical fiscal policies was already quite apparent before Schiller's resignation, and, more significantly perhaps, the support by the cabinet for Klasen against Schiller represented the *abandonment of Keynesianism* and the adoption of a policy subordinate to central bank control.

The episode of Keynesian experimenting also demonstrates the 'negative' influence of electoral considerations on economic policy formulation and thus the problem of policy continuity. Keynes himself had recognised the problem of marrying long-term demand management with democratic electoral cycles and hence the potential 'virtue' of a unitary, non-democratic state for implementing a consistent economic policy.[51] Such specific political continuity could not be offered by any government in West Germany's parliamentary system of democracy. However the Bundesbank, as a non-elected body, could provide that elusive continuity and specifically as an "institutionalised counterweight to governmental or fiscal policy".[52] Neoliberals were thus guilty of considerable humbug when they inferred the "totalitarian", non-democratic, anti-constitutional nature of demand management[53] and then demanded the "primacy of monetary policy",[54] since this primacy in West Germany effectively precludes even a half-way legitimated and effective fiscal policy: the primacy of monetary policy in West Germany, as it emerged in the early 1970s, was thus *fundamentally undemocratic* (see below pp. 220ff.). The objective need for effective and increasing state interventionism was however not served by the abandonment of "global steering"; future crises were thus allowed to accumulate below the confident political/electoral surface.

Trade Policy and Demand Management – the Economics of Ostpolitik

The predominant historical interpretation of Ostpolitik among West German political commentators in the media and in academics has emphasised its implications either for the national 'German question', or for the wider problems of political co-existence in Europe, the liberalisation of travel, human and cultural exchange and for electoral politics. On closer analysis such stress emerges as a *misconstruction*, because political phenomena are seen as ends rather than means, concealing the less glamorous economic purpose of intensified relations with Eastern Europe.

German capital developed strong links with the economies of central and eastern Europe before the turn of the century. These links were cultivated by successive German states through conventional trade missions, export credit guarantees, etc. and more significantly by two world wars, the main territorial thrust of which had been towards the East, its markets and its huge reserves of raw materials. The integration of West Germany into an exclusive Western block made the maintenance of such interests both difficult and, because of the 1950s trade boom, largely unnecessary. However, with the slowing down of growth at the end of the 1950s, the slower relative growth of domestic demand and the increasing importance of exports to overall growth, and with the increasing instability of western markets, the neglect of East European trade became all the more problematic for the representatives of German industry. The embargo politics of the cold war became increasingly dysfunctional, because they no longer corresponded to the interests of large sections of German capital – notably of the structurally weak iron and steel industries, but also of heavy engineering and the electro-technical industry. There was particular resentment about the sacrifices demanded of German industry through the Hallstein-doctrine, through COCOM and through NATO (with particular respect to the pipeline embargo of 1962), while the more pragmatic policies of France, Britain and Italy allowed rules to be bent and contracts to be signed in the absence of competition from the more scrupulous Germans.[55]

In the wake of the Pipe Line Embargo, trade with the Soviet Union was liberalised to some degree and trade missions were established in Hungary, Rumania and Bulgaria. But, in the absence of a trade treaty with Russia which was conditional on West Germany recognising post-war borders and the East German state, there was little prospect of extending trade links to a significant level, compared with western trade. However, moves to regularise European political relations were rendered more urgent by the susceptibility of the steel and heavy engineering industries to demand fluctuations, firstly in 1963 and then particularly in the recession of 1966/67.[56] The recession demonstrated the particular export dependency of certain branches of industry: while overall export dependency between 1965 and 1970 rose from 15.6 per cent to 18.3 per cent (ratio of export turnover to GNP), the chemical, engineering and motor-vehicle industries developed individual export quotas of over 30 per cent of turnover.[57]

Table 5.10   Branch export quotas (export sales as per cent of turnover), 1965–74

Branch	1965	1970	1973	1974
Chemical industry	25.0	30.9	33.9	36.2
Automobile industry	37.7	38.9	43.9	46.5
Electrical industry	18.8	21.8	22.9	25.7
Engineering	30.4	35.6	39.3	44.1
Economy as a whole (Exports as per cent of GNP)	15.6	18.3	19.2	23.2

Source: H. Hopf and G. Mayr, 'Destabilisierung durch den Weltmarkt' in *Gesellschaft im Konkurs?*, op. cit., pp. 104ff.

For certain firms this export dependency was even higher: by 1970 Volkswagen was turning over 68 per cent of its sales in exports, Hoechst 56 per cent, Bayer 66 per cent, Siemens 41 per cent and Mannesmann 41 per cent.[58] Thus when the chairman of the 'Eastern Committee' and steel industrialist, Otto Wolff von Amerongen, called for the 'depoliticisation' of Germany's foreign trade,[59] he was implicitly stressing the vital importance of new, largely untapped, markets for Germany's exporting industries in Eastern Europe.

The background to the sudden intensification of efforts to improve East–West relations in the mid-1960s was informed in large measure by the specific interests of German capital, but also by the failure of American embargo politics to hinder the steady growth of the economies in Eastern Europe, and hence the recognition that COMECON was both a stable and powerful economic block and a potentially strong customer for technologically advanced western products. Recession and 'national government' in West Germany triggered the rapid process of trade liberalisation and diplomatic progress which took place between 1967 and 1972. Industry was clearly strongly behind the acceleration of negotiations under the Grand Coalition and as such was a step ahead of the nationalist wing of the CDU, for whom recognition of East Germany and the Polish borders was a bitter pill to swallow. The treaties with Russia and Poland in 1970 and later with Czechoslovakia, Bulgaria and Hungary were welcomed by industry.[60] In 1972 Amerongen stressed that non-ratification of the Trade Treaty with Russia – which was linked to the inter-German 'Basic Treaty' – would be 'a clear setback for us',[61] which clearly implied criticism of CDU opponents of the Trade Treaty.

The keenness of industrialists to embrace COMECON markets had in fact been shrewdly fostered by the Russians by dangling the prospect of massive orders for German investment goods in front of the German negotiators. The main precedent for the 'large scale order' with which Moscow was 'beckoning'[62] was the Natural Gas-Pipeline deal which was struck in 1970 and involved the construction of a transcontinental pipeline from Siberia to Western Europe by a consortium led by Mannesmann which would supply natural gas to the Ruhrgas company, and which was financed by low-interest credit from German banks.[63] A supplementary contract from March 1972 increased the scope of trade such that by 1979 West German firms had delivered 6 million tons of wide bore pipe and Ruhrgas had purchased 35 billion cubic metres of natural gas. In the wake of this major co-operative venture and the trade treaty with Russia of July

1972, West Germany's trade with COMECON countries grew noticeably. By 1980 there were over 100 joint projects with Russia alone and German industry and banks had 53 permanent offices in Moscow. More significantly by 1980 West Germany had increased its 'Eastern' trade faster than any other OECD country and was by far the largest trading partner of the Soviet Union and its COMECON partners.

Table 5.11   Western exports to COMECON countries, 1980

	USSR	Poland	Rumania	E. Germany	Hungary	Czech	Bulgaria
Total ($ billion)	21.5	6.4	4.0	5.2	3.3	3.0	1.7
W. German share (per cent)	20%	23%	22%	52%	37%	34%	29%

Source: *Frankfurter Rundschau*, 24 May 1982.

Equally significant was that up to 1981 there had been constant very large payments surpluses with the Eastern bloc (e.g. DM8 billion in 1975).[64] The value of 'Eastern' trade to German capital and to the West German state thus appears self-evident and also appears to have justified high expectations:

(a) it represents reliable constant demand within the framework of planned economic strategy and contrasts with the severe fluctuations of demand in OECD markets; East European states (even Poland) are considerably more creditworthy than many developing states;[65] the general immunity of Eastern Trade to capitalist trade cycles allows the private bureaucracies of big capital to plan their future investment more securely;

(b) for particular branches and particular firms East European trade guarantees a high level of capacity utilisation within otherwise stagnating markets. In 1973 over 30 per cent of Mannesmann's exports (12 per cent of its total turnover) went to East European markets, 10 per cent of Thyssen's and nearly 15 per cent of the Gutehoffnungshütte;[66]

(c) the scope for expanded trade in the East is potentially higher than in the West, where markets are more saturated (note the current feverish activity to conquer Chinese markets);

(d) the large trade surpluses help to offset the cost of raw materials imports – particularly vital in the period of extreme rises in oil prices;

(e) the natural gas deal reduces West German dependence on oil imports; close trade links with the Soviet Union also give West Germany greater access to vital minerals for the production of fine steels and potentially to Russia's 'less expensive' uranium,[67] which would reduce West Germany's dependence on the (conditional) monopolised supply of the USA.

East European trade for West Germany would thus appear to have a potentially *stabilising effect on both cyclical and structural economic problems*, thereby alleviating the increasing problem of capital reproduction in West Germany particularly in relation to specific sectors. While the extent of this trade is still limited (it represented only 7.9 per cent of total export trade in 1975), particular firms could not survive without it. The cultivation of trade must therefore be seen as a significant contribution by the state towards the maintenance and expansion of external markets for German capital. One commentator asserts that the Grand Coalition achieved more in the area of trade policy (in particular with East Germany) than in any other (political) field,[68] which would suggest that trade liberalisation ran parallel to fiscal policy as a means of expanding demand.

Despite warnings of a dangerous dependence on Eastern Europe – in particular on energy supplies – the vital interests of capital have maintained government support (with credit guarantees, etc.) to a degree where US demands for renewed embargos and an end to the latest pipeline deal have been scornfully rejected by industry and state alike.[69] Rather the argument that interdependence secures peaceful co-existence is deployed to justify the maintenance of strong trade links and strong state support.[70]

Similarly the protests of ordo-liberals that Eastern trade distorts market forces, reduces competition and encourages monopolisation,[71] have fallen on deaf ears: neither industry nor state are concerned with the formal aesthetic conditions of competition, but with the maintenance of profits, investment and economic growth.

A more significant critical observation on Eastern trade was made by the Bundesbank in its monthly report of July 1982, when it was observed that the growth of Eastern trade was slowing down and more importantly that the hitherto positive balance of trade in favour of West Germany had changed to a trade deficit.[72] This inferred, correctly, that there was a built-in dependency in the natural gas-pipeline deal which would require a continuing expansion of German exports to Eastern Europe in order to counteract the potential high payments deficit. While over-capacity persists in heavy engineering, steel production and motor vehicles, and while West Germany remains dependent on expensive imported energy, both capital and central government will be keen to maintain strong Eastern trade links; conversely the Soviet Union has a modest lever for influencing economic and strategic decisions in the West. There is already evidence of considerable tensions within NATO countries over the 'transfer of technology' and the extended COCOM list of embargoed products,[73] which reflect the differing degrees of export dependency between Europe and the USA and the greater material interest of West European capital in trade with Eastern Europe. The prospect of an expansion of sales, for example through the proposed KATEK project in South West Siberia,[74] will only strengthen European resistance to US embargo tactics. This is reinforced by the fact that, despite considerable CDU/CSU criticism of Eastern trade policy by the Schmidt/Genscher government,[75] the Kohl government has retained a firm commitment to West Germany's Eastern trade flank.[76]

STAGFLATION, 1974/75

Classical theories of the market assert that mass unemployment and high inflation are mutually exclusive. The famous Phillips-Curve which 'demonstrated' this, did indeed correspond to the experience of the Depression in the 1930s, where prices fell in relation to the rise in unemployment (and fall in effective demand). However, the cyclical downturn which ended in the recession of 1975 in West Germany (and in other countries) showed classical market theories to be fundamentally flawed, and the Phillips-theory to be a grand illusion:[77] recession and growing unemployment developed parallel to high inflation:

In the trough year of 1975, with a real fall in GNP of 1.9 per cent, not only was unemployment at a higher level than for 20 years at 1 074 000 but price inflation stood at over 6 per cent for the third year running. In the recovery year of 1976 GNP grew by 5.1 per cent in real terms but general unemployment fell by only 0.1 of a percentage point (while it rose in industry) and bankruptcies continued to accelerate. The 'magic triangle' of stable growth, prices and employment had more or less become a thing of the past.

Table 5.12   Stagflation in West Germany, 1973–76

	1973	1974	1975	1976
1. *GNP* (real) per cent change over previous year	4.9	0.4	–1.9	5.1
2. *Private investments* (real) per cent change over previous year	0.3	–13.2	–4.5	2.3
3. *State investments* (real) per cent change over previous year	–0.5	7.7	–3.0	–3.9
4. *Prices* per cent change	6.9	7.0	6.0	4.5
5. *Unemployment* total (per cent of working population)	1.3	2.6	4.7	4.6
6. per cent Change of *industrial employment*	1.2	–3.6	–6.2	–2.5
7. *Employed population* (in millions)	22.9	22.6	22.0	21.9
8. Productivity increase (per cent)	7.1	4.6	4.4	8.8
9. Capacity utilisation (per cent) (WSI)	86.7	81.7	77.7	81.7
10. Bankruptcies	5 515	7 772	9 195	9 362

Source: *Statistisches Jahrbuch*, WSI-Mitteilungen
            SVR report (1977/78).

Origins of the Crisis

The establishment response to the crisis was, in one form or another, to blame factors external to the market economic order – OPEC, the trade unions or particular state authorities (see below). This exclusion of the market order from critical diagnosis was both intellectually untenable and politically opportunistic. Above all it pre-determined a set of prescriptions which could not hope to prove adequate.

The Arab–Israeli war of October 1973, the Arab oil 'boycott' and the subsequent rise in the fixed price of OPEC crude oil were clearly one chain of events which determined the recession in OECD countries. But these combined with a complex set of determinant factors to produce the severe reduction of GNP, high unemployment, inflation, low investment, high bankruptcies, etc. which characterised the stagflationary crisis of 1974/75. It is useful here to present a set of heuristic categories through which the nature of the crisis can be better understood. Accordingly the crisis can be analysed in terms of a combination of *cyclical economic*, *structural economic*, *structural political*, *process-political* and *demographic* factors. The descriptive value of the analysis is limited because it does not attempt either to

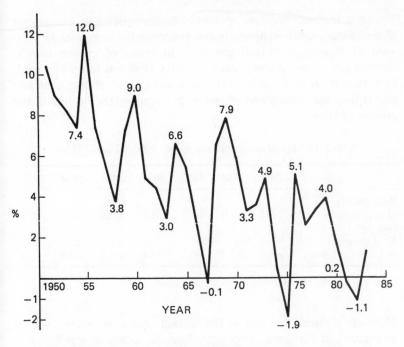

Fig. 5.3   Real growth p.a. of GNP (per cent), 1950–84

quantify/weigh each factor or to develop an elaborate mathematical model, but it does try to avoid the tabuisation of particular features.

Cyclical Economic Factors

A brief glance at the development of West Germany's cyclical development reveals a gradual decline in the average rate of growth. Even if one discounts the 1950s as a period of exceptional growth, which distorts the trend, the decline in the rate of growth may flatten out slightly in the 1960s and 1970s but it still continues.

Table 5.13   Average rates of growth over 5-year periods (real)[78]

	per cent
1951–55	9.4
1956–60	6.6
1961–65	4.9
1966–70	4.5
1971–75	2.1

Sources: *Statistisches Jahrbuch*; own calculations.

The same is true of the development of domestic demand, except that its decline in growth is slightly faster, reflecting the increasing importance of exports to overall growth.[79] In terms of growth trends, therefore, a second deeper recession after 1967 was to be expected. Investments show a similar cyclical development although at key points they are slightly out of phase, pre-figuring the decline in the growth of GNP:

Table 5.14   Investments and recession, 1965–67 and 1972–75

	1965	1966	1967	1972	1973	1974	1975
Real growth of investments (per cent)	+6.5	–0.9	–9.0	–0.1	+2.0	–8.1	–9.6
Real growth of GNP (per cent)	+5.5	+2.5	–0.2	+3.6	+4.9	+0.4	–1.9

Sources: *Statistisches Jahrbuch*; own calculations.

This was particularly clear in the second recession, when average investment in the three years preceding the recession was lower in real terms than in 1970 or 1971. All these general factors point to a *relative saturation of demand* within the economy for basic commodities such as food and housing[80] and for particular consumer durables:

Table 5.15   Selected consumer durables in private households, 1968 and 1978

	1968 (per cent)	1978 (per cent)
Car	43.3	79.8
Fridge	92.9	95.4
Automatic washing machine	32.0	65.0
Telephone	12.5	69.3
Colour TV	2.0	60.9
Deep freeze	7.4	68.3
Tape recorder	25.5	62.9

Source: Peter Czada, *Wirtschaft*, op. cit. p. 80.

The slowing down of domestic demand growth, which is also subject to demographic fluctuations, has clearly not been compensated for by the above average growth in export demand, nor have saturated markets been replaced quickly enough by new areas of "elevated demand".[81] The cyclical crisis which was evident in the general indicators for 1973 and 1974 (see Table 4.37 above) can also be taken to indicate a structural crisis of reproduction, of persistently lower rates of growth and deeper recessions for future cycles.

Structural Economic Factors

When Werner Abelshauser suggests that in the German economy there was somehow a 'return to the classic cycle',[82] he implies a return to the long-term *critical trend of capital reproduction*. Taking the global indicators of rate of profit, capital productivity marginal capital coefficient and capital intensity, it is possible to see 1975 as confirmation of an intensifying, general *structural crisis of reproduction*. Although there are periods of recovery, the trend for the rate of profit is clearly downwards, as is demonstrated even by those who identify the possibility of reversing the process.[83]

Table 5.16   Rate of profit and capital coefficient, 1960–74

	Rate of[a] profit on gross capital	*Rate of*[a] profit on net capital	*Capital*[b] Coefficient (whole economy)	*Capital*[b] Coefficient (manufacturing)
1960	20.9	34.9	3.06	1.29
1961	19.5	31.3	3.06	1.31
1962	17.7	28.1	3.07	1.34
1963	16.6	26.0	3.11	1.37
1964	16.9	26.4	3.17	1.41
1965	16.4	25.7	3.20	1.43
1966	15.6	23.7	3.22	1.44
1967	14.2	22.1	3.28	1.46
1968	16.4	25.8	3.34	1.48
1969	16.2	25.6	3.41	1.50
1970	15.3	24.1	3.43	1.51
1971	14.0	21.8	3.46	1.53
1972	13.5	21.0	3.48	1.54
1973	13.3	20.7	3.52	1.55
1974	12.3	19.1	3.57	1.56

[a] *For all businesses. Source*: Elsenhans, op. cit.
[b] Capital Coefficient here = ratio of capital stock to productive potential. *Source*: Görzig/Kirner *et al.*, *Daten zur Entwicklung des Produktionspotentials*, (DIW, Berlin, 1977).

Even with the fictitious ratio of capital stock to productive *potential* (rather than to domestic product),[84] the marginal gain from additional investment is increasingly smaller, as is the rate of return on that investment. This is evident from 1959 onwards and expresses itself in an intensification of production, the replacement of labour by machines and the acceleration of the labour process in an attempt to raise absolute profits. However, increasing capital intensity produces increasing susceptibility to demand fluctuations. The relatively high levels of capacity utilisation of the late 1950s and early 1960s were not matched in the 'super cycle' 1967–75, since the growth of aggregate investment far exceeded the growth of output.[85]

Table 5.17   Capacity utilisation of German industry in the super-cycle, 1967–75 (Ifo-Institut)

	1967	1968	1969	1970	1971	1972	1973	1974	1975
Capacity utilisation *in per cent of productive potential*	78	84	90	92	89	86	88	83	76

Source: Ifo-Institut (Munich).

This in turn reinforces the trend in investment to consolidate industrial operations through rationalising-out labour rather than extending capacity (see above pp. 183f). The structural crisis of capital reproduction manifests itself in structural unemployment and high levels of bankruptcy even in years of strong general growth (namely 1976, when despite 5.1 per cent growth employment levels fell by a further 100 000 over the recession year 1975 and bankruptcies rose from 9195 in 1975 to 9362 in 1976, see Table 5.12).

Within the general structural crisis of reproduction there are specific sectoral problems. The *building industry*, apart from being historically highly susceptible to cyclical fluctuations and irregular private and state investment, experienced a marked long-term drop in business from the early 1960s onwards. The textile and clothing industries only survived the long-term structural crisis by specialisation and low wages,[86] but have not been able to avoid either a decline in nominal turnover or increasing import penetration:

Table 5.18   Turnover and import penetration in textile and clothing industries, 1970–76

	1970	1972	1974	1976
Textile industry turnover (DM billion)	21.0	22.9	18.3	18.3
Clothing industry turnover (DM billion)	13.2	14.6	12.6	12.3
Import penetration – textiles (per cent)	24.1%	28.3%	29.5%	33.8%
Import penetration – clothing (per cent)	15.4%	20.3%	26.5%	31.1%

Source: *Statistisches Jahrbuch.*

The same is true of the leather, shoe and pottery industry. The structural weakness of the coal industry persisted, steel and ship-building were increasingly subject to cheap competition from the Far East. Even the electro-technical giant AEG experienced a critical drop in profits (averaging only 5 per cent of share capital between 1973 and 1975 compared to 51 per cent for Siemens),[87] as a result of loss of markets.

These and other sectoral weaknesses (e.g. Agriculture) had considerable consequences for state economic policy, largely inducing increased or new subsidies. However, the exponential decline in the number of small artisan businesses continued without countervailing measures by the state (903 000 in 1949, 615 000 in 1968 and 519 000 in 1975) reflecting not simply the development within agriculture, but the general structural effect of the crisis of reproduction: increased concentration of capital.

By whatever yardstick one applies, the acceleration of concentration in the super-cycle 1967 to 1975 was dramatic: within 8 years the number of industrial firms fell by 7.3 per cent from 103 853 in 1966 to 93 308 in 1974, reflecting both industrial bankruptcies and in particular a wave of mergers after 1968. In the eleven years from 1958 (the first year of the Cartel Law) to 1968 there were a total of 404 mergers which required registering with the Cartel Office. In the eight years 1969–76 there were no less than 2423 such mergers. Oligopolies strengthened their position at the expense of non-monopolised markets and firms (see above, Chapter 3), because of their ability to minimise costs (as customers) and maximise income (as sellers). The disproportionately high profits of oligopolies compared to non-monopolised firms is clear evidence for the recognised advantage of large accumulations of capital which is quite distinct from the

advantage of economies of scale. Within the framework of a general
reduction in the rate of profit the oligopolies are able to redistribute
the profit mass, increasing their share and reducing the share of
non-monopolised firms:

Table 5.19   General rate of net profit compared to rate of net profit of 10
largest firms, 1973–74

	1973	1974
General rate of net profit	20.7	19.1
Average rate of net profit of 10 largest firms (per cent of share capital)	31	36

Source: J. Huffschmid, 'Monopolisierung in der Krise' in *Gesellschaft im
Konkurs*, op. cit.; K. G. Zinn, *Der Niedergang des Profits*, (Cologne, 1978).

The first OPEC oil price 'shock' of 1974 is essentially one aspect of
a *general monopolisation of supply* which reduced the elasticity of
market forces still further in the 1970s. Raising oil prices from $2.70
per barrel in 1973 to $9.76 in 1974 was in fact only a partial reversal of
the low terms of trade suffered by developing countries for years as a
result of the monopolised power of the developed world. (These
terms of trade had been effectively frozen for two decades after the
Korea-boom.[88] In the case of West Germany the level of its export
prices rose in real terms by around 50 per cent between 1950 and
1972, while import price levels had fallen by some 10 per cent in the
same period.[89]) The oil price rise clearly had a considerable knock-on
effect through increased energy costs, but price inflation in West
Germany was high before 1974 and the oil-price rise was in part offset
by the rise in the exchange rate of the Deutschmark against the dollar
(1972 = 100, 1974 = 131, 1976 = 135, 1978 = 171, 1979 = 185).[90] It
was the multi-national oil corporations, which had exploited the
cheap Gulf oil for years that now also contributed to the price
explosion of oil products by general profiteering on the back of crude
oil prices.[91]

The general rigidity of real prices was reflected also in the price of
labour. After the unhappy experiences of Concerted Action and the
September strikes of 1969, the trade unions reverted to collective
bargaining on 12 month wage contracts, and during the inflationary
boom from 1970 to 1974 achieved *considerable improvements in
general rates of pay and in marginal benefits*.[92] The adjusted wages

quota rose from 53.5 per cent in 1968 to 58 per cent in 1974, while unit labour costs rose faster than labour productivity.[93] Within the inflationary spiral and the framework of the monopolised supply of manufactured commodities, union representatives were obliged *and able* to demand a higher price for increasingly skilled labour, which could in turn be passed on by the employer in the purchase price, but which at the same time implied increased consumer demand. The spiral of commodity prices (goods and labour) which were not flexible downwards, as in the 1930s, but only upwards, destabilised market forces critically and further weakened the credibility of market economics.

The West German economy was also subject to critical structural developments within the world economy, apart from cartellised oil supplies. The emergence of new developed economies in the Far East and to a lesser extent in South America coincided with rapidly improved world communications, far shorter lead-in times for industrial and commercial innovations and an increasing mobility of international capital, all of which demanded rapid and flexible responses from private competition as well as effective national and transnational political action. The combination of the Bretton Woods system of fixed exchange rates and liberal exchange controls could not survive the pressures of unequal national economic development or the anarchic behaviour of vast amounts of rogue capital. However the transition to flexible exchange rates (Floating) in 1973 increased rather than decreased the de-stabilising potential of world capital markets – particularly in the wake of the 1975 recession.

Structural Political Factors

The weaknesses of West Germany's national political structures have already been examined in relation to the failure of Keynesianism (above pp. 185f): the existence of three independent levels of fiscal authority (with differing expenditure patterns and priorities) and the increasingly dominant role of the unelected independent Federal Bank as agent of monetary policy, made the formulation of a coherent and adequate national economic policy virtually impossible. However, even assuming that this were possible West Germany's high export profile required some degree of transnational political control to ensure a stable foreign economic flank. This control was absent long before the 75 recession – the World Bank, the IMF, the OECD and the EEC were impotent (or indifferent) in the face of evident structural weaknesses in the world economy and growing concern about the 'limits of growth'. The EEC demonstrated the dysfunctional character of its policies when it failed to reform its agricultural policy along the lines of the Mansholt-Plan (1968), proving itself incapable of effecting even one of the many structural economic reforms to which it was supposed to attend. Equally dysfunctional was the role of NATO in as much as it both initiated an economically wasteful escalation of arms production and deployment and did not make the increased real expenditure conditional on anti-cyclical budgetary constraints.[94]

Process-Political Factors

In West Germany as elsewhere there seems to be a general assumption that electoral politics makes particular demands on the expenditure behaviour of the party/coalition in power: i.e. that in the run-up to an election the governing parties expand their expenditure to win votes,[95] and that budgets are consolidated in the year(s) immediately following a return to power. This *seems* to be confirmed by a glance at expenditure and revenue statistics for central government for 1953/54, 1961/62, 1965/66 and 1972/73.[96] What is also evident from the pattern of Bund budgets is that it matches the *electoral cycle* more than the business cycle. The natural non-correspondence of electoral cycles with economic cycles provides an additional factor for the destabilisation of the West German economy even though the precise effects cannot be properly calculated.[97]

Demographic Factors

More evident than any postulated economic effects of an electoral cycle are the demonstrable effects of demographic fluctuations on a whole number of areas of the economy: on government expenditure (for education, social security and recreation), on the labour market, on domestic demand, on social insurance funds, etc. West Germany's demographic 'bell' (see below) shows severe deviations from the normal age-related curves of population development. In addition to the effects of direct losses of the male population through the First and Second World Wars, which produced a considerable excess of women in particular generations, the shortfall of births in the two wars and in the Great Depression had a marked and irregular influence on the replacement of labour on the labour market, on

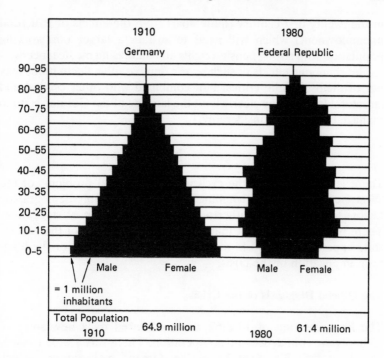

Fig. 5.4   The changing demographic structure of Germany

Sources: *Statistisches Jahrbuch für das deutsche Reich* (1913); *Statistisches Jahrbuch der Bundes republik* (1983).

pensions and on educational provision. Furthermore the baby boom of the 1950s and early 1960s was followed by a dramatic reduction of the birth rate in the 1970s which was virtually equivalent to the reductions caused by the wars and the depression, but now as a result of choice and the advances in contraception. The expansion of the school and university population in the 1960s and early 1970s made necessary a vast infusion of additional resources (new schools, universities and teachers), but, with the gradual reduction of the educational population after 1976, the spare capacity in education produced inverse problems of redistributing resources, shedding teachers and sustaining or selling expensive property, which continues up to today. The fall in the birth rate has led some research institutes to predict a severe reduction of the employable population in the twenty-first century (quite apart from the effects of structural unemployment) which will need to sustain a larger non-working population with strong pension rights and increasing medical needs.[98]

The economic effects of such severe demographic fluctuations may not of themselves be critical but, combined with other cyclical and structural factors they clearly limit the latitude of the German state to manage crises very considerably.

* * *

There is no doubt that the cyclical and structural problems of the West German economy combined with other, notably demographic factors to produce the hitherto unique phenomenon of stagflation. There is equally no doubt that the selective response of the various state apparatuses failed to master either the symptoms or the long-term implication of the crisis.

The Official Diagnosis of the Crisis

The first recession of 1966/67 was confronted by a new spirit of technocratic confidence and co-operation. There was a wide consensus about the efficacy of Keynesian demand management, which encompassed not just Karl Schiller and the SPD but also his Finance Minister Franz-Josef Strauss, the Academic Sub-Committee of the Economics Ministry, the 'five wise men' of the Council of Experts and, to a lesser extent, even the Federal Bank. At the outbreak of the second stagflationary recession this consensus had dissolved; equally the specific institutional instruments for implementing an anti-cyclical policy had either broken up (national coalition government) or had lost any semblance of co-ordinated behaviour (Concerted Action and the Conjunctural Council).

Nevertheless in 1974 a form of consensus did emerge from state institutions and from its quangos (the SVR and the Academic Sub-Committee), which, however, reflected the experience of the intervening years and demonstrated a radical reversal of theoretical approaches to the economy and economic management. A major role in the process was played by the SVR. The five economics professors, who made up this government-appointed body, clearly had a considerable influence on government thinking, right from the first year of their operating in 1963. Its recommendations for a co-ordinated anti-cyclical policy of fiscal intervention and its criticism of the shortcomings of the Federal Bank and the regional and local authorities were acted upon in 1967 and 1968. In 1972 the SVR however effectively abandoned Keynesianism and adopted a fundamentally ordo-liberal approach which sought to reduce the fiscal role of the state and maintain stability through monetary controls.

Just as in 1967, the SVR's diagnosis of the crisis was highly selective and teleologically pre-determined the prescribed cure, but, by adopting an essentially supply-side approach the SVR had to ignore not just a consideration of socialist options but also the accumulated wisdom of those western academics who, while conceding the structural flaws of the market economy, still believed in the possibility of active crisis-management. The common denominator of the 1967 and the 1974 annual reports of the SVR is the implied sanctity of the market. The explanation of the stagflationary crisis in 1974 is however reduced to three major factors which are 'external' to the market: excessive wage settlements, OPEC and the extension of state activities beyond acceptable limits.

In paragraph 1 of the 1974 Annual Report the price agreement of OPEC countries is described as 'a crude contravention of the rules of the division of labour within the world economy', which, by rendering energy supply 'deliberately unstable' forces the rest of the world to make wasteful adjustments to its energy policies. The 'oil-crisis' represents an external abuse of market power of which domestic concerns are not guilty: 'there is no doubt [sic],[99] that the strong acceleration of inflation in recent years cannot be explained by a lack of competition' (para. 375). On the other hand the 'labour market is dominated' by 'market power' (ibid.) (by implication trade-union power) which hinders the self-regulation of an otherwise reliable market. Furthermore the state has made wage inflation worse by agreeing to excessive wage settlements for its own employees and has destabilised the economy in general by appropriating an increasing share of the national product since 1969 (para. 406).

By singling out three inflationary villains (OPEC, the unions and the state) and exonerating the big corporations (proven abusers in fact of monopoly power),[100] the SVR can recommend a cure which *conforms to the market* and does not touch the autonomy of private companies:[101] regulation of the money supply as a primary determinant of other supply factors. This was intended to limit both state and private borrowing and hence restrict the latitude of the state to expand its expenditure (i.e. pressurise the fiscal authorities to consolidate their finances) and also the latitude of private companies to award wage rises beyond an *appropriate level*. Confronted by stagflation therefore the SVR recommended the control of inflation as the primary goal of the state (1974, para. 7), at the expense of employment, short-term economic growth and the social liberal reform programme. By checking state expenditure and the rise of the wages quota, the willingness to invest – as the "the heart muscle of a growing economy" – was to be stimulated (1974, para. 35).

The SVR's 1974 programme thus resembles the 1967 package in that profits and investments are given priority over wage growth, but in this second crisis the state has to play a marginal role. The common thread in the prescribed cures of the SVR is the notion of an absolute limit for the wages quota, beyond which private investment and enterprise will be completely discouraged. This was expressed in the 1967 report in terms of '*a wages policy which has a neutral effect on cost levels*' (*JG*, 1967, paras 248ff) and in 1976 in the desire to abolish '*minimum wage unemployment*' (*JG*, 1976, para. 278). 'Minimum wage unemployment' is the fault of unions who simply price their members out of jobs by preventing the anti-cyclical use of cheap labour, and of the state which cushions the effects of unemployment with indexed, generous benefit; as a concept it can thus neatly replace 'structural unemployment' (*JG* 1976, para. 278), which implies fundamental flaws in the capitalist system.

The view of a 'cost-neutral wages policy' which helps to prevent 'minimum wage unemployment' is the result of both political opportunism and intellectual cowardice, because it brushes aside a vast body of conflicting evidence and constructs a logic which must above all conform to the political requirement of affirming the sanctity of the market.[102] By the abrupt and crude jettisoning of Keynesian demand theory for a naive and 'radical market' version of supply theory,[103] the SVR, with the exception of the minority votes of Köhler, then Glastetter[104] and recently Mertens, demonstrated not so much their wisdom, according to one commentary, as their collective 'cluelessness'[105] concerning effective economic management, in the face of a stagflationary crisis which, in classical market theories (of either demand or supply persuasion) was not possible.

Nevertheless, the new monetarist orthodoxy of the SVR was broadly accepted by the national social–liberal cabinet and strongly supported by opposition and by employers. The liberal Economics Minister, Friderichs (who took over the post from the then 'double minister' Helmut Schmidt in December 1972) stressed the dangers of an excessive wages quota on a number of occasions,[106] and demanded the 'weeding out' of excessive social expenditure as a precondition for increasing the confidence of private enterprise.[107] Despite resistance from SPD cabinet members, especially the Finance Minister Apel, who argued for a degree of demand management through state investment, the junior coalition partner clearly won the ideological battle within the cabinet. The 'pragmatism' of the new Chancellor (after 1974), Helmut Schmidt, forced him to recognise the constraints of coalition government combined with a self-willed central bank and an increasing state debt, and to accept a deflationary approach.

The historical dilemma of Social Democracy in power – caught between its reformist goals and its duty as the fire brigade of capitalism – expressed itself again in political paralysis: the much vaunted 1975 *Long-Term-Programme* (The Orientation Framework for the Years 1975–85) was in essence *highly fatalistic*, because its ambitious economic and social policy aims were qualified by the recognition of the 'narrow limitations of our potential political actions'[108] set by world economic problems, by the severe separation of domestic political institutions[109] and the subsequent 'limited capacities for (economic JL) management'.[110] The commitment to the primacy of full employment[111] was thus neutralised by the realisation of the SPD's fiscal impotence. 'Schmidt's' crisis-management was nevertheless applauded by numerous industrialists, among them Peter von Siemens, who recorded the view 'that, when it comes to economic insight, we could not wish ourselves a better Chancellor or a more suitable Economics Minister'.[112]

The official diagnosis of the crisis thus corresponded to the general view of private enterprise which stressed the need for wage restraint, tax cuts and tight monetary control of state expenditure.[113] There were some dissenting voices within hard-hit branches, like the building sector and the motor vehicles industry, and among small firms in general,[114] who called for state-assistance and an end to restrictive policies, but the dominant view of the BDI, BDA and the DIHT favoured deflationary policies.

A feature of many commentaries of the 1975 crisis, which is implied by the strong demands for deflation, is the view that unemployment and bankruptcies have a salutory, cleansing and disciplining effect which somehow facilitates a strong recovery.[115] The new phenomenon of structural unemployment was thus seen in part as an acceptable instrument of economic policy which would help to control the price of labour and sustain a flagging rate of profit.

The Official Response to the Crisis

In contrast to the 1966/67 recession, the crisis in the 1970s was not limited to the one year of recession in 1975 but persisted in the shape of abnormally high unemployment, constant (if comparatively low) inflation and high levels of bankruptcies right up until the arrival of the next recession in 1981. The state's response to 'the' crisis must therefore be seen within a broader time span to the end of the 1970s, even though this overlaps chronologically with later sections of this study.

The first important observation about state policy after 1974 was that it was not co-ordinated à la Global Steering. Rather the fiscal policies of the area state authorities were predetermined by the autonomous pursuit of monetary stability by the Federal Bank. The self-subordination of central and regional governments to this regime was well-mannered and rarely produced significant conflicts.[116] However, it represented a highly significant development in West Germany's political economy which requires close scrutiny.

The Federal Bank and the Primacy of Monetarism

It was clear to most observers that it was impossible to control both elements of stagflation (recession/unemployment and inflation) simultaneously with the traditional instruments of state policy – be they fiscal or monetary or a combination of both. *Reflation* (through cheaper money and/or through state investment) might compound inflation, while *deflation* (through a credit squeeze and/or expenditure reductions) might reinforce unemployment and bankruptcies by increasing investment costs. Whereas all other European countries had the 'luxury' of choosing between the two (conflicting) priorities of controlling inflation or unemployment, the autonomy of the West German Bundesbank dictated, by dint of its statutory obligations, the priority of deflation (Bundesbank Law, para. 3). From this perspective 'a real alternative to a policy of stabilisation did not exist,' claims the 1974 Annual Report of the Bundesbank even though this involved some 'general economic costs' and 'individual sacrifices'.[117] The primacy of monetary stability had to be accepted as if the paramount economic crisis was that of inflation: the simultaneous appearance of additional crises of a cyclical, structural and demographic nature was not allowed to deflect the Federal Bank from its central duty.

The restrictive policies of the Central bank resumed in late 1972, after a brief respite, as a result of continued rises in domestic inflation. The Discount Rate was raised from 3 per cent in October 1972 to 7 per cent in June 1973 and the Lombard Rate from 4 per cent to 9 per cent, while minimum reserve levels were raised severely across the board.[118] Combined with the controversial exchange controls of 1972 and the introduction of flexible exchange rates in 1973 there was a staged process of deflation, beginning with a dramatically low increase in the money supply (M1) in 1973 of 2.6 per cent compared to 12.3 per cent in 1971 and 14.7 per cent in 1972. Bankruptcies rose by 25 per cent in 1973 and by nearly 50 per cent in 1974, while the rate of unemployment rose from 1.3 per cent in 1973 to 4.7 per cent in 1975. The oil-price rises of 1974 meant that the inflation targets of the Federal Bank were not met: prices rose faster in 1974 (by 7 per cent) and only slowed down in 1975 (6.0 per cent) and 1976 (4.5 per cent). In terms of economic growth, Federal Bank policy was pro-cyclical throughout 1974, compounding other recessionary effects of the national and international economy to create the severe drop of real GNP in 1975 of 1.9 per cent.

The high interest rates in 1973 and 1974 (see Fig. 5.5) also had an important negative influence on state finances and the state debt. The

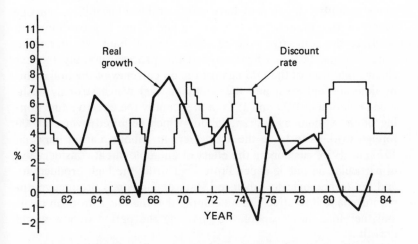

Fig. 5.5   Real growth of GNP and Federal Bank discount rate, 1960–85

Sources: Bundesbank *Monthly Bulletins*.

overall effort to consolidate state budgets in 1973, when the borrowing requirement of central, regional and particularly local government was reduced, not only functioned pro-cyclically by reducing
state investment (down 0.5 per cent in real terms) but availed little
since interest charges for 1973 amounted to nearly as much as the
borrowing requirement (DM10.2 billion to DM11.7 billion); rather
than helping to consolidate state budgets, the credit squeeze increased the pressure to extend the state debt merely to cover increased debt charges. This in turn increased the pressure on all the
spending authorities to limit expenditure, regardless of possible
anti-cyclical expenditure aims. Simply the current expenditure commitments in the recession year combined with the shortfall of revenue
and higher interest rates produced the sudden leap in the borrowing
requirement from DM24 billion in 1974 to DM64 billion in 1975.[119]

Despite some of these negative effects of deflation the development of the main indicators in the German Economy between 1973
and 1976 *compared favourably* with that of its European neighbours
and led one commentator to speak of an 'object lesson in economic
management'[120] Klasen, the Federal Bank president, claimed
the crucial role of having saved West Germany from 'English
conditions'[121] and Helmut Schmidt used the relative health of the economy in 1976 to fight the general election under the banner of 'Model
Germany'. In comparative terms the hard monetarist line on currency stability appeared to have considerable plausibility, but one
cannot ascribe the relative stabilisation and return to growth in 1976
solely to the restrictive policies of the central bank. Rather there
were external factors which assisted the process, notably the exchange rate rises of the DM against the oil currency of the dollar (hit
by domestic upheaval and the Vietnam war) which strongly cushioned inflation in 1974 and 1975, and secondly the effective functioning of the system of migrant labour which required over 500 000
foreign workers to leave the West German labour market between
1973 and 1976, cushioning the effect of unemployment considerably,
in particular on public expenditure.[122] Thirdly the high productivity
and the technologically advanced state of industry's productive apparatus made it relatively more competitive than its European rivals
and therefore more capable of surviving the period of low world
growth.

Even if one accepts the state's pride in the comparative stability of
the West German economy in 1976, there remained fundamental
economic problems (not to mention problems of democratic control

vis-à-vis the Federal Bank) which exercised the minds of many commentators through the period of Bundesbank control in the 1970s and the 1980s, which related to the theoretical assumptions of monetarist practice. These deserve brief scrutiny.

The Theoretical Assumptions of West German Monetarist Practice after 1973

Implicit in the view of there having been no 'real alternative to a policy of stabilisation'[123] in 1972 and 1973 is the *belief in the adequacy and effectiveness of the instruments of money supply control*. The main instruments deployed in the 1970s were:

(a) the interest rates charged on the discounting of bills of exchange (Discount Rate) and other securities (Lombard Rate);
(b) the proportion of bank assets to be deposited with the Central Bank (the Minimum Reserve Rates);
(c) open-market buying and selling of currencies and securities by the central bank; and
(d) the (occasional) obligation to deposit a given proportion of foreign loans with the central bank (Cash Deposit Duty).

By the correct manipulation of these instruments (particularly the first two), it is thought possible to be able to control the supply of money to the economy sufficient to sustain stable growth but also to control the price levels of the commodities produced – by matching 'money supply' to productive potential.

This hypothesis *assumes above all the responsiveness of users of credit finance to the instruments of control*. It has been argued that this assumption is severely flawed: that in fact the instruments of interest rates' and minimum reserves are '*blunt weapons*' which cannot and do not illicit a unitary response,[124] according to Kohler, credit demand is clearly influenced by the rate of interest but in relation to the expected return on investment[125] and the level of financial security enjoyed by the firm. Profit expectations vary widely from branch to branch, year to year, but very significantly according to the *timescale of investment* and the *size of the firm*. Kohler argues that long-term investment is not affected by short-term credit conditions but by research, development strategy and long-term capacity predictions.[126] Such strategies are however only plausible for larger enterprises; the higher profitability of larger firms (see above Table 5.8) makes investment more secure for both borrower and lender, and if domestic credit is not available the large firm has access to (often cheaper) foreign loans which the small business does not – the latter is dependent (if he is lucky) on expensive domestic credit. Not unexpectedly therefore 92 per cent of bankruptcies in 1973 were of firms employing less than 200 people,[127] while foreign credit to (larger) West German firms more than trebled in 1973 to DM17.5 billion.[128] Simply at this level restrictive monetary policies do not illicity a unitary response, rather they further accelerate concentration.[129] By thus failing to affect the investment plans of industry in boom periods[130] and the expenditure commitments of state budgets in periods of low revenue,[131] restrictive monetary policies achieve 'exactly the opposite of what is intended', compounding both inflation and more recently recession and unemployment.[132]

The assumptions about the adequacy of national instruments of monetary policy imply assumptions about the world economy which many argue are equally flawed. Before and especially after 1973 monetary policy pursued the double aim of securing the *internal and external* value of the currency, but with the tendency of national economies to develop unequally the pressure on external currency values may not correspond to the internal pressures. The increasingly volatile world capital markets reflect the differing conditions in individual national economies, such that a combination of varying interest rates, currency speculation and national budget deficits disallow the equilibrium which Friedmann and others assumed possible with flexible exchange rates.[133] The increasing mass of capital, which seeks not productive investment but mere credit interest income on European and other international capital markets[134] both subverts national monetary strategies and demonstrates the contradictory (non-unitary) nature of investment, as well as the virtual 'privatisation' of the international 'monetary order'.[135] To assume the benign influence of capital market speculators on exchange rates and interest rates[136] has been shown to be naive by the experience of the years after 1973, where exchange rate fluctuations caused confused and dysfunctional central bank responses.[137] In the case of West Germany the Central Bank repeated the pro-cyclical imposition of high interest rates in 1979 as in 1972–74, which effectively throttled the recovery and accelerated the growth of unemployment.[138] The 'stabilisation crisis' which the new Federal Bank president, Pöhl, denied in 1980[139] set in with a vengeance in 1981 and 1982.

The Political Implications of Central Bank Autonomy after 1973
Exchange rate floating increased the power of central banks and

correspondingly weakened the power of government in West Germany.[140] The central bankers of West Germany became for some 'a secondary government'[141] for others 'the real masters of the economy'.[142] *Electoral answerability however remained with the central government* which was the ostensible guardian of the economy, but yet objectively hamstrung by monetary constraints. And yet, apart from individual SPD representatives, there was very little public criticism of the Federal Bank by government representatives or others in the early years of its crucially new regime.[143] There were regular press reports of internal cabinet anger and concern about high interest rates, but significantly Helmut Schmidt waited until after his resignation in 1982 to make 'drastic' and 'urgent' warnings of the consequences of Federal Bank policy.[144] Earlier SPD plans to limit the power of the central bank through legislation were pushed aside in the face of the reality of the bank's increased power. The criticisms of economists and trade unionists concerning the dysfunctional role and the recessionary effect of central bank policy and of its 'blocking of government policy',[145] have in more recent times been diverted by references to the overiding role of American interest rates by German and other European central bankers. However, the problem of the effective subservience of elected governments to the unelected autonomous Federal Bank remains, particularly if the latter's policies weaken the economy and bring down governments.[146] The realisation that there was 'no place for Keynesianism',[147] let alone more rigorous modes of economic control, have raised severe doubts about the nature of West German democracy which supply theorists often reinforce. At a conference on economic policy in Mannheim in January 1983 Gerhard Fels, a former member of the SVR, recommended the dominance of the Federal Bank and monetary policy in economic policy making, while Otmar Issing, an economics professor from Würzburg, bemoaned the 'Damocles sword of the next elections' which hangs over the economic policy makers.[148] It would seem vital that in a period of economic and social upheaval, as at present, the historically justified qualms about the misuse of central bank power by particular central governments should be forgotten in the face of the potentially greater dangers of central bank autonomy, and that the Federal Bank should be brought into line with all other West European central banks and submitted to the control of elected federal authorities.

State Expenditure and the State Debt

The factors determining the 1975 recession outlined above directly influenced the real and perceived needs for state expenditure. However both the failure to consolidate the state debt during the super-cycle (1967–75) and the restrictive policies of the Federal Bank were seen to impinge upon the fiscal policy of all authorities during the stagflationary crisis. The Federal Economics Minister, Friderichs (FDP), in accepting the monetarist diagnosis of the crisis, predetermined the shape of central government policy: a recipe of tight budgets and wage restraint, combined with indirect aid to industrial investors. He allowed some room for an anti-cyclical growth stimulus in 1974/75 but little scope to tackle the economy's structural problems.

The general expenditure pattern from 1974 to 1980 shows a belated attempt to halt the recessionary decline between 1973 and 1975 with two years of expanded budgets (1974 and 1975), after the budget cuts of 1973, but accompanied by and partly neutralised by restrictive monetary policies until mid-1975. After the consolidation of state budgets in 1976 expenditure growth reverted to a fundamentally pro-cyclical path (see Fig. 5.6), hastening the 1981/82 recession.

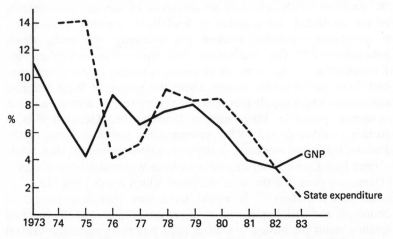

Fig. 5.6   State expenditure and nominal GNP growth 1973–83

Concealed within this general development were significant *shifts in expenditure away from state investment towards direct and indirect subsidies and towards debt servicing* (See Table 5.20). State investment fell from 16.4 per cent of state expenditure (without the social insurance funds) in 1970 (17.3 per cent of national Net Investments) to 10.2 per cent in 1977 (15.2 per cent of Net Investments) with a slight interruption in the decline in 1974. State building investment fell consistently as a proportion of total expenditure, from 11.8 per cent in 1973 to 9.0 per cent in 1977 and 7.6 per cent in 1982. Interest charges on the other hand rose from DM10.5 billion in 1973 (3.8 per cent of total expenditure) to DM20.9 billion in 1977 (5.2 per cent) and to DM45.0 billion in 1982 (7.9 per cent). While direct subsidies rose roughly in proportion with the total budget, indirect subsidies shot up to unprecedentedly high levels.

These shifts in expenditure reflect the real abandonment of Keynesian fiscal management, which was signalled in the emergency budgets after 1974. The central government's *Programme for Employment and Growth with Stability* (12 December 1974) contained only DM1.13 billion worth of additional building investment to add to the regional programmes of the previous September of DM50 million. The remainder of the package contained wage cost subsidies to employers of DM500 million, mobility assistance to unemployed workers of 100 million and most importantly a 7.5 per cent subsidy for private investments valid until the end of June 1975. In addition tax allowances were extended to some second homes. Friderich's budget ran counter to proposals by the Trade Unions and some SPD ministers and the building industry for additional direct public investments of up to DM10 billion[149] to reduce unemployment (particularly in the building sector), and relied largely on the goodwill of employers to take on additional labour. Accordingly the *investment subsidy was general, it was not limited to specific weaker sectors, nor by conditions for expanding the workforce*,[150] with the result that it was pocketed by those firms 'who would have invested even without government assistance'[151] and had little apparent effect on the trend of unemployment and short-time working in 1975. Statistics from the engineering sector show that the investment subsidy produced a surge of orders only in June 1975 after two years of consistent decline,[152] in time to qualify for state help but obviously avoiding the higher interest rates of early 1975. The investment subsidy cost some DM8 billion but achieved little;[153] the real decline in investments continued (1974: −8.1 per cent, 1975: −7.8 per cent). More was achieved in the short term by the introduction of tax and child benefit measures on 1 January 1975 which cost the public purse DM18 billion in the first year. However, overall demand in the economy stagnated through 1975, forcing the central, regional and local governments to

Table 5.20   State finances 1973–83

	1973	1974	1975	1976	1977	1978	1979	1980	1981	1982	1983
GNP (Nominal) in DM billion	918.6	987.1	1031.8	1123.0	1198.5	1290.0	1395.3	1485.7	1545.2	1599.1	1671.6
per cent change p.a.	+7.4	+7.4	+4.3	+8.8	+6.7	+7.6	+8.1	+6.4	+4.0	+3.5	+4.5
State expenditure (all authorities exc. soc. ins.)	277.6	316.5	361.5	376.7	396.3	433.1	469.9	510.1	542.9	563.1	571.5
per cent change p.a.		+14.0	+14.2	+4.2	+5.2	+9.2	+8.4	+8.5	+6.4	+3.7	+1.4
Bund expenditure in DM billion	125.6	136.4	160.0	166.4	174.1	190.8	205.1	217.6	234.9	246.6	248.3
per cent change p.a.	+12.3	+8.5	+17.3	+4.0	+4.6	+9.5	+7.5	+6.0	+7.9	+4.9	+0.6
Länder expenditure DM billion	115.8	134.0	146.3	154.4	161.6	176.5	191.8	208.6	216.6	224.2	227.6
per cent change p.a.		+15.7	+9.1	+5.5	+4.6	+9.2	+8.6	+8.7	+3.8	+3.5	+1.5
Local Auth. Expenditure in DM billion	84.0	97.1	101.2	100.4	108.4	118.2	130.4	145.6	152.1	153.1	151.4
per cent change p.a.		+15.5	+4.2	-0.8	+8.0	+9.0	+10.3	+11.6	+4.4	+0.6	-1.1
State expenditure on investments (Bill)		47.7	47.7	45.8	45.0	49.4	55.3	62.2	59.2	54.2	50.4
as per cent of total expend.		15%	13%	12%	11%	11%	11%	12%	11%	9.6%	8.8%
on Construction (Bill)	32.9	36.5	38.6	37.4	35.8	39.0	43.3	48.9	46.8	43.1	

as per cent of total expend. on Interest (Bill)	11.8%	11.5%	10.6%	9.9%	9.0%	9.0%	9.2%	9.6%	8.6%	7.6%	
	10.5	12.7	14.8	18.1	20.9	22.0	25.0	29.6	36.7	45.0	51.5
as per cent of total expend. on Subsidies (Bill)	3.8%	4.0%	4.1%	4.8%	5.2%	5.0%	5.3%	5.8%	6.7%	7.9%	9.0%
	14.9	14.8	15.2	16.6	19.2	23.8	24.8	23.7			
as per cent of total expend.	5.3%	4.6%	4.2%	4.4%	4.8%	5.4%	5.2%	4.6%			
Bund Expenditure											
on Investment (Bill)	5.3	7.2	7.9	7.1	7.4	7.8	8.1	8.3	7.4	7.1	
on Construction (Bill)		5.7	6.0	5.5	5.8	6.2	6.6	6.4	5.7		
on Interest (Bill)	3.6	4.8	5.8	7.4	9.0	10.0	11.5	14.4	18.6		
Länder Expenditure											
on Investment (Bill)	5.2	8.6	8.6	8.1	8.3	8.7	9.3	10.5	10.0	9.9	9.6
on Construction (Bill)		6.1	6.3	5.9	6.1	6.4	6.7	7.2	6.9		
on Interest (Bill)	2.7	3.1	3.8	5.2	6.3	6.8	7.9	8.9	10.8		
Local Authorities' Expenditure											
on Investment (Bill)	22.3	31.9	31.2	30.6	29.3	32.9	37.9	43.4	41.8	37.2	33.7
on Construction		24.5	24.1	23.4	21.7	24.4	27.9	31.2	30.3		
on Interest	4.2	4.8	5.2	5.5	5.6	5.2	5.6	6.3	7.3		

Source: Statistisches Jahrbuch, Bundesbank Monthly Reports, own calculations.

adopt an emergency building programme in August 1975 which amounted to some DM5.8 billion. Again, however, this was followed by the Budget Restructuring Law of September 1975 which raised unemployment contributions from 2 per cent to 3 per cent (of gross income) and made substantial cuts in training programmes, savings assistance and student finance. The building programme itself had a marginal direct effect and could not prevent a further decline in building activity in 1976.[154]

The year 1976 saw a return to real GNP growth but no return to full employment (unemployment hovered around the million mark until 1979). Attempts by SPD ministers to introduce substantial job creation measures were watered down to a DM300 million programme to combat youth unemployment (January 1976) and DM430 million programme to promote the mobility of the unemployed (November 1976). On the other hand Friderich's controversial tax relief measures for industry, resisted by Finance Minister Apel, were introduced bit by bit: in April 1976 *retrospective relief on profit income* was introduced allowing the commercial losses of one year to be set against the profits of the following year; in January 1977 the duplicate taxation of corporation tax and income tax was abolished and in January 1978 degressive depreciation was extended, wealth tax rates were lowered and the allowances for several commercial taxes were raised.[155] Meanwhile the tax burden for the mass of wage and salary earners increased, despite the 1977 tax reforms, largely through 'cold progression' (of nominal earnings into higher tax brackets). The much vaunted 'Programme for Future Investments' of 1977 which amounted to over DM20 billion in largely infrastructural investments came on stream between 1978 and 1980 when there was general growth in the economy and specifically in the building sector, such that not only did it function *pro-cyclically* but also '*practically three quarters of the additional investment expenditure evaporated in price rises*'.[156]

The results of Friderich's economic management where a redistribution of income burdens from the company sector to private households, increasing state commitments which could only be financed by an increasing state debt and a continuing crisis of structural unemployment, bankruptcies and monopolisation. The inequitable development of income burdens is quite evident from Table 5.21.

The net burden on private households was nearly trebled from 1970 to 1980 (DM59.6 billion to DM167.8 billion) whereas the net relief

Table 5.21   Net burden on private sector (DM billion), 1970–80

Year	Private households Burden (direct taxation and transfer payments)	Relief (social payments other transfer payments)	Balance	Businesses Burden (direct taxation wealth & other transfers)	Relief (subsidies wealth and other transfer payments)	Balance
1970	144.0	84.4	+ 59.6	15.1	19.1	− 4.0
1971	169.2	96.2	+ 73.0	14.6	20.0	− 5.4
1972	189.7	109.7	+ 80.0	15.4	23.6	− 8.2
1973	230.9	121.6	+ 109.3	19.5	28.2	− 8.7
1974	258.3	139.9	+ 118.4	20.2	30.8	− 10.6
1975	268.3	173.1	+ 95.2	19.4	31.1	− 11.7
1976	305.0	185.0	+ 120.0	24.1	37.5	− 13.4
1977	331.9	199.1	+ 132.8	30.1	41.1	− 11.0
1978	346.8	208.1	+ 138.7	31.1	47.3	− 16.2
1979	367.6	218.7	+ 148.9	34.2	50.9	− 16.7
1980	399.0	231.2	+ 167.8	33.2	51.2	− 18.0

Source: Glastetter et al., *Die wirtschaftliche Entwicklung in der Bundesrepublik Deutschland 1950–1980* (Frankfurt, 1983).

for businesses more than quadrupled from DM4–18 billion. The gross income burden on businesses fell in the same period as a proportion of the gross income burden on private households from 10.4 per cent to 8.3 per cent.

Even so the increased taxation burden on wage and salary earners was not enough to reverse the widening deficit in state budgets:

Table 5.22   The public debt, 1950–80 (DM billion)

	Total	Bund	Länder	Local authorities
1950	20.6	7.3	12.8	0.5
1960	52.8	17.9	15.5	4.7
1965	83.7	33.7	17.4	25.8
1970	125.9	49.7	27.8	40.3
1973	167.0	61.4	39.5	59.9
1975	256.4	108.5	67.0	74.4
1976	296.7	128.4	81.8	79.8
1977	328.5	150.2	89.6	83.3
1978	371.6	177.5	102.1	87.5
1979	413.9	202.6	115.9	90.4
1980	435.3	232.3	137.8	95.2

Source: Bundesbank *Monthly Reports*.

Whereas in 1970 78.5 per cent of state expenditure (without social insurance) was covered by taxation, this fell to 67 per cent in 1975 and averaged about 72 per cent in the period of 'recovery' 1976–80. In absolute terms the net borrowing requirement of the three levels of government remained at very high levels throughout the period between the two recessions (1975, 1981/82).

Table 5.23   Net borrowing requirement of the State (without social insurance), 1970–80

	1970	1975	1976	1977	1978	1979	1980
Borrowing requirement (DM billion)	7.9	64.0	40.3	31.8	43.1	48.4	

Source: Bundesbank *Monthly Reports*.

The ratio of state debt to gross national product rose from 18.5 per cent in 1970 to 24.8 per cent in 1975 and to 37.0 per cent in 1980, which provoked increasing comment from economists. At the centre of the debate was the fundamental dilemma of stagflation: whether the state should stimulate growth and employment or consolidate its budgets and reduce the dangers of inflation. In contrast to the consensus of the mid-1960s the academic and political establishment was split between fiscalists (e.g. the DIW, WSI and the SPD) and monetarists (e.g., the SVR, Bundesbank, HWWA, Ifo, WWI, RWI, and both FDP and CDU/CSU), favouring expansionism and consolidation respectively.

The arguments of the 'consolidation'-camp[157] can be reduced to the following assertions:

(a) the politico-economic crisis of stagnating rates of growth and rising state deficits was 'pre-programmed' by excessive state expenditure in the period 1969 to 1972;

(b) the increasing borrowing requirement of the state creates 'crowding-out' effects on the capital market: by absorbing an increasing proportion of GNP (*qua* state quota) and specifically of the nation's liquid capital assets, the state increases credit demand to a degree which raises credit discount rates and squeezes out potential private investment, thereby inhibiting growth;[158]

(c) tax increases are unacceptable, therefore the only way out of the debt crisis is to make cuts in the budget provisions for social expenditure, state personnel and state subsidies; this will moderate general expectations of limitless social provisions and income rises, liberate resources for private investment and restore the confidence of private investors.[159]

The reflation camp, on the other hand, denied the assumed causal links between state debt/state quota and stagflation and unemployment:

(a) the 'opposite conclusion is more convincing' – that 'rather, since 1975 the state accepted less deficits than would have been appropriate to both trade cycle and growth';[160] the reductions in planned state budgets in 1976 (of some DM9.5 billion) had in fact cost some 220 000 jobs;[161]

(b) there is no evidence of significant 'crowding-out' effects; either in general terms of potential credit-based private investment being squeezed out,[162] or of there being a significant interest rate effect from increased state absorption of liquidity,[163]

(c)   since there was 'no realistic alternative to the state debt policies',[164] or more specifically since state investment 'evokes [sic] private investment' by signalling the desire to stabilise demand,[165] there were (according to the DIW) also weighty arguments for a short-term *increase* in state expenditure (from 1978 to 1985) of DM130 billion, financed by increased indebtedness, but creating directly and through various multiplicator effects both a considerable reduction in unemployment and an actual reduction in the planned state debt by 1985.[166]

Each set of arguments proceeded from insubstantiable assumptions of the expected indirect growth effects of respective policies. In terms of the logic of the increasing problems of capital reproduction, and hence the increasing fire-brigade duties of the state, the 'reflation' arguments appear more plausible, the arguments of state withdrawal more unrealistic and dangerous to the maintenance of employment. It is important here, however, to note that, despite an acceleration of net borrowing in 1977/78 the thrust of social–liberal fiscal policy was towards minimising expenditure and relying on export-led, supply-induced growth. It is, therefore, highly misleading to talk of additional expenditure by state authorities between 1974 and 1979 of DM160 billion 'for the purpose of stimulating conjunctural growth' and equivalent to a *7 per cent annual increase in state budgets.*[167] *Total* expenditure by the state (excluding social insurance) only rose by DM153 billion in the six years 1974 to 1979, a very high proportion of which was due not to crisis management plans but to recurrent commitments in defence, education, transport, health and debt servicing, which had increased due to inflation, population trends, international agreements and not the least high interest rates. If one includes the 1977 medium-term 'Programme for Future Investments' of DM16 billion, it is still only reasonable to talk about a total of DM32.2 billion pinpointed for additional expenditure towards economic growth in the whole period – i.e. DM5.37 billion per annum in nominal terms,[168] compared to an average interest bill of DM18.9 billion over the same period. Thus, *far from being profligate*, as conservative critics like Biedenkopf, Miegel, the SVR and the Bundesbank directors would have us believe, *the state authorities forewent any significant anti-cyclical measures and effectively endeavoured too eagerly to implement the restrictive policies demanded of them by their critics*, with predictable negative effects for *state revenue* and hence for the state debt: consolidation can be seen as having achieved indirectly the opposite of its intended effects, therefore, namely to have increased budget deficits and thereby the borrowing requirement.[169]

GROWTH AND UNEMPLOYMENT, 1976–80

The Primary Determinants of Growth

West Germany's GNP grew in real terms by 12.7 per cent between 1976 and 1980 or by 2.5 per cent per annum. The working population rose by some 700 000 from 25.6 million to 26.3 million. Wage and salaried employment rose from 21 939 000 in 1976 to 22 960 000 in 1980; unemployment fell by only 161 000 in the same period from 1 060 000 to 889 000, the unemployment rate from 4.6 per cent to 3.8 per cent. In 1980 industrial production was 10.2 per cent higher in real terms than in 1976 (consumer goods production up 6.5 per cent, investment goods up 12.9 per cent). Investments rose by an average of 5.4 per cent in real terms per annum, private consumption by a mere 2.4 per cent per annum, and state consumption by only 2.8 per cent p.a.[170] The most significant indicators here relate to investments, growth and jobs and these suggest that, despite a rising investment quota (Investments: GNP = 1976: 20.4, 1980: 23.0), the marginal gains in national production were not sufficient to absorb the workers shed by declining industries and the additional numbers of school leavers who entered the labour market from 1976 onwards. 27 per cent more investments (in real terms) had produced an increase of 12.7 per cent in GNP and only 2.8 per cent in the working population.

This trend reflected the rationalisation of the domestic productive apparatus which was undertaken to raise labour productivity and to *reduce both labour costs and the need for labour*, but which also raised the marginal capital coefficient. The need for *extensive* investment (which could have created more jobs) was in part neutralised by the sluggish improvement in capacity utilisation after 1976 which, according to the DIW, had not been restored to 'normal' levels even by 1979.[171]

Thus even in the best year of the 1975–81 cycle (1979) the

Table 5.24   Employment in West Germany, 1975–81

	1975	1976	1977	1978	1979	1980	1981
Working population (1000s)	25 810	25 591	25 547	25 699	26 039	26 302	26 101
Dependent workers	22 014	21 939	22 029	22 264	22 659	22 986	22 846
(blue-collar)	11 029	10 824	10 813	10 910	11 011	11 042	10 817
(white-collar)	8 784	8 862	8 936	9 067	9 334	9 614	9 681
(Civil Servants)	2 201	2 253	2 280	2 287	2 314	2 330	2 348
Unemployment (1000s)	1 074	1 060	1 029	992	876	888	1 271
Vacancies (1000s)	236	234	231	245	304	308	207
Short-time workers (1000s)	773	277	231	190	87	137	346

Source: Statistisches Jahrbuch.

Table 5.25   Age structure of the unemployed, 1979 and 1983

	1979	Male	Female	1983	Male	Female
U–20	9.3	7.2	10.9	9.5	8.3	10.9
20–25	16.8	14.1	18.8	19.7	18.3	21.3
25–30	14.8	12.2	16.7	15.6	14.2	17.1
30–35	9.8	9.4	10.1	11.0	11.5	11.7
35–40	9.1	9.8	8.7	8.9	9.6	8.2
40–45	8.4	9.4	7.6	8.9	9.7	8.0
45–50	7.1	8.2	6.2	8.0	8.7	7.3
50–55	8.0	8.6	7.6	6.7	7.1	6.3
55–60	12.6	14.3	11.4	8.4	9.0	7.6
60–65	4.1	6.7	2.1	2.6	3.6	1.5

Source: *Statistisches Jahrbuch.*

number of unemployed was nearly three times higher than the number of vacancies (see Table 4.49).

The effect of this *structural unemployment* was particularly noticeable on the younger age groups within the working population. The age structure of the unemployed population in 1979 showed that 40.9 per cent of all unemployed were in the age groups under 30 (46.4 per cent of all unemployed women were within this range); this unequal distribution of unemployment had worsened by 1983, when 44.8 per cent of all unemployed were 30 or under (49.3 per cent of all unemployed women) – see Table 5.25

If one breaks down the development of employment by sector and compares this with the sectoral distribution of national wealth creation, a number of important features of this period become apparent. Firstly the *importance of the tertiary (service) sector both as an employer and as a creator of wealth increases sharply throughout the period*, while the relative importance of the primary and secondary sectors declines. There is still however a marked difference between the level of employment and the level of wealth creation in each sector. In 1976 the primary sector still employed 6.5 per cent of the working population but contributed only 3.3 per cent to national wealth; equally the tertiary sector employed 48.6 per cent of the working population in 1976 but contributed only 41.8 per cent to national wealth. On the other hand the secondary sector (industry, small manufacturing) contributed 55 per cent of additional national wealth but maintained only 44.7 per cent of the working population. These ratios altered in the five years 1976 to 1980 in favour of the

Table 5.26   Sectoral distribution of the working population, 1975–83

	1975	1976	1977	1978	1979	1980	1981	1982	1983
Primary									
sector (1000s)	1 773	1 682	1 589	1 536	1 479	1 430	1 405	1 381	1 371
(per cent of total)	(6.8)	(6.5)	(6.2)	(5.9)	(5.6)	(5.4)	(5.4)	(5.4)	(5.4)
Secondary									
sector (1000s)	11 686	11 459	11 395	11 421	11 523	11 633	11 369	10 950	10 567
(per cent of total)	(45.2)	(44.7)	(44.6)	(44.4)	(44.3)	(44.2)	(43.5)	(42.7)	(41.9)
Tertiary									
sector (1000s)	12 351	12 450	12 563	12 742	13 007	12 233	13 327	13 301	13 249
(per cent of total)	(47.8)	(48.6)	(49.1)	(49.5)	(49.9)	(50.3)	(51.0)	(51.8)	(52.5)

Source: *Statistisches Jahrbuch*.

Table 5.27   Sectoral production structure, 1975–83

		(Contribution to GDP in per cent)								
	1970	1975	1976	1977	1978	1979	1980	1981	1982	1983
Primary	3.8	3.4	3.3	3.1	3.0	2.6	2.5	2.5	2.7	2.4
Secondary	58.2	54.4	55.0	52.9	52.5	52.7	52.1	51.2	49.6	49.3
Tertiary	38.0	41.8	41.8	43.9	44.4	44.7	45.2	46.2	47.6	48.2

Source: *Statistisches Jahrbuch*.

tertiary sector, but although the latter increased its share of wealth creation by 8.1 per cent from 41.8 per cent to 45.2 per cent it only increased its share of the working population by 3.5 per cent (from 48.6 per cent to 50.3 per cent). Thus despite (or because of) being more labour intensive than the secondary sector, the tertiary sector is subject to the same pressures to increase labour productivity and hence cannot absorb labour at anything like the rate at which it creates additional wealth. If one looks beyond 1980 it is clear that *the expansion of employment in the service sector is beginning to stagnate* (see Table 5.28); after an increase of 976 000 jobs from 1975 to 1981 the working population in the service sector begins to decline along with the other sectors, both in the year of recession 1982 and in the year of recovery 1983, reflecting in part the effect of automation on clerical and other work. This has clearly compounded the problem of structural unemployment in the early 1980s.

Table 5.28   Index of gross wealth creation (in prices of 1970, 1970 = 100), 1970–80

	1970	1975	1976	1977	1978	1979	1980
All Industry	100	105	111	114	116	122	123
Energy	100	115	120	121	127	133	134
Motor vehicles	100	103	119	128	133	–	–
Building	100	100	103	104	107	114	119
Electro-technical	100	123	132	145	144	–	–
Chemicals	100	113	134	137	140	–	–
Service sector	100	124	130	136	143	150	156
Banking	100	128	136	147	156	168	174
Insurance	100	131	137	140	142	151	157
Health	100	144	149	151	154	159	–

Sources: *Statistisches Jahrbuch der Bundesrepublik* (1983); own calculations.

The primary determinants of growth between 1976 and 1980 were an expansion of domestic demand for particular services (banking, insurance, publishing, health) and of general demand for particular industrial products, notably investment goods and capital goods.

Within the increased general demand for industrial goods, it was above all the *expansion of exports* that helped to sustain the modest rates of growth in the period. Whereas GNP only increased by 12.7 per cent in real terms from 1976 to 1980, exports grew by 17.6 per cent increasing their share of GNP from 27.8 per cent (1976) to 29.0 per cent (1980).[172] The accelerated growth of the export quota (it was only 22.6 per cent in 1970) was complemented by a *significant increase in capital exports*. The value of West German direct investments abroad rose from DM48.3 billion in 1976 to DM84.3 billion in 1980 or by 63 per cent in real terms, and whereas in 1976 West Germany's holdings of foreign assets amounted to only 61.3 per cent of foreign holdings in West Germany, by 1981 this ratio had altered to 103.7 per cent.

The distribution of these investments grew increasingly unequal in regional terms. The increasing concentration of West German direct investments in developed industrial countries – in particular in the USA – indicates the desire to maintain and increase secure levels of profit within relatively stable markets, with investment operations either matching export operations or linked geographically to the processing of localised materials, rather than the simple desire to

Table 5.29   West German direct investments abroad, 1955–81
(Total Value in DM million)

1955	421	1964	7,205	1973	32,935
1956	831	1965	8,317	1974	36,765
1957	1,349	1966	9,995	1975	41,982
1958	1,859	1967	12,057	1976	48,377
1959	2,422	1968	14,349	1977	52,120
1960	3,162	1969	17,617	1978	60,085
1961	3,843	1970	21,113	1979	69,537
1962	4,956	1971	23,781	1980	84,364
1963	6,071	1972	26,597	1981	101,152[a]

[a]provisional
Source: *Statistisches Jahrbuch* (1984).

Table 5.30   Regional distribution of direct investments, 1976 and 1980

	1976 *(per cent)*	1980 *(per cent)*
Western industrialised countries	74.6	77.2
USA	(13.6)	(21.6)
Developing countries	15.9	15.0
Africa	(1.5)	(1.1)
Latin America	(12.6)	(11.8)
OPEC countries	3.8	2.6
Others	5.7	5.2
Total	100.00	100.00

Source: *Statistisches Jahrbuch*.

avoid high domestic wage rates. The increasing neglect of the poorest developing countries (e.g. in Africa, which could offer very low wage rates) in favour of the emerging countries in South America and the Far East as locations for invesment, reflects the relative and absolute impoverishment of these regions after the two oil 'shocks' of 1974 and 1979 and their (partly related) political instability.[173]

West German direct investment is concentrated in a few sectors, led by holdings in general trading companies (19.6 per cent of all holdings in 1980), the chemical industry (17.2 per cent), engineering (11.8 per cent) and the electro-technical sector (6.9 per cent) – the four sectors thus making up over 55 per cent of all foreign holdings.

Another important reason for the faster growth of direct invest-

Table 5.31   External value of DM and balance of trade and payments
(DM billion), 1972–84

(1972 = 100)	Against $	Against 14 currencies	Real value against 14 currencies[a]	Balance of trade	Balance of payments
1972	100	100	100	+ 20.2	+ 2.7
1973	121.7	110.4	109.2	+ 32.9	+ 12.3
1974	124.7	116.9	108.5	+ 50.8	+ 26.5
1975	131.3	118.6	103.5	+ 37.2	+ 9.9
1976	128.1	125.6	104.0	+ 34.4	+ 9.9
1977	138.9	134.6	105.5	+ 38.4	+ 9.4
1978	160.7	140.7	105.9	+ 41.2	+ 18.1
1979	175.9	147.8	106.5	+ 22.4	− 11.0
1980	177.6	148.2	100.4	+ 8.9	− 28.6
1981	143.1	140.2	91.3	+ 27.7	− 13.1
1982	132.9	147.3	93.0	+ 51.2	+ 8.6
1983	126.5	151.9	93.1	+ 42.0	+ 10.3
1984	113.6	149.8	88.9	+ 53.9	+ 17.8

[a]Takes into account respective rates of inflation in the fourteen countries
Source: Bundesbank *Monthly Report* (Apr. 1985).

ments compared to exports in the period 1976–80 – indeed throughout the 1970s – was the *gradual appreciation of the Deutschmark against most other currencies* and particularly against the US Dollar, which, despite the higher domestic inflation rates of competitors, still rendered German goods and services internationally less competitive on price.

The trade balance was clearly affected by the two big oil price increases but trade volume was high enough to maintain a consistent surplus. The deficit on invisibles,[174] however, increased from DM16.9 billion in 1972 to DM33.6 billion in 1979 and DM37.4 billion in 1980, creating a three year payments deficit from 1979–81 and reflecting the combined effect of lower trade surpluses and the exchange rate peak in 1979 and 1980.

In summary the relative international performance of the West German economy between 1976 and 1980 was strong, but the persistance of high structural unemployment, the lower marginal gains of domestic investment and the extreme fluctuations of world commodity prices and exchange rates made the economy more susceptible to structural and cyclical crises. This becomes increasingly evident in the early 1980s with the acceleration of export dependency (see below).

State Reform Politics

It would be incorrect to claim that the social–liberal coalition completely retreated from its reform programme in the late 1970s, but it is clear that it was under increasing pressure from industry and opposition to reduce the financial burden of social provisions and to minimise the effect of industrial relations reforms. The reform of child benefit (1975), Youth Labour (1976), Pensions (1978) and Maternity Leave (1979) were only possible on the basis of higher absolute and relative contributions by the working population to both tax revenue and social insurance funds. Judged in terms of the net per capita distribution of income the late 1970s showed a significant fall in the relative share of the wage and salary dependent in national income and an increase in the share of owners of capital,[175] a trend which clearly ran counter to social-liberal promises, even though Friderichs and later Lambsdorff (both FDP) consistently asserted their position of increasing business income as a means of recovery.

One of the other main platforms of the social–liberal cabinet in 1972 was the implementation of *general parity co-determination* in West German industry and commerce to match the system in operation in the Coal and Steel industry since 1951. The passage of the 'Codetermination Law' of 1976 was a significant indicator or the impotence of the Social Democratic Party within the coalition. The initial draft of 1974 envisaged parity representation for the workforce on the supervisory boards of most companies with a payroll of more than 2000, similar to the 51 Law but not including a neutral arbitrator for situations of stalemate. During the next two years, after a vigorous campaign of opposition from the business community, the FDP pushed through two significant modifications of the original draft: the representation of the workforce was split into four categories, including senior managers, each of which would be guaranteed a seat on the board, regardless of voting support, and in the unlikely event of a stalemate (given the self-interest of senior managers and their answerability to the shareholders) the leader of the shareholders' representatives would have a casting vote: *formal parity of numbers was transformed into an actual guaranteed majority for the representatives of capital.*[176] Despite this elimination of real parity and the various other means of limiting the power of worker representatives, the 1976 law was the subject of an appeal to the Federal Constitutional Court by employers' organisations in 1977 which, though it was rejected, gave many people the impression that the law was a significant advance for the interests of labour, which it quite clearly was not. There is no evidence to demonstrate that the commercial operations, investment or rationalisation decisions of capital have been hampered by the existence of the new Co-determination Law. Structural unemployment has increased, the distribution of net per capita income has grown less fair and more recently the 35-hour week issue has been conducted not through supervisory board discussions but through strike action by key unions.

RECESSION AND MASS UNEMPLOYMENT, 1980–83

West Germany's third and worst recession began in 1981 with a fall of 0.3 per cent in real GNP and accelerated in 1982 with a fall of 1.1 per cent. It was signalled by the general decline from the previous peak of +4 per cent in 1979 to +1.8 per cent in 1980, by the severe sectoral setback for the car industry in 1980 after a 5-year boom and by a slight rise in unemployment and bankruptcies in the same year. In general, however, the recession was not expected and certainly not in such a severe form. The five economics institutes in their Spring Report of 1980,[177] the Federal Bank ('we are not heading for a stabilisation crisis'[178]) and even the SVR in its 1980 annual report, expected stagnation at worst and some growth at best. However the worst forecasts were exceeded with a rise of nearly 400 000 in the level of registered unemployed in 1981 and a further 561 000 in 1982, along with a rise of over 460 000 in those on short time. The figures would have been worse but for the loss of some 240 000 migrant workers. On the other hand the level of employment dropped by only 600 000 between 1980 and 1982 to 22.3 million, compared to the 900 000 fall in 1975; this is evidence for the increased number of school leavers swelling the unemployment figures (1975: 1.07 million or 4.7 per cent, 1982: 1.83 million or 7.5 per cent).

Cyclically-determined unemployment was thus compounded by demographic factors in 1981 and 1982, which then, together with structural economic factors, continued to force unemployment levels up even in the recovery years 1983/84/85.

What is just as significant and perhaps more striking about the 1981/82 recession is the dramatic increase in bankruptcies and

Table 5.32   Comparison of the labour market in the two recessions
1975 and 1981/82

	Employed popu-lation (1000s)	Migrant workers (1000s)	Unemployed (1000s)	Rate of unemployment (per cent)
1973	22 906	2 459	273	1.2
1974	22 640	2 328	582	2.6
1975	22 014	2 061	1 074	4.7
1980	22 986	2 018	889	3.8
1981	22 846	1 912	1 272	5.5
1982	22 395	1 787	1 833	7.5
1983	21 962	1 694	2 258	9.1
1984	21 870	1 593	2 266	10.2
1985	(Feb.)		2 611	10.5

Source: Bundesbank *Monthly Reports*: various.

insolvencies; excluding personal bankruptcies the number was some
85 per cent higher than the peak of 1975 and continued to rise through
1983 and 1984.[179] The figure of over 20 000 commercial bankruptcies
in the two years of recession reflects very clearly the particular crisis
of reproduction with its increasing pressure on the general rate of
profit and on the liquidity of individual (especially small) firms.

The trading slump was reflected in the decline in the *rate of
utilisation* (1981: 79; 1982: 75, according to Ifo and the OECD) and in
gross investments. The latter rose in real terms by only 0.5 per cent in
1980 and fell sharply by 9.0 per cent in 1981 and 3.4 per cent in 1982.
What investments were implemented served primarily for rationalisation and replacement and not for an extension of capacity.[180] Industry was particularly hard hit, such that its share of GDP fell from 43.1
per cent in 1980 to 41.5 per cent in 1982, with real falls in the value
creation of many industrial sectors, including textiles, refineries,
iron, special steels and even the electro-technical and chemical industries. The decline of industrial production was eased considerably by
a continued real rise in exports (1980: +5.5 per cent, 1981: +8.7 per
cent, 1982: +3.7 per cent).[181]

The Official Diagnoses of the Crisis

The origins of the 1981/82 crisis and the now ongoing crisis of mass
unemployment are the subject of considerable controversy. One

common feature of all analyses is the second wave of oil price rises starting in 1979 which, like the first wave in 1974, took some time before it worked its way through the system. There is general agreement that the need to absorb heavy increases in primary energy costs placed a considerable burden on all western economies. Not only were there inflationary pressures to absorb, but also the effects of the re-distribution of global wealth. In 1980 already the wealth transfer from West Germany to the oil-producing countries was equivalent to DM30 billion,[182] or 2 per cent of GNP. The development of the balance of payments from a deficit of DM28.6 billion in 1980 and DM13.1 billion in 1981 to a modest surplus of DM8.6 billion in 1982 reflects both this effect and the time-lag between the initial capital transfers and their return in the form of export orders.[183]

It is significant that once again 'official' opinion (represented by the SVR, the Federal Bank, the Academic Sub-Committee of the Economics Ministry and others) dealt with the oil-price rises as an isolated external factor and not as one feature of a general structural crisis of monopolisation (see above, p. 208). In the first paragraph of its 1974 report the SVR had already implied that OPEC contravened rules which everyone else kept to, [184] in all subsequent references, oil prices are thus abstracted from the market and accepted fatalistically as an external factor beyond national control. On the other hand this conveniently allows the exculpation of the market both practically and theoretically, since any failures can be blamed on such 'external' factors. It also allows the reiteration of other reasons for the cumulative crises which are also external to capitalism but far more accessible to remedial action within the national economy: inflexible wages and excessive state expenditure.

> More investments, through which alone new jobs and new sources of income can be created, presuppose the confidence in firms that neither excessive state revenues or expenditure, nor wages will produce unexpectedly high cost burdens which will render their investment calculations futile.[185]

However, since the 'excessive' state expenditure is located primarily in the state consumption fund, i.e. in its personnel costs (salaries, pensions and an increasing workforce), the central target is essentially the 'unfair' distribution of national income in favour of labour and the 'disadvantage' of capital, the high quota of private consumption and the low investment quota. Thus it is wage levels that remain at the centre of all considerations of employment policy.[186]

The attack on wage costs has become more differentiated since the first round of crisis management in 1967. On the one hand the anti-inflationary position of recommending 'cost-neutral' or 'inflation-neutral' wage settlements has been modified to a recommendation of a 'wage policy which is appropriate to employment' or 'a remuneration which is close to market conditions';[187] this new position implies the direct responsibility of trade unions for unemployment, by dint of 'inflexible' 'unitary' wage agreements,[188] and is flanked by references to productivity and unit labour costs rather than to absolute wage costs as a proportion of total (including capital) costs. On the other hand increasing attention is being given to *marginal labour costs* as a vital factor in the deterrence of investment. This can be explained in part tactically, because of the consistent decline in real net wages in the five years 1980–84,[189] but it is difficult to deny that marginal labour costs (social insurance, works facilities, holiday money, severance pay, etc.) have risen as a proportion of gross wages. Statistics from the employers' 'Institute of the German Economy' claim that marginal wage costs have risen from 47 per cent of gross wages in 1970 to almost 69 per cent in 1983.[190] Above all at present the 'severance commitments' imposed on firms by trade unions and the labour courts are seen to paralyse both the shedding and the re-employment of labour,[191] or at worst they encourage firms to declare bankruptcy rather than meet their severance liabilities.[192]

The practical political conclusions are that the unions can help their redundant colleagues back to work by foregoing a portion of the wage mass: 'In small and medium sized firms there is a sum x which is allotted to personnel costs. If it is divided by 30, a wage rate of y results. If the wage rate falls, 35 or 40 people can perhaps be served from the same wages pot' (thus FDP general secretary Haussmann).[193]

This 'wages pot' theory is a common feature of many (albeit more refined) analyses of supply-side economists, and often goes hand in hand with 'crowding-out' theories: if enterprises can mobilise sufficient capital (without the crowding-out effect of state expenditure) and have the prospect of lower unit wage costs (i.e. higher unit returns) there will be an inevitable boost to investment, production, employment and income with corresponding multiplicator effects. This is certainly the position of the Federal Bank and the previous Economics Minister Lamsdorff. However, the crowding-out theory has been questioned not just by Keynesians and socialist economists, but more recently by orthodox neo-liberal economists.[194] For example, the five economic research institutes (and the SVR) have implied that any limitations on the supply of capital have derived not so much from excessive state expenditure but from the excessively restrictive monetary policies of the Federal Bank.[195] Both bodies stress the critical influence of high interest rates in the wake of the 79 oil price rises on the domestic economy, with their resultant 'additional costs' for both private enterprises and state expenditure. The attacks on the Federal Bank in 1980, 1981 and 1982 reflected on the one hand the need to identify further political factors which were external to the market but they were also evidence for the increasing official confusion regarding economic policy.

One of the main reasons for this confusion is the evident *failure of supply-side policies* to reproduce the elusive magic square of stable growth, prices, employment and balance of payments. For, despite a consistent fall in the value of real wages between 1979 and 1984[196] and a more recent surge in company profits, growth has been sluggish and has in no way been sufficient to prevent the steady rise in unemployment to over 2.5 million in 1985.[197] As far back as 1977 the employers' 'Institute of the German Economy' had asserted that only with a maxi-cycle of a decade or more with an average real rate of growth of 5 per cent could unemployment be reduced to below 600 000; as it is, its most pessimistic forecast of 11.3 per cent unemployment in 1988/89 seems to have been far more realistic.[198] As a result there has been a fatalistic theoretical and practical *withdrawal from full employment as a primary commitment within the magic square*.[199] More critically there has been an implied (and occasionally open) recognition of the impotence of national economic policy[200] in the face of the increasing disequilibrium of world capital markets. There is no doubt that the Federal Bank, by imposing the longest and severest squeeze since the war, contributed to the most severe economic crisis since the war. However, the recommendation by the Five Institutes and the SVR to ignore international capital movements (and their implications for exchange rates and balance of payments) and to concentrate on the domestic money supply would probably not have affected the level of domestic investment, since 'as long as the interest yield from money investments is higher than the return on fixed capital assets, the capital investors will prefer the purchase of gilts to fixed investments'.[201] The surge of capital outflows to the USA after 1978 was due in large part to the increasing attraction of US gilts, many of which were financing the US budget deficit, with their *uniquely high real interest rates* – the yield on long-term government bonds in the USA rose from 2.5 per cent (12 per cent minus 9.5 per cent inflation) in 1981 to 8.1 per cent (10.7 per cent minus 2.6 per cent inflation) in the second half of 1983.[202] The transformation of the USA from the major source of surplus capital in the post-war period to a net importer of capital in 1983 and the related capital flow deficit of DM16.2 billion in West Germany in 1983[203] thus made supply-side investment calculations à la SVR quite irrelevant.

Thus, linked to the failure of supply-side economic policy, is the consistent failure of its proponents to forecast adequately the future trends of the economy. In terms of the size of its research departments and its politico-economic dominance the Federal Bank is the most significant official forecasting body in West Germany; it forecast a rise of 3 per cent in real GNP for 1980, of up to 1 per cent for 1981 and 1 per cent for 1982, while the real results were +1.8 per cent –0.3 per cent and –1.1 per cent respectively.[204] This degree of inaccuracy reflects the growing elusiveness of world capital movements and trends, as well as an inherent blindness to demand factors. The reverse side of the reduction in real wages is a (for many) predictable fall in domestic consumer demand, the loss of which, even given the rapid expansion of exports, represents not a stimulus but a disincentive to the majority of firms dependent on the home market. The same demand arguments have been deployed to oppose the cuts in social expenditure.[205]

Although the proponents of deregulation, privatisation of state property and services and export-led growth have dominated the ideological arena in the 1980s, they have done so in the absence of any empirical justification, with considerable disagreement among each other and – not the least – at considerable expense. However, they dominate, among other things, because of equal confusion among the opposition.

Alternative Diagnoses of the Crisis

In West Germany there are broadly three main streams of political economy which are opposed to neo-liberal supply-side theories and which proceed either from the primacy of *demand* in economic analysis or from other expressions of socially articulated *need*. There are the Keynesians, who, in one shape or another, assert the viability of the market and the need for growth but under the guiding hand of an active interventionist state. There are socialists who eschew the market, but who nevertheless argue practically for state sponsored management of demand and social need, again within the framework of economic growth. Finally there is an increasingly articulate body of opinion which, in a wide variety of ways, questions the ideology of growth and stresses 'qualitative' aspects of human and social need – to be found not simply among the 'Green' movement but within mainstream socialist and even conservative circles.

The Keynesian Alternative

It is significant that since the early 1970s, when it was still the dominant school of establishment economic thinking Keynesianism in West Germany has become a marginal ghetto populated almost exclusively by Social Democrats and adherents of the broad labour movement. Of the five major economics research institutes only the DIW (Berlin) – whose president, Hans-Jürgen Krupp was one tipped as a future SPD economics minister – has maintained a Keynesian stance. The WSI (Economic and Social Science Institute of the German Federation of Trade Unions), a leading member of which, Werner Glastetter, was briefly in the SVR, is also strongly Keynesian in its approach. Otherwise supply-side theories have taken over as establishment wisdom.

The immediate cause for the demise of Keynesianism has clearly been ten years of stagflation, a condition which defied interventionist anti-cyclical cures of traditional crisis-management. However, in the face of the evident failure of neo-liberalism to counteract stagflation, the fiscalists have been able to mount effective and plausible attacks on current wisdom. Proceeding from the assumption of the fallibility but viability of the market, they postulate the necessity of both state monitoring of growth and the flexible deployment of state investment as a means of anti-cyclical control. The new Left-Keynesians within the labour movement also include the need for tripartite co-operation (state–industry–unions) in their programmes.[206]

In their critique of neo-liberal policies they stress the danger for growth and particularly employment of large budget cuts and debt-consolidation with warnings of 'saving to death' ('kaputtsparen'), arguing, with Hankel, that the 'thrifty state fleeces its citizens', by compounding the long-term fiscal crisis of the state through a failure to stabilise demand and subsequently needing to resolve the resulting crisis by higher taxation rather than through interest yielding bonds.[207] The crowding-out arguments are countered either by reference to empirically verifiable cyclical and other shortfalls in private investment[208] or by *extolling the virtue of crowding-out as a means of sensible investment control* (namely, infrastructure) in contrast to the implied chaos of uncontrolled private investment.[209] While clearly not denying the dangers of debt-expansion, the Keynesians argue that an effective anti-cyclical budgetary policy should neither rule out the expansion of key areas of expenditure – namely, the DM140 billion programme recommended by the DIW (above) – nor simply make savings where particular deficits emerge, as in the finances of the Federal Institute of Labour after 1975.[210] While neo-liberal institutions openly welcome the decline in state investments as a proportion of state expenditure and GNP[211] and recommend the concentration of state investment on the external economies of the private sector and withdrawal from 'consumptive' expenditure,[212] Keynesians demand the specific maintenance of state investment as a key instrument of fiscal policy and a more differentiated view of what constitutes productive investment. Ehrenberg (SPD) argues very plausibly that the 'social-state' is not merely socially essential but also equivalent to a 'factor of production';[213] equally it is argued that education expenditure, including teachers' salaries, constitutes social investment *qua* human capital.[214]

The saturation of demand in certain areas of individual and social consumption can be compensated for, according to Scharpf, by state assistance in developing new areas of 'elevated demand', particularly in the recreational sector;[215] economic growth is fundamental, particularly for the realisation of environmental and social improvements: 'it is pure romanticism to believe that these tasks can be solved without strong growth impulses'.[216]

The main Keynesian critique of neo-liberals – that they simply repress those factors of economic life which are uncomfortable[217] – is clearly right. The recommendations for a differentiated policy which combines flexible state investment with job-creation strategies and a shorter working week are clearly more adequate than the blind faith of market theologians. There are some, however, who would claim that both Keynesian diagnoses and prescriptions are guilty of repressing certain other features of West Germany's political economy.

'No Growth' or 'Qualitative Growth' – Green Political Economy

The confidence of Keynesians and neo-liberals in the possibility, efficacy and necessity of growth is being challenged by a growing body of opinion internationally and nationally, and in particular through the mobilisation of environmental movements and organisations. Apart from the 'Green'-Party, which has strong eco-socialist leanings, the notion of the limits of growth have also begun to influence thinking within both social-democratic and conservative circles. They all have one common assumption: namely that *growth – in its historical form – is increasingly less likely, less necessary and less desirable*. They differ in terms of the nature and degree of growth which is acceptable and above all in relation to the organisation of and distribution within a future society which rejects traditional growth patterns.

The diminishing likelihood of growth in West Germany is a highly plausible argument and can be demonstrated by reference to the *long-term trend* of post-war trade cycles (see above, pp. 203ff). The increasing stagnation of real growth is not merely a reflection of the increasing problems of capital reproduction, capital export and world recessions but also of relative saturation on domestic markets. The optimism of some Keynesians in the potential of sailing and tennis clubs [sic][218] as vehicles of growth, appears to be hardly realistic, not just because the *recreational service sector* has hitherto failed to compensate for the decline in manufacturing growth (and jobs) but also because it *represents more volatile demand* than that for basic commodities and amenities. Equally the theory which Mensch develops from Kondratieff, Schumpeter and others of long waves which reflect bunched innovations and bunched saturation in a seemingly endless dynamic cycle hypostasises 'demand' as an historical category of constant value, and postulates a technological imperative which seemingly overrides collective reason.[219]

The saturation argument reinforces the view that growth is less necessary, since the current national product not only satisfies a broad range of by no means merely basic needs already, but includes surplus agricultural production which is often destroyed, while a consistent (and in certain cases growing) proportion of productive capacity is left unused. Where basic needs in other parts of the world are not satisfied and where an inordinate proportion of global production is committed to armaments and forces of repression, the perceived need to expand social consumption willy-nilly has to be superseded by some measure of international redistribution, according to the eco-socialists, including 'the conscious renunciation' of increased consumption in the industrialised countries.[220] Above all the necessity argument is most plausible in relation to the finite nature of basic material resources. The rapid consumption/

destruction of certain resources (minerals, forests, etc.) and the desertification of certain areas make the 'necessity for growth' argument synonymous for many with the 'necessity for suicide'.

The desirability of a break with the ideology of growth is expressed in a wide variety of forms: pragmatic self-interest, moral conservatism, neo-Malthusian pessimism, the socialist rejection of consumer-fetishism, etc. – all however stress the importance of replacing the quantitative yardstick of living standards with the yardstick of the *quality of life*, which, it is claimed, is damaged by growth and its negative environmental effects. The most telling, if obvious, argument of both conservative and eco-socialist critics of growth, centres on the whole *system of national auditing* with GNP as the bottom line: 'we have to ask whether everything which is included in the Social Product actually contributes to general welfare, whether the social costs of increasing industrial production do not in fact exceed the individual benefits';[221] the reduction/abolition of 'senseless goods' as an element of national wealth creation would enrich rather than empoverish.[222] Kruppa (a policy advisor to the CDU) estimates that the social costs of environmental pollution effectively already reduce the real rate of growth (qua socially useful values) by 2 per cent.[223] He proposes the concept of *qualitative growth* which would require a social audit (welfare, quality of life) rather than a quantitative audit in which 'growth' conceals both quantifiable costs and qualitative decline. This reinforces the positive potential of environmental protection as an agent of 'qualitative' growth and job creation.[224]

For eco-socialists the organisational preconditions for change include both the decentralisation and (radical) deconcentration of production (= optimal restoration of individual control of the product of labour) as well as the reduction of the state's share of social resources and responsibility for the repressive state apparatus, for economic management and for social welfare.[225] For Kruppa, whose influence within the CDU is admittedly marginal, the 'Social Market Economy' has to jettison the 'fetish of growth', absorb more strongly elements of Christian social doctrine and encourage the transformation of labour into paid labour and unpaid work in the home and in the community.[226]

The concept of 'qualitative growth' is increasingly evident within the SPD, but with a few exceptions, like Lafontaine, the necessity of growth is not denied but merely qualified by an increasing insistence on social controls on the nature of growth. Accordingly a *greater responsibility* for managing both economy and ecology is demanded for the state, since 'the so-called self-healing powers of the market frequently do not solve but aggravate economic and ecological problems'.[227] While conceding that the critique of purely quantitative growth is in part correct, H. J. Krupp (DIW), asserts that an expansion of state activity is 'unavoidable' and that the necessary investments for environmental protection require real GNP growth; otherwise they can only be effected by reducing private consumption and social provisions which would run the risk of 'an incalculable catastrophe'.[228]

In neither case – of 'qualitative *not* quantitative growth' or 'qualitative *only with* quantitative growth' is there a clear view of the politico-economic mechanics of the process of transformation. Conservative, eco-socialist and social-democratic conceptions imply (whether acknowledged or not) an increased interference by the state in the private disposition of wealth and a rigorous system of political controls on research, development and production. Furthermore the process of transformation would require the maintenance of mass loyalty (presumably through a campaign of public education), the maintenance of the loyalty of capital (the prevention of the expatriation of capital or investment strikes) and just as importantly a high level of international agreement and co-operation on strategy, means and ends. The realisation of these pre-conditions, given either the maintenance of market-economic relations by conservatives or social democrats or the relative de-industrialisation/deconcentration beyond capitalism of the eco-socialists, is regarded as extremely optimistic by the other major school of thought considered here, which can be characterised roughly as revolutionary socialist.

The Socialist Growth Model

The highest unemployment and the biggest decline in living standards in the history of the Federal Republic characterise the condition of the economy and of society this spring (1983 JL). It is being used by the employers to intimidate and discipline the workforce, to reduce wages and salaries and workplace benefits and to limit the rights of protection and co-determination. The Federal Government is also fostering a climate of confrontation towards the wage- and salary-dependent through economic and social policies which

– claim to be reducing mass unemployment, while in reality they increase it further,

– redistribute state expenditure contrary to their own declarations, at the expense of the areas of social welfare, education and infrastructure and to the advantage of armaments, large-scale technology and international expansion and

– redistribute taxes and other general levies at the expense of the dependent workforce, pensioners and social benefit recipients, in order to relieve the private economy.[229]

This diagnosis by the now established group of socialist economists, 'Alternative Economic Policy', reflects the dual view of a fundamental crisis of capitalism which has nevertheless been compounded by the authors of economic policy. This view informs their proposed remedies, which include the necessity for the (ultimate) socialisation of production, but largely preceded by a set of remedial measures within capitalism, (which brings them closer to some Left Keynesian views than might be otherwise expected). They attack the view of successive governments of the primacy of profits – as the precondition for an (*unproven*) causal chain: profits=investments =growth=jobs – by demonstrating correctly that investment is induced not by present profit levels but by future expected sales (and profits) and that the forcing of investment in a period of low private expectations simply destroys jobs by facilitating rationalisation. They too propose a programme of 'qualitative growth' but distinct from H. J. Krupp's Keynesian model, in that they stress the need to limit the power of capital. In other respects they share a good deal of common ground with Left Keynesians.

The reduction of unemployment cannot be achieved by 'traditional forms of economic growth': these would be 'socially and ecologically unsustainable at the required rates of growth'. This reduction can only be achieved by qualitative growth, accompanied by a reduction of the working week and the 'democratisation of the economic decision-making processes'. The growth should be stimulated by additional annual state expenditure of DM30 billion in areas similar to those highlighted by the DIW in its mammoth 1979 programme (DM130 billion up to 1985):

(a) development of innovations for saving energy and raw materials and for alternative energy sources;
(b) social housing developments;
(c) public transport;
(d) refuse recycling, water purification;

(e) education; and
(f) state social services.

The financial resources should come from higher taxation of top earners and of windfall profits and from a higher state debt. The 'Alternative Report' makes do with the socialisation of steel and shipbuilding.

The plausibility of the Alternative Report and its recommendations is only matched by the unlikelihood of its being implemented at national let alone international level. All such socialist programmes would have to overcome not just the prejudice which confronts 'planning' as such in the West but also (and perhaps more significantly) the inauspicious record of East European countries, particularly in relation to environmental pollution.[230] The objective advantages of planning for the optimal control of social and environmental affairs[231] have to be seen to operate or to promise success at least before it is accepted by the mass of people in the rest of the industrialised world. However there are signs that the common denominator of ecological awareness is leading towards a greater proximity of eco-socialists, left social democrats and socialists in Germany, which could at least produce a programme acceptable to the majority of the West German population, particularly if the present phase of neo-conservatism continues to fail.

Notes

1. *Stabilität im Wachstum – Jahresgutachten des Sachverständigenrats 1967/68*, (Stuttgart, 1967).
2. C. f. P. Czada, *Wirtschaft. Aktuelle Probleme des Wachstums und der Konjunktur* (Berlin, 1980) p. 227.
3. W. Glastetter *et al.*, *Wirtschaftliche Entwicklung in der Bundesrepublik 1950–1980*, op. cit., p. 62.
4. W. Glastetter, *Die wirtschaftliche Entwicklung der Bundesrepublik im Zeitraum 1950 bis 1975* (Berlin, 1977) p. 4.
5. E. Mandel, *Die deutsche Wirtschaftskrise* (Frankfurt/M., 1969) p. 14.
6. SVR *Jahresgutachten 1967/68*, op. cit., para. 3.
7. M. Welteke, Theorie und Praxis, op. cit., p. 140.
8. Ibid., p. 141.
9. Czada, *Wirtschaft* op. cit., p. 234.
10. Bundesdrucksache V/3630, pp. 110f.
11. Welteke, *Theorie und Praxis*, op. cit., p. 144.
12. Source: *Statistisches Jahrbuch der Bundesrepublik 1969*. The next highest figure was 44 431 in the metal-processing industries.

13. Welteke, *Theorie und Praxis*, op. cit., p. 144.
14. H. D. Hardes, *Einkommenspolitik in der BRD: Stabilität und Gruppe-ninteressen; der Fall Konzertiete Aktion* (Munich, 1974).
15. Karl Schiller in a debate in the Bundestag, 17 Feb. 1967, stenographische Berichte, vol. 63, p. 4330.
16. Cf. Otto Brenner, quoted in the *Frankfurter Rundschau*, 1 June 67.
17. Karl Schiller, *Reden zur Wirtschaftspolitik*, vol. I (Bonn, 1968) pp. 34f, cf. also Hanns-Martin Schleyer (BDA/BDI), quoted in the *FR*, 1 June 67.
18. Gross Wages Quota = proportion of gross income (from wages and salaries) to National Income.
19. Net Wages Quote = proportion of net income from wages and salaries to total net private income.
20. 'This Concerted Action . . . is concerned with wages policy, but not just with this.' Thus K. Schiller, *Reden zur Wirtschaftspolitik*, vol. 1, op. cit., pp. 34f.
21. This was in protest at the employers' constitutional appeal against the 1976 Co-determination Law.
22. Assuming the constancy of the gross wages quota of 1966 (= 66.6 per cent) savings for 1967 were DM0.7 billion, for 1968 DM6.7 billion and for 1969 DM2.3 billion (at market prices).
23. Figures from the DIW, quoted in Welteke, *Theorie und Praxis*, op. cit., p. 144.
24. See E. Hoppmann, 'Soziale Marktwirtschaft oder konstruktivistischer Interventionismus' and E. Tuchfeldt, 'Soziale Marktwirtschaft und Globalsteuerung', both in *Soziale Marktwirtschaft im Wandel* (ed. E. Tuchfeldt) (Freiburg, 1973) pp. 27ff and 159ff.
25. K. Schiller, 'Stetiges Wachstum als ökonomische und politische Aufgabe', in *Der Ökonom und die Gesellschaft* (Stuttgart, 1964) pp. 226f.
26. J. Huffschmid, *Die Politik des Kapitals*, op. cit., p. 126.
27. K. Schiller, 'Stetiges Wachstum als ökonomische und politische Aufgabe', op. cit., pp. 227f.
28. J. Huffschmid, *Die Politik des Kapitals*, op. cit., p. 126.
29. Ibid., p. 123.
30. K. Schiller, 'Konjunkturpolitik auf dem Wege zu einer Affluent Society' in *Jahre der Wende, Festgabe für Alex Möller* (Karlsruhe, 1968) p. 71.
31. The 'Society of Independent Entrepreneurs' (ASU) requested and were refused access to Concerted Action meetings; cited by Huffschmid, *Die Politik des Kapitals*, p. 126.
32. K. Schiller, 'Stetiges Wirtschaftswachstum . . .', op. cit., p. 222.
33. Abelshauser, *Wirtschaftsgeschichte der Bundesrepublik Deutschland 1945–1980*, op. cit., p. 107.
34. For example Czada notes the tendency by large and small firms to 'invest' in government stock and fixed interest bonds in times of stagnation rather than in real assets, *Wirtschaft*, op. cit., p. 77.
35. See J. Krack and K. Neumann, *Konjunktur, Krise, Wirtschaftspolitik* (Frankfurt, 1978) p. 194.

36. N. B. the regular annual transfer of postal revenues to the Bund, see above.
37. The annual maintenance costs for schools and kindergartens are as high as 31 per cent of original building costs, those of universities 18–23 per cent, hospitals 25 per cent, swimming pools 15–20 per cent and roads, etc. 9.5 per cent (See Welteke, *Theorie und Praxis*, op. cit., p. 166).
38. Cf. Helmut Müller, *Die Zentralbank – eine Nebenregierung* (Opladen, 1974); also F. Dörge, 'Macht ohne Mandat? Die Bundesbank – eine Nebenregierung' in *Die Zeit*, 31 Oct. 1969.
39. The high level of state expenditure increases (calculated according to *general inflation indicators*) must be set against higher than average price rises in investment goods in 1969–1971.
40. This is the polemical claim of K. Biedenkopf and M. Miegel, *Die programmierte Krise* (Bonn, 1979) p. 35.
41. In the first three weeks of November 1968, for example, DM9.4 billion worth of foreign currency poured into West Germany (*viz.* Krack/Neumann *Konjunktur, Krise*, op. cit., p. 218).
42. The Local Authorities' commitment to the Second Investment Programme represented on paper only 16 per cent of total planned expenditure by the state in the two programmes of 1967.
43. See above, Chapter 3.
44. See *Der Spiegel*, 5 June 1972. In a later edition (10 July 72) Der Spiegel quotes an 'SPD election analyst' who claimed that Schiller's loud checked suits had also damaged his reputation!
45. *Der Spiegel*, 3 July 1972.
46. Ibid.
47. In its July Monthly Report 1972 the Bundesbank stresses its reluctant preference for exchange controls as a faute de mieux in the face of chaotic world capital markets, p. 7.
48. Quoted in *Der Spiegel*, 10 July 72.
49. Walter Scheel apparently saw it in these terms (*Der Spiegel*, 3 July 1972).
50. Thus D. Dickertmann, 'Die Autonomie der Bundesbank unter dem Einfluß geldpolitischer Entwicklungen', in: *Wirtschafspolitische Chronik*, vol. I (1975,) p. 32.
51. See Keynes' introduction to the German Edition of his *General Theory of Employment, Interest and Money* (Munich/Leipzig, 1936) p. ix.
52. Thus Dickertmann, 'Die Autonomie der Bundesbank', op. cit., p. 24.
53. See footnote 24 above.
54. W. Eucken, *Grundsätze der Wirtschaftspolitik* (Tübingen, 1955) p. 256 and O. Issing, 'Währungspolitik im Spannungsfeld wirtschaftspolitischer Konflikte' in E. Tuchfeldt (ed.), *Soziale Marktwirtschaft*, op. cit., p. 204.
55. Claudia von Braunmühl, 'Ist die "Ostpolitik" Ostpolitik?' in Jahn/Rittberger (eds), *Die Ostpolitik der BRD* (Cologne, 1976) p. 165; also K. P. Tudyka, 'Gesellschaftliche Interessen und auswärtige Beziehungen – Das Röhrenembargo', in Varain (ed.) *Interessenverbände in Deutschland*.

56. Braunmühl, 'Ostpolitik', op. cit., p. 21.
57. Ibid., p. 18.
58. Source: H. Hopf/G. Mayr, 'Destabiliserung durch den Weltmarkt' in *Gesellschaft im Konkurs*, op. cit., p. 139. By 1974 Mannesmann's export dependency had risen sharply to 60 per cent.
59. In *Außenhandelsdienst*, no. 21 (1969) pp. 493f.
60. See *Der Spiegel*, 27 Mar. 1972, p. 23.
61. Ibid.
62. See *Handelsblatt*, 10 Aug. 1970.
63. The rate of 6.5 per cent interest was considerably lower than the current market rate of 10 per cent, whereby Braunmühl does not exclude the possibility of state subsidies on top of the export credit guarantees ('Ostpolitik', op. cit., p. 27, n59). Subsequent deals have not offered such generous interest conditions.
64. *See Bundesbank Monthly Report* (July 1982) p. 15.
65. Thus Hans Friderichs, former Economics Minister and Head of the Dresdner Bank, quoted in Stern, 1980 (n.d.), also in the FR, 30 May 1980. In any case West Germany's share of the Eastern European debt is much lower than its share of trade, see FR, 20 July 82.
66. Braunmühl, 'Ostpolitik', op. cit., p. 22.
67. See *FR*, 10 Apr. 1980 and Braunmühl, 'Ostpolitik', op. cit., p. 22.
68. Horst Lambrecht, 'Der Innerdeutsche Handel' in *apuzg* B40/1982.
69. See *Der Spiegel*, nos 27/1980 and no. 43/1983.
70. See Leading Article in *FR*, 26 Mar. 1981 and remarks by Genscher, Schmidt and Lamsdorff in the Bundestag debate on the 1978 German-Soviet Trade Agreement, quoted in *Das Parlament*, 21 Oct. 1978.
71. A. Schüller, 'Pragmatische oder marktwirtschaftliche Osthandelspolitik' in E. Tuchtfeldt (ed.), *Soziale Marktwirtschaft*, op. cit., pp. 207ff.
72. *Bundesbank Monthly Report*, July 1982, pp. 14ff.
73. See Wolfgang Hoffmann, 'Keine Freiheit für das Wissen' in *Die Zeit*, 10 Aug. 1984.
74. The KATEK project involves a massive scheme for the conversion of coal into oil and the development of related chemical industries in South West Siberia. Viz. Elfie Siegl on the background to Kohl's visit to Moscow in 1983 in *FR*, 2 July 1983.
75. See Karl-Heinz Narjes (CDU) and Franz Amrehn (CDU) in the Bundestag debate on the German-Soviet Trade Treaty, in *Das Parlament*, no. 42, 21 Oct. 1978.
76. It is likely that this commitment will increase rather than decrease, given not just projects like KATEK but also the expectations of large state orders from China, see press reports, as in *FR*, 11 Nov. 1983 with talk of an 'investment paradise' in China.
77. Phillips' Theory was expounded in 'The Relationship between Unemployment and the Rate of Change of Money Wages in the United Kingdom, 1861–1957' in *Economica*, vol. 25, 1958, pp. 281ff. Peter Czada talks specifically of the 'Phillips-Illusion', *Wirtschaft*, op. cit., p. 127.
78. This is confirmed by strict adherence to cycles, see Abelshauser, *Wirtschaftsgeschichte der Bundesrepublik Deutschland*, op. cit., p. 104.

79. Cf. Glastetter, *Die wirtschaftliche Entwicklung der Bundesrepublik 1950 bis 1975*, op. cit., p. 15.
80. Czada, *Wirtschaft*, op. cit., p. 79.
81. Fritz Scharpf talks of 'gehobener Bedarf', largely in the recreational and service sector, in: 'Die Rolle des Staates im westlichen Wirtschaftssystem', op. cit., pp. 38f.
82. Abelshauser, *Wirtschaftsgeschichte* . . . , op. cit., p. 103.
83. See H. Elsenhans', 'Lohnerhöhungen: Wachstumschance für den Kapitalismus' in *Forum – Zeitschrift für Theorie und Praxis des demokratischen Sozialismus*, no. 2 (1976) pp. 78–133.
84. The capital stock/domestic product ratio shows a higher capital coefficient but a similar rising trend, namely, *Statistisches Jahrbuch der Bundesrepublik* (1984).
85. Cf. Czada, *Wirtschaft*, op. cit., p. 58.
86. The 'Göggler' empire which attempted to disprove the pessimistic outlook for European textile producers, got into difficulties in part through speculative holdings in the (likewise) structurally threatened building industry, see J. Huffschmid, 'Monopolisierung in der Krise', in: Huffschmid/Schui (ed.), *Gesellschaft im Konkurs*, op. cit., pp. 88f.
87. Ibid., p. 96.
88. Glastetter *et al.*, *Die wirtschaftliche Entwicklung in der Bundesrepublik 1950–1980* op. cit., p. 486.
89. Ibid., p. 489.
90. See Bundesbank Monthly Reports.
91. Exxon's profits rose from $1.53 billion in 1972 to $2.44 billion in 1973, those of Royal Dutch Shell from $0.7 billion to $1.79 billion and Texaco's from $0.89 billion to $1.29 billion. The 'oil-crisis' reflected the flaws of earlier West German energy policy which allowed a rapid transition from coal to relatively cheaper oil at the end of the 1950s without calculating the long-term implications of a rapid consumption of oil as a rarer commodity than coal.
92. Marginal benefits relate to pensions, recreational facilities, holiday pay, 13th monthly salary, canteen facilities, etc.
93. Czada, *Wirtschaft*, op. cit., p. 67.
94. NATO countries agreed to annual rises of 3 per cent in real terms at their plenary session in May 1977.
95. See Czada's oblique reference to the CDU's tax cuts and expenditure boost in 1965, *Wirtschaft*, op. cit., p. 227, and Biedenkopf/Miegel on the SPD/FDP government's tripling of the borrowing requirement in 1972, *Die programmierte Krise*, op. cit., p. 34.
96. See above Chapter 4, Graph on Bund expenditure; the case for 1972/73 is more evident in the borrowing requirement figures.
97. Cf. Miller/Mackie, 'The Electoral Cycle and the Asymmetry of Government and Opposition Popularity' in *Political Studies*, vol. XXI (1973) and K. G. Zinn, *Der Niedergang des Profits*, op. cit., p. 156.
98. Their conclusion is that there will be a greatly increased demand for migrant labour, see Reinhardt Ebert, 'Braucht die Wirtschaft weiterhin Ausländer? in *Das Parlament*, no. 35/36, 1981, Ebert quotes

the DIW, which had calculated a migrant population of over 10.3 million in 2030.

99. In fact there was considerable doubt which was confirmed in empirical studies of price movements in the 1970s, where highly concentrated branches were seen to be able to impose far higher price increases on their less monopolised customers; see H. Schui, article in *FR*, 25 Nov. 1978.

100. See above Chapter 3. The exclusion of the oil corporations from any blame is particularly disingenuous, see above note 91.

101. F. Manske states quite correctly the 'the inclusion of monopolies in the analysis would lead the SVR to quite different conclusions about the causes and effects of the crisis'; F. Manske, 'Die Suche nach den Schuldigen' in Huffschmid/Schui (ed.), *Gesellschaft im Konkurs*, op. cit., p. 277.

102. The singling out of trade-union power as the primary cause of economic instability (inflation and recession) which is external to the market economic order has been the subject of considerable criticism, not the least because it denies the labour market the same 'freedom' as other commodity markets, where values fluctuate according to supply constraints (scarcity, abundance, quality, etc.). Manske thus describes the SVR's analysis as 'contravening market principles', (ibid., p. 292). The increasing skill, productivity, but also scarcity of labour in the 1960s can be seen as quite natural factors contributing to the rise in the price of labour, just as the widespread introduction of a system of migrant labour in the same period can be seen as a deliberate political (market-external) measure to resist the market power of labour.

There are a large number of critiques of the work of the SVR, of which the following are more noteworthy: R. Hickel/Mattfeldt (ed.), *Millionen Arbeitslose – Streitschrift gegen den Rat der fünf Weisen* (Reinbek, 1983); Hickel/Mattfeldt, 'Die "Fünf Weisen" in der Krise, 20 Jahre Rat der Ratlosen' in *GM*, Nov. 1983, pp. 699ff; H. Baisch, 'Kritik an der Sachverständigenkonzeption' in Markmann/Simmert (ed.), *Krise der Wirtschaftspolitik* (Cologne, 1978) pp. 57ff; Ch. Roberts, *Konjunkturprognosen und Wirtschaftspolitik* (Cologne, 1981).

103. See Hickel/Mattfeldt, 'Die "Fünf Weisen" in der Krise', op. cit., pp. 700ff.

104. Glastetter resigned from the SVR in mid-1981 after only 2-years service.

105. The Subtitle of the article by Hickel and Mattfeldt, is 'Twenty Years of Counselling by the Clueless' (20 Jahre Rat der Ratlosen).

106. See *FAZ*, 30 Aug. 1975, 17 Sept. 1975, *Die Welt*, 4 Aug. 1975.

107. *Der Spiegel*, 11 Aug. 1975 and *FAZ* 4 Aug. 1975.

108. SPD, *Zweiter Entwurf eines ökonomisch-politischen Orientierungsrahmens für die Jahre 1975–1985* (Bonn, 1975) § 2.1.2.

109. Ibid., § 2.4.7.

110. Ibid., § 2.6.5.

111. Ibid., § 2.3.3.

112. *Spiegel*-Interview with Peter von Siemens, 24 Nov. 1975.

113. See H., Abromeit, 'Interessendurchsetzung in der Krise' in *apuzg*, B11/1977, op. cit., pp. 29ff.
114. Ibid., pp. 29f.
115. Ibid., p. 30.
116. The appearance of unanimity between Schmidt and successive heads of the Bundesbank was only put in doubt by revelations by Schmidt after his resignation, see interview in *FR*, 10 Dec. 1982.
117. *Annual Report of the Bundesbank* (1974) p. 1.
118. *Monthly Reports of the Bundesbank* (1972) *passim*. In the reserve class I for liabilities over DM1 billion, for example, the reserve rate was raised from 15.45 per cent in July 1972 to 20.1 per cent in November 1973.
119. Debt servicing as a proportion of state expenditure and the state debt has increased exponentially since the mid-1960s (see above).
120. See K. Zweig, *Germany through Inflation and Recession: an Object Lesson in Economic Management* (London, 1976).
121. *Der Spiegel*, 17 Feb. 1975.
122. It is noteworthy that *these* external factors were given little credit by state spokesmen in contrast to the frequent citing of external factors to explain failure – e.g., the SVR 1974 Report in relation to oil prices.
123. *Bundesbank Annual Report* (1974) p. 1.
124. Thus Reinhard Kohler, 'Die Bremspolitik der Bundesbank hat noch nie richtig funktioniert' in *FR*, 27 June 1979, p. 13; Kohler was assistant to the later Bundesbank director Claus Köhler from 1972 to 1974.
125. Thus Hans-Joachim Rüstow (adviser to the Free Democrats) in *FR*, 9 Apr. 1980.
126. Kohler, op. cit., p. 13.
127. See Verband der Vereine Creditreform Neuss, *Insolvenzenanalyse III* (Neuss, 1974) p. 3.
128. H. Schui, 'Opfer für die Stabilität – die krisenverschärfende Politik der Bundesbank' in Huffschmid/Schui (ed.), *Gesellschaft im Konkurs*, op. cit., p. 368. In 1980 the proportion of foreign loans to all short-term loans to German industry was 40 per cent, see *FR*, 16 Oct. 1980.
129. Ibid., p. 369.
130. Thus Kohler, 'Die Bremspolitik der Bundesbank', op. cit., p. 13.
131. Thus Rüstow, *FR*, 9 Apr. 1980.
132. Kohler, 'Die Bremspolitik der Bundesbank', op. cit., p. 13.
133. Milton Friedman, 'The Case for Flexible Exchange Rates' in *Essays in Positive Economics* (Chicago, 1953) pp. 157ff.
134. In 1974 already the Euro-Dollar markets represented over $200 billion worth of stateless capital, see *Der Spiegel*, no. 34 (1974).
135. Thus W. Hankel, 'Shylock gesucht: Hockzinspolitik und internationale Kreditmärkte' in *Blätter für deutsche und internationale Politik* (May 1982).
136. See Friedmann, 'Flexible Exchange Rates', op. cit., p. 175.
137. See Viktor Schoofs, *Flexible Wechselkurse und Zentralbankpolitik* (Göttingen, 1983) pp. 28ff.
138. Rüstow, *FR*, 9 Apr. 1980.
139. Pöhl interviewed in *FR*, 18 July 1980.

140. Thus Dickertmann, 'Die Autonomie der Bundesbank', op. cit., p. 32.
141. See above, note 38.
142. See *Der Spiegel*, 17 Feb. 1975.
143. Thus Klauss-Dieter Arndt, before his death, quoted in *Der Spiegel*, ibid.
144. Interview with Schmidt in *FR*, 10 Dec. 1982, see also several essays by Schmidt in *Die Zeit* and the *FR* on the need for international action on interest rates. (e.g. *FR*, 24. & 28. Feb. 1983).
145. See Kohler, Hankel, Schoofs, Rüstow, quoted above and the DGB spokesman Heinz Markmann, quoted in *Der Spiegel*, 17 Feb. 1975 on the policy-blocking of the Bundesbank.
146. This problem is only occasionally aired in the critical media, as in 1975 when *Der Spiegel* gave a lengthy article the title 'Will tight money bring down the SPD?' (17 Feb. 1975). Whether the suspicion is founded or not, the effect on policy formulation in all elected cabinets must be very considerable.
147. See Abelshauser, *Wirtschaftsgeschichte* op. cit., pp. 106ff.
148. Quoted in *FR*, 1 Feb. 83.
149. See Abromeit, 'Interessendurchsetzung in der Krise', op. cit., p. 32.
150. See Krack/Neumann, *Konjunktur, Krise . . .* , op. cit., p. 228.
151. Ibid., p. 228.
152. Cited in *FAZ*, 10 Dec. 1975.
153. A survey of investment aims in 1975 (Ifo-Institut) showed that 46 per cent of investments were for rationalisation, 26 per cent for replacement and only 28 per cent for extending capacity; quoted in Welteke *Theorie und Praxis*, op. cit., p. 191. The Programme for Employment and Growth (and the Investment Subsidy) could have clearly contributed to an increase in unemployment through the encouragement of the rationalisation of production.
154. See *SVR Annual Report* (1976) para. 78.
155. For details see Krack/Neumann, *Konjunktur, Krise . . .* , op. cit., p. 239.
156. See *Bundesbank Monthly Report* (Nov. 1984) p. 29. The Bundesbank uses this fact to justify the subsequent reduction in state investments, because 'they cannot be controlled in a sufficiently flexible way', ibid., p. 28.
157. These are gleaned primarily from the annual reports of the SVR and Biedenkopf/Miegel, *Die programmierte Krise*, op. cit.
158. *SVR* 1979/80, para. 38, Biedenkopf/Miegel, *Die programmierte Krise*, op. cit., pp. 64ff.
159. Biedenkopf/Miegel, ibid., pp. 80ff.
160. Glastetter *et al.*, *Die wirtschaftliche Entwicklung*, op. cit., p. 449.
161. DIW weekly report, quoted in Czada, *Wirtschaft*, op. cit., p. 147.
162. Glastetter *et al.*, *Die wirtschaftliche Entwicklung* (pp. 447f), demonstrate the natural tendency of firms to reduce their borrowing in cyclical downturns, and the completely 'unrealistic' expectation that private investors could have absorbed the estimated average shortfall in investments of DM38 billion p.a. between 1976 and 1980 (ibid. fn 250, p. 591).

163. Thus Rüdiger Pohl, 'Staatsdefizite, Kreditmärkte und Investitionen' in: *Vierteljahreshefte zur Wirtschaftsforschung*, no. 4 (1981).
164. Glastetter *et al.*, *Die wirtschaftliche Entwicklung*, op. cit., p. 452.
165. Thus Rudolf Hickel in *FR* (documentation on the State Debt), 26 Jan. 1980, p. 14.
166. For details see DIW, *Monthly Bulletin* (Apr./May 1978) pp. 7f.
167. Thus Biedenkopf/Miegel, *Die programmierte Krise*, op. cit., p. 82; in the footnote this assertion is qualified dramatically by stating that, of the increase in the state debt, an average of DM30 billion per annum was 'determined by cyclical developments', which is quite different from saying that these DM30 billion were specifically deployed for anti-cyclical purposes.
168. If one takes account of the effects of inflation, which were on average higher in the housing and civil engineering sector than household inflation, the significance of state reflation is even further reduced.
169. It is important to point out that the local authorities pursued consolidation most successfully, increasing their debt from DM66.4 billion to DM95.2 billion between 1974 and 1980 whereas the debt of the cental government more than tripled in the same period from DM72.1 billion to DM232.3 billion and that of the Länder nearly tripled from DM47.3 billion to DM137.8 billion.
170. Sources for calculations: *Statistisches Jahrbuch*, various years; *Bundesbank Monthly Reports*, various years.
171. *DIW Weekly Report* no. 36 (1979).
172. Source: *Bundesbank Monthly Reports* (various); the export quota includes intra-German trade.
173. The attractiveness of (white) South Africa as a 'safe' location for investment is reflected in the fact that West German companies and banks maintain larger holdings there than in the whole of the rest of Africa (1981: DM1.85 billion compared to DM1.31 billion for the whole of Black Africa) – provisional figures from *Statistisches Jahrbuch* (1984).
174. A hefty proportion of the invisible deficit was created by the net outflow of money through tourism (1980: –DM25.5 billion) and the money transfers of migrant workers (1980: DM7.2 billion).
175. Cf. the extensive analysis of Glastetter *et al*, *Die wirtschaftsliche Entwicklung*, op. cit., pp. 303ff.
176. The provisions of the 1976 law on Co-determination were comically tortuous in relation to the casting vote. They involved firstly the prerogative of the Chairman of the supervisory board to an additional vote, but secondly, when the chair changes from the shareholders' to the employees' side the casting vote passes over to the Deputy Chairman (or the head of the shareholders' group)!
177. Reprinted (in abbreviated form) in the *DIW Monthly Bulletin*, no. 4 (May/June 1980).
178. Pöhl interview in *FR*, 18 July 1980.
179. See Creditreform statistics, cited in *FR*, 4 Dec. 1984.
180. According to an Ifo-Institut survey in 1981, 34 per cent of new investments served to extend capacity and 66 per cent either for rationalisa-

tion or replacement; in 1982 only 19 per cent served to extend capacity and 81 per cent to rationalise or replace the existing apparatus.
181. Exports to the developing countries (including OPEC) rose by a startling 36.5 per cent in 1981 and a further 2.8 per cent in 1982, wiping out the sudden deficit which arose in 1980 after the second oil shock. See *Bundesbank Monthly Report* (Oct. 1983).
182. *SVR Annual Report* (1980), cited in *FR*, 21 Nov. 1985.
183. Ibid.
184. See above § 5.3.2
185. Otto von Lamsdorff at the Frankfurt Spring Fair, quoted in *FR*, 5 Mar. 1983.
186. *SVR Annual Report* (1984), quoted in *FR*, 28 Nov. 1984.
187. *Autumn Report of the Five Economic Research Institutes* (1982), reprinted (in abbreviated form) in the *DIW Monthly Bulletin* (Dec. 1982) p. 6.
188. Ibid., p. 6.
189. Real wages fell by 0.3 per cent in 1980, 1.4 per cent in 1981, 2.2 per cent in 1982, 1.0 per cent in 1983 and 0.5 per cent in 1984; source: *FR*, 19 Nov. 84.
190. Iw-Institut quoted in *Der Spiegel*, no. 16 (1985); cf. Czada, *Wirtschaft*, op. cit., p. 155.
191. OECD-Report quoted in *Der Spiegel*, no. 14 (1985).
192. See article by Roland Bunzenthal in *FR.*, 17 Nov. 1981.
193. FDP General Secretary Haussmann in a *Spiegel*-Interview, Nr. 16/1985.
194. Viz. the *Spring Report of the Five Economic Research Institutes*, 1980, reprinted in the *DIW Monthly Bulletin*, Nr. 4, 1980, p. 57.
195. Both bodies have stressed the need to base the expansion of the money supply on a generous estimate of the expected expansion of productive potential (plus inflation) rather than on exchange rate and balance of payments considerations; viz. *Spring Report of the Five Economic Research Institutes*, op. cit. and the *SVR special Summer Report* 1981 (reprinted extracts) in *FR*, 8 July 1981.
196. See note 189 above.
197. In the *SVR 1984 Report*, Dieter Mertens – in a minority report – stresses that the promise of employment has not been realised, despite 'years of improving the conditions for supply policies'; extracts in *FR*, 28 Nov. 1984.
198. Findings recorded in *SDZ*, 7 June 1977.
199. This commitment was contained in both the 'Law on the Establishment of the SVR', 1963 and in the 'Stability Law' of 1967.
200. Thus Helmut Hesse, chairman of the Academic Sub-Committee of the Economics Ministry, at a conference on Economic Policy in Mannheim, quoted in the *FR*, 1 Feb. 1983.
201. Iw-Institut, quoted in *Der Spiegel*, no. 43 (1983).
202. Statistics from the Bayerische Landesbank, quoted in *FR*, 4 Jan. 1984.
203. See H. Ehrenberg 'Ist vergessen, daß Konjunktur nicht ohne Nachfrage auskommt?' in *FR*, 19 Nov. 1984, and statistics cited in *FR*, 26 Jan. 1984.

204. See the critical commentary on the Bundesbank forecasts in *Der Spiegel*, no. 43 (1983); the optimism of the Bundesbank was echoed by Lamsdorff at the Frankfurt Book Fair in 1981, when he predicted growth for 1982; quoted in *Die Zeit*, 6 Nov. 1981.
205. Herbert Ehrenberg, the former SPD Minister of Labour, stresses the vital role of the 'social state' as a 'factor of production' in *FR*, 19 Nov. 1984.
206. Cf. Fritz Scharpf, *Die Rolle des Staats*, op. cit. and 'Sozialliberale Beschäftigungspolitik – keine Erfolgsbilanz', in *GM*, no. 1 (1983).
207. W. Hankel (Bologna/Frankfurt), quoted in *FR*, 3 June 1981.
208. Glastetter *et al.*, *Die wirtschaftliche Entwicklung*, op. cit., p. 449.
209. Thus H. J. Krupp (DIW), 'Staatsverschuldung – noch kein Grund zur Sorge', reprinted in abridged form in *FR*, 4 June 1980; 'Crowding-out effects can be completely desirable from the point of view of growth policy. . . . If one wishes to liberate resources for absolutely necessary infrastructural investments, certain crowding-out effects are necessary, in order to avoid inflationary state indebtedness.'
210. This policy is heavily criticised by Scharpf, 'Sozial-liberale Beschäftigungspolitik', op. cit., pp. 27f.
211. See the article 'Sachinvestitionen, Darlehen und sonstige Finanzierungshilfen der Gebietskörperschaften seit Mitte der siebziger Jahre' in *Bundesbank Monthly Report* (Nov. 1984) p. 28.
212. Ibid., p. 28. This implies the financing of research and development by universities and research institutes as a 'new' category of investment, ibid., p. 32.
213. Cf. note 205 above.
214. Ibid.
215. Scharpf, *Die Rolle des Staats*, op. cit., p. 38n53.
216. H. J. Krupp, in one of two contrasting articles on 'No-Growth' in *FR*, 6 Jan. 81.
217. Thus Glastetter, in interview with *FR*, 2 Sept. 1981, notably his reference to the market 'creating problems as well as solving some', an obvious observation which the supply theorists in the SVR would want to deny.
218. Thus Scharpf, *Die Rolle des Staats*, op. cit., p. 38.
219. See Gerhard Mensch, *Das technologische Patt. Innovationen überwinden die Depression* (Frankfurt/M., 1978); Cesare Marchetti, 'Swings, Cycles and the Global Economy' in *New Scientist*, 2 May 1985. Karl-Georg Zinn remarks that the 'innovation-wave-theory' ignores that the 'quality of these innovation spurts changes', *Niedergang des Profits*, op. cit., p. 152.
220. See 'Zwölf Thesen der Ökosozialisten' in Bickerich (ed.), *SPD und Grüne* (Hamburg, 1985) p. 107.
221. Professor Adolf Kruppa, adviser to the CDU-Social Committees, in one of two articles 'Nullwachstum 1981 – Ende eines Fetischs oder soziale Katastrophe' in *FR*, 6 Jan. 1981.
222. Thesis 7, in 'Zwölf Thesen der Ökosozialisten', op. cit., p. 108.
223. Kruppa, *FR*, 6 Jan. 1981.

224. Peter Czada cites the findings of the Ifo-Institut of an increasing number of jobs created by both industry and the state as a result of investments for environmental protection: 1972–74: 111 300; 1978–80: 145 100, *Wirtschaft*, op. cit., p. 84.
225. Die Grünen, *Das Bundesprogramm* (Bonn, 1980).
226. Kruppa, *FR*, 6 Jan. 1981.
227. SPD Party Programme 1983.
228. H. J. Krupp, 'Nullwachstum', *FR*, 6 Jan. 1981.
229. *Memorandum 83*, (Alternative Report of 4 Economics Professors – Rudolf Hickel, Jörg Huffschmid, Herbert Schui and Axel Zerdick) reprinted in full in *FR* (Whitsun 1983).
230. See Martin Jänicke, 'Umweltpolitik in Osteuropa' in *apuzg*, B23 (1977).
231. Ibid., p. 3.

6 State and Economy in Germany beyond the 1980s – 'Model Germany' or 'A Colossus on Feet of Clay'?

The theology of market economics demands above all a fundamental faith in the dynamic nature of capitalism and the inevitability of growth. Its ideological systems are littered with absolute categories which only allow a linear vision of increasing prosperity. When this linear view is interrupted by world-wide stagnation, debt crises, mass unemployment and inflation, the automatic response is to blame 'external' factors: OPEC, the trade unions, the flawed policies of the state. These, according to some, are the culprits for the present 'sclerosis' of the German economy[1] and it is their neutralisation/reform which promises a return to the traditional path of growth and full employment. Such faith, however, would seem to be empirically unverifiable and theoretically suspect, not the least because it does not admit an alternative to its own forms of organisation.

There are two fundamental limitations to the vision of limitless growth:

(a) the finite nature of the world's resources, which defy even the ingenuity of high-tech man and should dictate the limits of human consumption – there can never be enough asses' milk for everyone to bathe in;
(b) the internal laws of capitalism itself: this book has attempted in part to illustrate the operation of these laws, particularly in the period after 1959.

Accordingly the long-term growth trend is to be seen not as a function of external factors but of the increasing problems of the reproduction of 'national' capital: an increasing marginal capital coefficient and correspondingly lower rates of capital productivity and profit; increasing capital intensity and the related marginalisation of (living) labour as a factor in the valorisation of capital *and* as a factor of domestic demand. These are features of the general increase in capital concentration which in Germany has created a command structure dominated by the universal banks and the branch-based oligopolies which determines almost exclusively the fate of small capital and as significantly both the duties and the latitude of national and regional economic policy. It is specious to assert that the state, the unions or even OPEC are factors which are external to (and which paralyse) the market; these are integral factors of a system which predetermines their modes of operation. Any 'sclerosis' of the German economy would be inherent in the general and particular nature of its political economy.

To announce the imminent demise of West German capitalism would, however, be hasty and just as specious. For all its structural economic flaws, it remains the wealthiest economy in Europe with a prodigious productive capacity, a world reputation for precision and reliability in capital goods (heavy engineering, electro-technical and heavy chemical goods) and in motor vehicles and pharmaceuticals, a strong research base and a highly skilled and disciplined labour force. West Germany is the second largest trading nation in the world and has recently outperformed its European partners in its penetration of the expanding markets of the USA.

This said, there a number of voices which sound warnings for the future. The American economics journalist, Bruce Nussbaum, singles out West Germany as the 'one nation which will stumble' in the 'post-OPEC era', claiming its inability to compete when it comes to high technology.[2] Hamish McCrae, of the Guardian, sees West Germany as the 'prisoner of the world's failures', by dint of its very success in expanding its exports (of capital goods) which has rendered it more susceptible to international recessions than any other country.[3]

Without belittling the strength and adaptability of German capital, the highlighting of West Germany as a focus of particular problems over and above the general problem of Western capitalism and the global economy has a degree of plausibility. West Germany's particular politico-economic problems would seem to be a function of both its ostensible economic strengths and its organisational – political weaknesses. These can be dealt with in terms of its place in the world economy and the potential for national and international economic policy co-ordination.

WEST GERMANY IN THE WORLD ECONOMY

West Germany's recovery after the Second World War was due in large measure to its successful re-integration into the world economy and its correspondingly successful expansion of exports through the exploitation of favourable terms of trade *and* the underpriced currency. Within the general expansion of world trade between 1950 and 1970 West Germany's exports grew at a faster rate than average. The export quota (ratio of exports to Net Social Product) rose rapidly from 9.3 per cent in 1950 to 17.2 per cent in 1960 and to 23.8 per cent in 1970. This was perceived generally as an indicator of the economy's international strength – losing the war but winning the peace. Since the early 1970s, however, the growth of exports (and imports) has, if anything, accelerated,[4] but this time against the background of falling terms of trade,[5] international stagflation and flexible (uncontrolled) exchange rates. Exports, therefore, have always been, and are increasingly the dominant element of West German economic growth. The adoption of supply-side economic theories by the state since 1972 has reinforced the foreign economic flank of growth by seeking to limit the growth of domestic consumer demand. The 'offensive strategy' of boosting exports was clearly determined by the need to maintain a healthy balance of payments after the sudden rises in import costs of 1974 and 1979, and judged by this yardstick alone the strategy has succeeded (despite the upheavals of 1979–81). Critics, however, regard the export offensive as a potentially 'dangerous speculation'[6] which exposes the national economy to an increasingly volatile world market – in terms of dependence on both foreign demand and foreign supplies.[7] The necessary corollary for state economic policy is that an ever increasing proportion of domestic production is directed at markets which are outside its direct influence.[8]

The growth of the *export quota* is limited in a far more obvious way than economic growth as such (even though growth is itself limited if exports are its dominant element): i.e. with an export quota of 34.3 per cent in 1984 (including exports to the GDR), exports as the dynamic vehicle of general growth can only expand proportionately into the 65.7 per cent of GNP still consumed domestically. Quite apart from this blindingly obvious fact it is clear that West German exports appear to be limited by the ability of world markets to absorb exports (namely, their respective balance of payments and currency reserves), by the rivalry of other exporting nations (West Germany's share of world trade fell from 11.5 per cent in 1973 to 9 per cent in 1981) and by the emergence of new industrial capacity in former client nations. The ineptitude of monetarism (as a major element of supply-side economics) in contributing to the empoverishment of the potentially dynamic national economies of the developing world through high interest rates, has led to an increased trading inter-dependence of the developed world which in turn is threatening to provoke protectionism and further recession, despite or because of the arms-led boom in the USA. Helmut Schmidt was clearly correct when he referred to the two ticking time-bombs of third-world debt and balance of trade inequalities.[9] With such a high foreign trade commitment, autarky is clearly no longer a plausible bolt-hole.

It is therefore no surprise that the question of West German inter-national *competitiveness* has been raised recently, in particular at state level and that it has effectively replaced concern for domestic *competition* and control of domestic economic concentration.[10] In a situation where the German economy is seen in an intense struggle for the high ground in the new industrial revolution with the two other dominant economies of the USA and Japan, the *state is obliged to help maximise the effectiveness and strength of the major exporting oligopolies*. This they attempt to achieve with a combination of tax relief measures, trade diplomacy, pressure on wage levels as direct costs of production and increased support for scientific research as external costs of production, through investment grants (which pre-dominantly serve the purpose of rationalisation) and other means including domestic deflation and budget cutbacks. The victims of this intensified export orientation of state policy are not merely the domestic consumers – whose real incomes have fallen over the first half of this decade – but also those branches of capital which supply domestic consumers (private households and the state). Thus the employers' own 'Institute of the German Economy' recently com-plained that the local authorities had cut back too severely on their investment expenditure, to the tune of DM6 billion and had com-pounded the malaise of the construction industry, among others.[11]

The question of West German international competitiveness re-appears in the commentaries of those critical of the supply-side export offensive. Jörg Becker (Marburg) asserts that West Germany would do well 'to withdraw as far as possible from the suicidal technological race between the USA and Japan'[12] and to align itself closer to the interests of the Third World while moving out of wasteful arms production and away from the one-sided support of large firms. Glastetter recommends the strengthening of the 'domestic economic flank' in the face of ominous world economic developments.[13] The danger of West Germany, as a high wage economy, venturing further and further into cut-throat export markets (especially with its capital goods bias)[14] is of overstretching a competitiveness which is based as much on quality and promptness of delivery as on price, and then being confronted by a further world trade recession and losing out in a trade war.

What is clear is that West Germany's foreign economic policy has had a significant effect on the nature and scope of domestic economic policy. In a period of economic history which objectively places greater and greater demands on the state as a direct economic agent, the export offensive has obliged the state in West Germany to relinquish important elements of direct (anti-cyclical) control in favour of indirect fiscal and monetary manipulation and subsidies which in the long run favour German oligopolies rather than the whole German economy.

There seems to be little reason to believe that the German state is capable of responding to this increasing national politico-economic crisis without a radical modification of its organisational and fiscal structures.[15]

NATION STATE AND CRISIS MANAGEMENT

In previous chapters the general constraints on policy-making for the capitalist state and the specific constraints of West Germany's political economy and political apparatus have been dealt with quite fully. The response of the West German state to the extended period of crisis from 1973 through to the present day has been largely determined by those constraints. However, rather than address the constraints as problems, policy has tended to reinforce them. In the absence of effective international policy co-ordination (within the OECD, GATT, the EEC, etc.) indeed in the wake of the exchange rate anarchy since 1973 most policy initiatives have been national-political in nature – which represents a fundamental weakness of crisis management in itself. But while there is an objective need for, a) increased state control over capital flows, investment and wealth distribution, b) an increased democratisation of political structures (namely Federal Bank) and c) the centralisation of fiscal control, successive governments looked on while the international monetary order was 'privatised' (Hankel), abandoned exchange controls and presided over a reduction in state control over national investments and a renewed inequitable trend of income and wealth distribution. There has been a degree of centralisation of fiscal control in the increased pressure on local authority finances (with the progressive reduction of taxation revenue through the reform of commercial rates and the abolition – in 1980 – of the Payroll Tax),[16] but this has been negative centralisation, as part of a deflationary reduction of state expenditure.

Moreover, the fundamental issue of reforming the Federal Bank Law has never been seriously considered. The strategy of deregulation and state withdrawal would appear to have little chance of stabilising West German capitalism, quite simply because private capital (as is assumed) cannot solve 'its' crisis of reproduction itself – the uncontrolled drift of private investments *towards interest income* and *away from sales income* is evidence of this inability. Unless there is a change towards greater political control of social reproduction and towards new modes of collective planning and collective co-ordination (of fiscal, monetary, wage, environmental, social and regional policies) there is little prospect of solving the national/ international crisis of stagnation. Maintaining the present orthodoxy will most likely lead to a reinforced 'feudalisation' of production and distribution[17] under the aegis of international oligopolies and a continued worsening of national and international wealth distribution.

Notes

1. Renate Merklein, 'Die Sklerose der deutschen Wirtschaft' in *Der Spiegel*, no. 1 (1985).
2. Bruce Nussbaum, *The World After Oil – The Shifting Axis of Power and Wealth* (New York, 1983), quoted in *Der Spiegel*, no. 52 (1983).
3. Hamish McCrae in *The Guardian*, 4 Feb. 1983.
4. Werner Glastetter *et al.*, *Die wirtschaftliche Entwicklung in der Bundesrepublik Deutschland 1950–1980*, op. cit., p. 474.
5. The decline in the terms of trade was of the order of 15 per cent between 1972 and 1981 (Glastetter *et al.*, ibid. p. 481) which effectively reduced the real income of the national economy – according to the Federal Bank (Geschäftsbericht 1984, p. 26) a 2 1/2 per cent decline of the terms of trade reduces the real income of the national economy by half a per cent.
6. Glastetter *et al.*, op. cit. p. 551.
7. Ibid. p. 469.

8. Werner Abelshauser, *Wirtschaftsgeschichte der Bundesrepublik* 1945–1980, op. cit. p. 164.
9. Helmut Schmidt, quoted in *Frankfurter Rundschau*, 26 Sept. 1985.
10. See above Chapter 3.
11. Thus the Information Service of the Institut der deutschen Wirtschaft quoted in *Fr. Rundschau*, 25 Apr. 1984.
12. Jörg Becker, 'Bundesrepublik: Besser starker Zweiter als schwächlicher Primus' in *Fr. Rundschau*, 2 Mar. 1985.
13. Glastetter *et al.*, op. cit., p. 472.
14. Hamish McCrae, op. cit.
15. Werner Abelshauser, *Wirtschaftsgeschichte* . . ., op. cit. p. 170.
16. See Günter Samtlebe, 'Städtische Finanzen unter Druck von Bund und Ländern' in *Gewerkschaftliche Monatshefte*, no. 6 (1984,) pp. 368ff.
17. Karl-Georg Zinn stresses the dangers of a 're-feudalisation' of consumption as a potential capitalist strategy for growth and counterposes this with recommendations for a selective expansion of mass-consumption, *Der Niedergang des Profits*, op. cit., pp. 151f; a 're-feudalisation' of contractual relations is already evident – see above Chapter 3.

Bibliography

Abelshauser, Werner, 'Rekonstruktion der deutschen Wirtschaft' in Scharpf/Schröder (eds), *Politische und ökonomische Stabilisierung Westdeutschlands 1945–1949* (Wiesbaden, 1977).

____, *Wirtschaftsgeschichte der Bundesrepublik 1945–1980* (Frankfurt, 1983).

Abraham, David, *The Collapse of the Weimar Republic. Political Economy and Crisis* (Princeton, 1981).

Abromeit, Heidrun, 'Zum Verhältnis von Staat und Wirtschaft im gegenwärtigen Kapitalismus' in *Politische Vierteljahresschrift*, no. 1 (1976).

____, 'Interessendurchsetzung in der Krise' in *aus politik und zeitgeschichte*, B11 (1977).

Adenauer, Konrad, *Erinnerungen 1945–53* (Stuttgart, 1965).

Altvater, Elmar, 'Zu einigen Problemen des Staatsinterventionismus' in *Probleme des Klassenkampfs* no. 3, (1972).

Ambrosius, Gerold, *Der Staat als Unternehmer* (Göttingen, 1984).

Arndt, Helmut, *Die Konzentration in der westdeutschen Wirtschaft* (Pfullingen, 1966).

Augstein, Rudolf, 'Waffen statt Politik' in *Bilanz der Bundesrepublik* (Cologne, 1961).

Autorenkollektiv, Der Imperialismus der BRD (Berlin, 1973).

Badstübner, Rolf/Thomas, Siegfried, *Restauration und Spaltung. Entstehung und Entwicklung der BRD 1945–55* (Cologne, 1975).

Baisch, H., 'Kritik an der Sachverständigenkonzeption' in Markmann and Simmert (eds), *Krise der Wirtschaftspolitik* (Cologne, 1978).

Baring, Arnulf, *Außenpolitik in Adenauers Kanzlerdemokratie* (Munich, 1970).

Bergsdorf, Wolfgang, 'Besatzung und Wiederaufbau Deutschlands' in *aus politik und zeitgeschichte*, B/20 (1979).

Besson, Waldemar, *Die Außenpolitik der Bundesrepublik* (Munich, 1970).

Bickerich, Wolfram (ed.), *SPD und Grüne* (Hamburg, 1985).

Biedenkopf, Kurt/Miegel, Meinhard, *Die programmierte Krise* (Bonn, 1979).

Blanke, Bernhard, 'Formen und Formwandel des politischen Systems in der bürgerlichen Gesellschaft' in Volkhard Brandes *et al.* (eds), *Handbuch 5 Staat* (Cologne/Frankfurt, 1977).

Blanke, Bernhard/Jürgens, Ulrich/Kastandiek, Hans, *Kritik der Politischen Wissenschaft*, 2 vols (Frankfurt, 1975).

____, 'Zur neueren marxistischen Diskussion über die Analyse von Form und Funktion des bürgerlichen Staates' in *Politische Vierteljahresschrift, Sonderheft*, 6 (1976) pp. 19–60.

Bloch, Friedrich, 'Steuern und Konzentration' in Grosser, Dieter (ed.), *Konzentration ohne Kontrolle* (Opladen, 1974).

Böhm, Frank, *Kartelle und Monopole im modernen Recht* (Karlsruhe, 1961).

Borchardt, Knut, 'Die Bundesrepublik Deutschland' in G. Stolper, K. Häuser and K. Borchardt (eds), *Deutsche Wirtschaft seit 1870* (Tübingen, 1966).

Bower, Tom, *A Blind Eye to Murder: Britain, America and the Purging of Nazi Germany – a Pledge Betrayed* (London, 1981).

Brandt, Gerhardt, *Rüstung und Wirtschaft in der Bundesrepublik* (Witten/Berlin, 1966).

Braunmühl, Claudia von, 'Ist die "Ostpolitik" Ostpolitik' in Rittberger/Jahn (eds), *Die Ostpolitik der BRD* (Opladen, 1974).

——, 'Weltmarktbewegung des Kapitals, Imperialismus und Staat' in Braunmühl, Funken, Cogoy and Hirsch (eds), *Probleme* einer materialistischen Staatstheorie (Frankfurt, 1973).

Bundesverband der deutschen Industrie, *10 Jahre Kartellgesetz 1958–1968: Eine Würdigung aus der Sicht der deutschen Industrie* (Bergisch-Gladbach, 1968).

Butterwegge, Christoph, *Probleme der marxistischen Staatstheorie* (Cologne, 1977).

CEPES, *Wirtschaftpolitische Grundsatzfragen beim Aufbau einer Rüstungswirtschaft in der Bundesrepublik Deutschland* (Frankfurt, 1957).

Clay, Lucius D., *The Papers of General Lucius D. Clay*, 2 vols (ed. J. E. Smith) (Bloomington/London, 1974).

Czada, Peter, *Wirtschaft – Aktuelle Probleme des Wachstums und der Konjunktur* (Berlin, 1980).

Czichon, Eberhard, *Wer verhalf Hitler zur Macht* (Cologne, 1967).

Deppe, Frank (ed.), *Die Europäische Wirtschaftsgemeinschaft. Zur politischen Ökonomie der westeuropäischen Integration* (Hamburg, 1975).

——, *Kritik der Mitbestimmung* (Frankfurt, 1972).

Deutsches Institut für Wirtschaftsforschung (DIW), *Handbuch DDR-Wirtschaft* (Hamburg, 1977).

Dickertmann, D., 'Autonomie der Bundesbank unter dem Einfluß geldpolitischer Entwicklungen' in *Wirtschaftspolitische Chronik*, no. 1 (1975).

Dörge, F., 'Macht ohne Mandat? Die Bundesbank – eine Nebenregierung' in *Die Zeit*, 31 Oct. 1969.

Dreesbach, Lutz, *Die kleinen Seitensprünge großer Unternehmen* (Düsseldorf, 1983).

Ebbighausen, Rolf (ed.), *Monopol und Staat. Zur Marx-Rezeption in der Theorie des staatsmonopolistischen Kapitalismus* (Frankfurt, 1974).

Ebert, Reinhardt, 'Braucht die Wirtschaft weiterhin Ausländer?' in *Das Parlament* nos 35/36 (1981).

Ehrenberg, Herbert, *Die Erhard-Saga* (Stuttgart, 1965).

Elsenhans, H., 'Lohnerhöhungen: Wachstumschance für den Kapitalismus', in *Forum – Zeitschrift, für Theorie und Praxis des demokratischen Sozialismus* no. 2 (1976).

Elsholz, Günter, *Die Wettbewerbsordnung der Bundesrepublik Deutschland* (Informationen zur politischen Bildung 121), (Stuttgart, 1967).

Erhard, Ludwig/Müller-Armack, Alfred, Die Soziale Marktwirtschaft: Manifest 72 (Frankfurt, 1972).

Erhard, Ludwig, *Deutsche Wirtschaftspolitik* (Düsseldorf/Vienna, 1962).

——, *Wohlstand für Alle* (Düsseldorf, 1957).

Eucken, Walter, *Grundsätze der Wirtschaftspolitik* (Tubingen, 1955).

Föhl, Carl, 'Stabilisierung und Wachstum bei Einsatz von Gastarbeitern' in *Kyklos*, vol. 20 (1970).

Franz, F., 'Die Rechtsstellung der ausländischen Arbeitnehmer in der Bundesrepublik Deutschland' in F. Klee (ed.), *Gastarbeiter* (Frankfurt, 1972).

Friedländer-Prechtl, Robert, *Wirtschafts-Wende. Die Ursache der Arbeitslosen-Krise und deren Bekämpfung* (Leipzig, 1931).

Friedmann, Milton, *Essays in Positive Economics* (Chicago, 1953).

Glastetter, Werner, *Die wirtschaftliche Entwicklung der Bundesrepublik Deutschland 1950–1975* (Berlin/Heidelberg/New York, 1977).

Glastetter, W., Paulert, R. and Spörel, U., *Die wirtschaftliche Entwicklung in der Bundesrepublik Deutschland 1950–1980* (Frankfurt, 1983).

Gossweiler, Kurt, *Grossbanken, Industriemonopole, Staat: Ökonomie und Politik des staatsmonopolistischen Kapitalismus in Deutschland 1914–1932* (Berlin, 1975).

Gough, Ian, *The Political Economy of the Welfare State* (London, 1979).

Grosser, Dieter (ed.), *Konzentration ohne Kontrolle* (Opladen, 1974).

Hallgarten, George/Radkau, Joachim, *Deutsche Industrie und Politik* (Cologne, 1974).

Hankel, Wilhelm, 'Shylock gesucht: Hochzinspolitik und internationale Kreditmärkte' in *Blätter für deutsche und internationale Politik* (May 1982).

Hardes, H. D., *Einkommenspolitik in der BRD: Stabilität und Gruppeninteressen; der Fall Konzertierte Aktion* (Munich, 1974).

Harms, Uwe, 'Wirtschaftliche Aspekte des Gastarbeiterproblems' in *Hamburger Jahrbuch* (1966).

Hartwich, H. -H., 'Entwicklung zum Lohnsteuerstaat?' in *Gegenwartskunde* no. 1 (1978).

——, *Sozialstaatspostulat und gesellschaftlicher Status Quo*, (Cologne/Opladen, 1970).

Hayter, Teresa, *Aid as Imperialism* (London, 1971).

Henning, F. -W., *Das industrialisierte Deutschland 1914 bis 1972* (Paderborn, 1972).

Hickel, R./Mattfeldt, H., 'Die "Fünf Weisen" in der Krise, 20 Jahre Rat der Ratlosen' in *Gewerkschaftliche Monatshefte*, no. 11 (1983).

——, (eds), *Millionen Arbeitslose – Streitschrift gegen den Rat der fünf Weisen* (Reinbek, 1983).

Hirsch, Joachim, 'Kapitalreproduktion, Klassenauseinandersetzungen und Widersprüche im Staatsapparat' in Brandes *et al.* (ed.), *Handbuch 5 Staat* (Cologne/Frankfurt, 1977).

——, *Staatsapparat und Reproduktion des Kapitals*, Frankfurt (1974).

Hoffman, Wolfgang, 'Keine Freiheit für das Wissen' in *Die Zeit*, 10 Aug. 1984.

Hopf, Hilmar and Mayr, Gaby, 'Destabilisierung durch den Weltmarkt?' in Huffschmid, J. and Schui, H., *Gesellschaft im Konkurs?* (Cologne, 1976).

Hoppmann, E., 'Soziale Marktwirtschaft oder konstruktivistischer Interventionismus' in Tuchfeldt, E. (ed.), *Soziale Marktwirtschaft im Wandel* (Freiburg, 1973).

Huber, E. R., *Wirtschaftsverwaltungsrecht* (Tübingen, 1953).

Hüttenberger, Peter, *Die Entstehung der Bundesrepublik Deutschland* (Informationen zur politischen Bildung), (Bonn, 1974).

Huffschmid, J. and Schui, H. (eds), *Gesellschaft im Konkurs?* (Cologne, 1976).

Huffschmid, Jörg, *Die Politik des Kapitals* (Frankfurt, 1972).
Huster, E. -U., Kraiker, G., Scherer, B., Schlotmann, F. -K. and Welteke, M., *Determinanten der westdeutschen Restauration 1945–1949* (Frankfurt, 1975).
Issing, Otmar, 'Währungspolitik im Spannungsfeld wirtschafts-politischer Zielkonflikte' in E. Tuchfeldt (ed.), *Die Soziale Marktwirtschaft im Wandel* (Freiburg, 1973).
Jaeggi, Urs, *Kapital und Arbeit* (Frankfurt, 1969).
Jänicke, Martin, 'Umweltpolitik in Osteuropa' in *aus politik und zeitgeschichte*, B23 (1977).
Keynes, J. M., *General Theory of Employment, Interest and Money* (London, 1936).
____, *Preface* to German edition *Allgemeine Theorie der Beschäftigung, des Zinses und des Geldes* (Munich/Leipzig, 1936).
Klingemann, H. -D., 'Volkswirtschaftliche Konsequenzen der Rüstung in der Bundesrepublik' in *Beiträge zur Militärsoziologie, Sonderheft, 12* (1968).
Knapp, Manfred, 'Deutschland und der Marshall-Plan' in Scharpf/Schröder (eds), *Politische und ökonomische Stabilisierung Westdeutschlands 1945–1949* (Wiesbaden, 1977).
Kohler, Reinhard, 'Die Bremspolitik der Bundesbank hat noch nie richtig funktioniert' in *Frankfurter Rundschau*, 27 June 79.
Krack, J. and Neumann, K., *Konjunktur, Krise, Wirtschaftspolitik* (Frankfurt, 1978).
Krüger, H., 'Staatsverfassung und Wirtschaftsverfassung' in *Deutsches Verwaltungsblatt* (1951).
____, 'Wirtschaftsverfassung, Wirtschaftsverwaltung, Rechtsstaat' in *Betriebsberater* (1953).
Krull, Christian, *Wirtschaft und Rüstung* (Frankfurt, 1955).
Krupp, H. J., 'Staatsverschuldung – noch kein Grund zur Sorge' in *Frankfurter Rundschau*, 4 June 1980.
Kühnl, R. and Hardach, G. (eds), *Die Zerstörung der Weimarer Republik* (Cologne, 1977).
Kuklik, Bruce, *American Policy and the Division of Germany* (New York, 1972).
Kurowski, Franz, *Deutsche Offiziere in Staat, Wirtschaft und Wissenschaft.*
Läpple, Dieter, 'Kapitalistische Vergesellschaftungstendenzen und Staatsinterventionismus' in *Handbuch 5 Staat* (Cologne/Frankfurt, 1977).
____, *Staat und allgemeine Produktionsbedingungen* (Berlin, 1973).
Lambrecht, Horst, 'Der innerdeutsche Handel' in *aus politik und zeitgeschichte*, B40 (1977).
Lampert, Heinz, *Die Wirtschafts – und Sozialordnung der BRD* (Bonn, 1976).
Lau, Joachim, 'Die Wettbewerbspolitik der EWG' in Deppe, F. (ed.), *Die Europäische Wirtschaftsgemeinschaft* (Hamburg, 1975).
Lesch, Manfred, *Die Rolle der Offiziere in der deutschen Wirtschaft nach dem Ende des Zweiten Weltkrieges* (Berlin, 1970).
Lowe, Adolph, *Politische Ökonomik* (Frankfurt, 1965).
Mandel, Ernest, *Die deutsche Wirtschaftskrise* (Frankfurt, 1969).

____, *Die EWG und die Konkurrenz Europa-Amerika* (Frankfurt, 1968).
Manske, Fred, 'Die Suche nach den Schuldigen' in Huffschmid, J./Schui, H., *Gesellschaft im Konkurs?* (Cologne, 1976).
Marchetti, Cesare, 'Swings, Cycles and the Global Economy' in *New Scientist*, 2 May 1985.
Maunz, Theodor, *Deutsches Staatsrecht* (Munich, 1973).
Mechtersheimer, Alfred, 'Der militärisch-industrielle Komplex in den USA und der Bundesrepublik Deutschland' in *aus politik und zeitgeschichte*, B28 (1971).
Mensch, Gerhard, *Das technologische Patt: Innovationen überwinden die Depression* (Frankfurt, 1978).
Merx, Volker, *Ausländerbeschäftigung und Flexibilität des Arbeitsmarkts der Bundesrepublik Deutschland* (Cologne, 1972).
Miller, W./ Mackie, M. L. 'The Electoral Cycle and the Assymmetry of Government and Opposition Popularity' in *Political Studies*, vol. XXI (1973).
Miliband, Ralph, *The State in Capitalist Society* (London, 1973).
Montgomery, Field Marshall Bernard, *Memoirs* (London, 1958).
Müller, Helmut, *Die Zentralbank – eine Nebenregierung* (Opladen, 1974).
Müller, Wolfgang/ Neusüß, Christel, 'Die Sozialstaatsillusion und der Widerspruch von Lohnarbeit und Kapital' in *Probleme des Klassenkampfs*, Sonderheft 1.
Müller-Armack, Alfred, *Wirtschaftsordnung und Wirtschaftspolitik* (Freiburg, 1966).
____, see above: Ludwig Erhard/ Alfred Müller-Armack.
Neelsen, Karl, *Wirtschaftsgeschichte der BRD* (Berlin, 1973).
Nipperdey, Hans-Carl, 'Freie Entfaltung der Persönlichkeit' Berlin 1962, reprinted in Denninger, Erhard (ed.), *Freiheitliche demokratische Grundordnung* (Frankfurt, 1977).
Nussbaum, Manfred, *Wirtschaft und Staat in Deutschland während der Weimarer Republik* (Vaduz, 1978).
OECD, *Monetary Policy in West Germany* (Paris, 1973).
Olle, Werner/Schoeller, Wolfgang, 'Weltmarkt, nationale Kapitalreproduktion und Rolle des Nationalstaats in *Handbuch 5 Staat* (Cologne/Frankfurt, 1977).
Opitz, R., 'Der große Plan der CDU: "Die Formierte Gesellschaft" in *Blätter für deutsche und internationale Politik* (Sept. 1965).
Pahl, W., 'Mitbestimmung in der Montanindustrie', in *Gewerkschaftliche Monatshefte* no. 5 (1951).
Perels, Joachim, *Kapitalismus und politische Demokratie. Privatrechtssystem und Gesellschaftsstruktur in der Weimarer Republik* (Frankfurt, 1973).
Phillips, A. W., 'The Relationship between Unemployment and the Rate of Change of Money Wages in the United Kingdom 1861–1957' in *Economica*, vol. 25 (1958).
Pirker, Theo, *Die blinde Macht* (Munich, 1960).
Pohl, Rüdiger, 'Staatsdefizite, Kreditmärkte und Investitionen', in *Vierteljahreshefte zur Wirtschaftsforschung*, no. 4 (1981).
Poulantzas, N., *Political Power and Social Classes* (London, 1973).
Roberts, Ch. C., *Konjunkturprognosen und Wirtschaftspolitik* (Cologne, 1981).
Röpke, Wilhelm, *Freie Welt und Totalitarismus* (Bremen, 1957).

____, 'Gemeinsamer Markt und Freihandelszone' in *ORDO*, vol. 10 (1958).

____, *Die Gesellschaftskrisis der Gegenwart* (Erlenbach, 1948).

Rosenmöller, Christoph, 'Volkswirtschaftliche Aspekte der Ausländer-beschäftigung' in *Bundesarbeitsblatt*, vol. 21 (1970).

Ruhl, Klaus-Jörg (ed.), *Neubeginn und Restauration: Dokumente zur Vor-geschichte der Bundesrepublik Deutschland 1945–1949* (Munich, 1982).

Scharpf, Fritz, Planung als politischer Prozess (Frankfurt, 1973).

____, 'Die Rolle des Staats im westlichen Wirtschaft-system' in *Staat und Wirtschaft* (Conference Proceedings), (Berlin, 1979).

____, 'Sozial-liberale Beschäftigungspolitik – keine Erforlgsbilanz' in *Gewerkschaftliche Monatshefte*, no. 1 (1983).

Schiller, Karl, 'Konjunkturpolitik auf dem Wege zu einer Affluent Society' in *Jahre der Wende, Festgabe für Alex Moeller* (Karlsruhe, 1968).

____, *Reden zur Wirtschaftspolitik, vol. 1* (Bonn, 1968).

____, 'Stetiges Wachstum als ökonomische und politische Aufgabe' in *Der Ökonom und die Gesellschaft* (Stuttgart, 1964).

Schmidt, Eberhard, *Die verhinderte Neuordnung 1945–1952* (Frankfurt, 1970).

Schmidt, Ute/Fichter, Tilman, *Der erzwungene Kapitalismus* (Berlin, 1975).

Schoofs, Viktor, *Flexible Wechselkurse und Zentralbankpolitik* (Göttingen, 1983).

Schüller, A., 'Pragmatische oder marktwirtschaftliche Osthandelspolitik' in E. Tuchfeldt (ed.), *Soziale Marktwirtschaft im Wandel* (Freiburg, 1973).

Schui, Herbert, 'Die hohe Wirtschaftskonzentration trägt die Schuld an der Wachstumskrise' in Frankfurter Rundschau, 25 Nov. 1978.

____, 'Opfer für die Stabilität – die krisenverschärfende Politik der Bundes-bank' in Huffschmid, J. and Schui, H. (eds), *Gesellschaft im Konkurs?* (Cologne, 1976).

Shonfield, Andrew, *Modern Capitalism* (London, 1965).

Siebels, F. and Lenke, H., 'Kapitalistische Vergesellschaftung der Land-wirtschaft und "Gemeinsamer Agrarmarkt" in der EWG' in F. Deppe (ed.), *Die EWG* (Hamburg, 1975).

Simon, Walter, *Macht und Herrschaft der Unternehmerverbände BDI, BDA und DIHT* (Cologne, 1976).

Sozialdemokratische Partei Deutschlands (ed.), *Zweiter Entwurf eines ökon-omisch-politischen Orientierungsrahmens für die Jahre 1975–1985* (Bonn, 1975).

Statz, Albert, 'Zur Geschichte der westeuropäischen Integration bis zur Gründung der EWG' in Deppe, F. (ed.), *Die EWG*, Hamburg (1975).

Stolper, Gustav et al., *Deutsche Wirtschaft seit 1870* (Tübingen, 1964).

Thalheim, Karl, *Die wirtschaftliche Entwicklung der beiden Staaten in Deutschland*, Berlin, 1978).

Tuchfeldt, Egon, 'Soziale Marktwirtschaft und Globalsteuerung' in E. Tuch-feldt (ed.), *Soziale Marktwirtschaft im Wandel* (Freiburg, 1973).

Tudyka, Kurt P., 'Gesellschaftliche Interessen und auswärtige Beziehungen. Das Röhrenembargo' in Varain, H. J. (ed.), *Interessenverbände in Deutschland* (Cologne, 1973).

Verband der Vereine Creditreform Neuss, *Insolvenzenanalyse III* (Neuss, 1974).

Vilmar, Fritz, *Rüstung und Abrüstung* (Hamburg, 1973).

Vogelsang, Thilo, *Das geteilte Deutschland* (Munich, 1966).

Wagemann, Ernst, *Geld-und Kreditreform* (Berlin, 1932).

Welteke, Marianne, *Theorie und Praxis der Sozialen Marktwirtschaft* (Frankfurt, 1976).

Wirth, Margaret, *Kapitalismustheorie in der DDR* (Frankfurt, 1973).

Wurm, Franz F., *Wirtschaft und Gesellschaft in Deutschland 1848–1948* (Opladen, 1975).

Zapf, Wolfgang, *Beiträge zur Analyse der deutschen Oberschicht* (Munich, 1965).

Zieschang, Kurt, 'Ursachen und Wesen des staatsmonopolistischen Kapitalismus' in Sozialistische Politik, vol. 24 (1973).

Zinn, Kurt-Georg, *Der Niedergang des Profits* (Cologne, 1978).

Index